The Perfect Pie

MORE THAN 125 ALL-TIME FAVORITE PIES AND TARTS

. . . .

Susan G. Purdy

BROADWAY BOOKS | NEW YORK

BROADWAY

Broadway Books titles may be purchased for business or promotional use or
for special sales. For information, please write to:
Special Markets Department,
Random House, Inc., 1540 Broadway, New York, NY 10036.

BROADWAY BOOKS and its logo, a letter B bisected on the diagonal, are
trademarks of Broadway Books, a division of Random House, Inc.

Portions of this work were previously published by Collier Books, a division of
Macmillan Publishing Company, under the title *As Easy as Pie*
by Susan G. Purdy, copyright © 1984 by Susan G. Purdy.

Lines from "Shoo-Fly Pie and Apple Pan Dowdy" by Guy Wood and Sammy
Gallop used by permission of Warock Corp.

Visit our website at www.broadwaybooks.com

Library of Congress Cataloging-in-Publication Data

Purdy, Susan Gold
The perfect pie: more than 125 all-time favorite pies and tarts /
Susan G. Purdy.—1st ed.
p. cm.
Includes index and line drawings.
1. Pies.   I. Title
TX773 .P98624   2000
641.8′652 21—dc21   99-045530

FIRST EDITION

Designed by Judith Stagnitto Abbate / Abbate Design

Illustrated by Susan G. Purdy and Sidonie Coryn

ISBN 0-7679-0262-9

00 01 02 03 04 10 9 8 7 6 5 4 3

THE PERFECT PIE

BOOKS BY SUSAN G. PURDY

The Family Baker

Let Them Eat Cake

Have Your Cake and Eat It, Too

A Piece of Cake

As Easy as Pie

Christmas Cooking Around the World

Christmas Gifts Good Enough to Eat

Jewish Holiday Cookbook

Halloween Cookbook

Christmas Cookbook

Let's Give a Party

Christmas Gifts for You to Make

Books for You to Make

Costumes for You to Make

Jewish Holidays

Festivals for You to Celebrate

Holiday Cards for You to Make

If You Have a Yellow Lion

Be My Valentine

Christmas Decorations for You to Make

My Little Cabbage

With Thanks . . .

For encouraging me to write this book in the first place, I want to thank my husband, Geoffrey, who with our daughter, Cassandra, enthusiastically participated in several years of pie eating and recipe testing. For introducing me in the first place to all the arts—including the art of creative baking—I am grateful to my mother and father, Frances Joslin Gold and Harold A. Gold. For generously sharing family recipes with me, I thank my sister, Nancy G. Lieberman, and my aunts, Phoebe Vernon, Sesyle Joslin Hine, and Bea Joslin. For suggesting literary quotations, I thank Alexandra Hine and my mother-in-law, Lucille Purdy.

The biggest thank-you of all goes to friends, relatives, neighbors, and food professionals who have tasted, tested, and/or shared recipes and pies, given me the benefit of their culinary judgment, and are still willing to visit our home again even though a "test" pie will most probably be on the menu. Most of you I have thanked in person, though a special "thank you" is gratefully extended to Susan "Charley" Kanas; Katia Kanas; Léo, Sam, and John Kanas Roberts; Dick Parks; Jim Garland; Elizabeth MacDonald; Joan Moore; Diana de Vries; Michele Peasley; Barbara W. Cover; E. Barrie Kavash; Kathleen and Howard Bronson; Susan Dunnington; the late Mrs. Ruth Lawrence; David and Delia Lawrence; Sandra Calder Davidson; Frances and Wally Sheper of Franni's, Montreal, Québec; and the students in all my baking classes at cooking schools across the country; Dede Ely-Singer; Dick Gackenback and C. O. Godwin; the late Maria Peterdi; Yves Atlanti, chef of the Restaurant Muscadin, Azay-le-Rideau, France; M. Gaudin, Pâtisserie-Confiserie, Fougères, Normandie, France; M. Apolda, Boulangerie-Pâtisserie, Azay-le-Rideau, France; and Chef Harvey Edwards, Café du Bec Fin, Old Greenwich, Connecticut. For her drawings on pages 54 and 56, 57, 58, top 59, 60, 61, 66 (curled lattice), and 70, I thank Sidonie Coryn. For creative guidance throughout this project, I thank my literary agent, Olivia Blumer. For skillful editing and organizing while cheerfully keeping me focused, kudos go to my Broadway editor, Harriet Bell. Special thanks to book designer Judith Stagnitto Abbate and copy editor Judith Sutton.

CONTENTS

. . . .

I love you as New Englanders love pie," wrote Don Marquis in his *Sonnets to a Red-Haired Lady.* "Pie in the sky," "as American as apple pie," "apple pie and motherhood"—pie quotations and clichés are as thick as berries in a homemade pie, and with good reason: They ring true. If a vote were taken, pie would be (and in many places has been) chosen hands down as the all-time great national dessert, with apple as the favorite flavor. Yet, oddly enough, when you ask most adults if they bake their own pies or whose pie they prefer, their response is often a nostalgic, even wistful, "Grandmother's."

Beloved, but never baked! Homemade pies of all flavors are on their way to becoming a lost art, and for a pleasure that is so close to our hearts (and stomachs), this possibility takes on the proportions of a national disaster. But it is my premise that pies are easy and fun to make, and anyone can do it. By "pies," I mean not only two-crust so-called American-style pies, but also tarts, strudel, and fruit dumplings—in fact, nearly any dessert enveloped in pastry. This book is not meant to be the ultimate pie recipe collection; rather, it is a selection of personal and student-tested favorites presented with the hope of restoring the art of pie and pastry baking to the everyday repertoire of the home baker. And, recognizing that the home baker's time is more limited today than ever before, this book offers jump starts, shortcuts, tips, and freezing hints that make baking a practicable skill.

I wrote this book in response to the questions and problems raised in the pastry- and pie-baking classes I have taught all over the country. Almost with one voice, beginner baking students implore: "I can't [or I hate to] make piecrust." "I'm afraid to handle pastry dough." Those with slightly more experience say, "I need recipes that are quick and easy to prepare but elegant enough to serve at dinner parties." Hardworking men and women with little free time ask, "What can I keep in the freezer for last-minute, impromptu desserts?" And *everyone* wants to know, "Why is my piecrust tough?" or "Why does my crust shrink when baked?"

The answers to these questions and many more are found in the recipes that follow. Years of studying with master chefs, teaching baking, writing, and working with professional colleagues have given me a wealth of expertise I am delighted to be able to share with you.

Pastry making is an art form and, like all art forms, it is built upon a foundation of techniques that can be learned; it is not magic. Sure, there is the added fillip that comes from individual talent, flair, and creativity (or genes)—but these develop and are enhanced by experience. The basic skills are there for us all to learn and enjoy.

Following the organization of my classes, I address piecrust and pastry dough as the first order of business, explaining the functions and interaction of ingredients so you can understand the *whys* of baking as well as the *hows*. I suggest that the beginner master the information in these introductory chapters and these basic techniques before experimenting with the other pastry recipes included in the Pastry Recipe Collection. The recipe chapters are divided by types of pastry—that is, fruit and berry pies, chiffon pies, custard and cream pies, cobblers, etc. Ingredients, such as blackberries, for example, may appear in several chapters, in pies and tarts as well as cobblers. To find a complete list of recipes using a particular ingredient, look in the Index. I hope you will dip into this collection, taste here and there, and find to your delight that you *really can* make a light, flaky piecrust or high-rising puff pastry, and that sharing these skills with those you love to bake for gives you as much pleasure as it gives me.

THE LANGUAGE OF PIES

Just exactly what is a pie? And when is a pie a tart or a tartlet? When is a pie a flan? The answers can be as confusing as the questions, but as so many types are mentioned in this book, some attempt at definition must be made.

An American-style *pie* generally is any pastry crust with a sweet or savory filling baked in a shallow round dish with slanted sides. Pies are served from their baking dishes. Open-faced pies have no top crust. Deep-dish pies have the same kind of fillings as other pies but more of it because they are baked in deeper plates and have no bottom crust. They always have an upper crust.

A *tart* is the European cousin of the pie. It generally contains sweetened fruit or preserves or a custard filling, though there are savory tart recipes as well. A tart looks like an open-faced pie: a filled pastry shell. Sometimes tarts, as well as open-faced pies, have pastry-strip lattice crusts. European-style tarts are baked in straight-sided rather than slope-sided pans, often with fluted edges. Before serving, tarts are removed from their baking pans, which are usually made with removable bottoms to facilitate this procedure. In England and France, the words *tart* and *flan* are used interchangeably, while in America, tarts and flans are either called tarts or open-faced pies. A *flan* is actually named for the round metal ring in which it is baked. It is basically a pastry case containing any one of a variety of fillings, like a tart. However, in Spain and parts of France, the term *flan* can also signify a pudding or molded egg-cream mixture.

A *galette* is, literally, a round flat French cake. However, any flat, free-form (as opposed to pan-baked) fruit tart can also be called a galette, or, in Italian, a *crostata*. The most widely known galettes in France are made for Twelfth Night celebrations and each one contains a good luck charm or tiny porcelain statue of Jesus. In the north of France, Twelfth Night galettes are made of puff pastry, while in the south, they are made with yeast dough.

Pâte is the French word for "paste," meaning dough. The word *pâté* refers to a totally enclosed pastry case containing a forcemeat, or filling, of meat, vegetables, or (less commonly) fruit. To be strictly correct, *pâté* should refer only to a pastry-enclosed meat or fish mixture baked in the oven and served hot or cold. By contrast, a *terrine* can be a sweet dessert layered in a rectangular mold or a savory forcemeat baked *without* a pastry case (usually in an earthenware vessel, also called a terrine), with strips of fat or bacon on top; terrines are served cold only. And while we are in the family, a *galantine* is also forcemeat, a terrine in fact, but baked inside boned poultry.

4

ABOUT THE RECIPES IN THIS BOOK

- Before baking, you may wish to read the sections on equipment and ingredients (pages 14 and 24), to familiarize yourself with information and techniques that will help you succeed.

- Before starting a recipe, be sure to read it through from start to finish, so you will know what ingredients and equipment to have on hand, and how to plan your time.

- To achieve success in baking, use the pan sizes specified. A pie plate or tart pan that is too large will not have enough filling; while a pan that is too small may cause the filling to overflow in the oven.

- All dry measurements are level.

- All eggs are U.S. Grade A large (2 ounces).

- I prefer to bake with butter (see Butter, page 27). If you choose to substitute margarine, the flavor will differ somewhat. Use only hard stick margarine, never soft spreads or tub margarines, which will almost always cause baking failures because they contain unspecified amounts of water and additives.

- Lemon or orange *zest* refers to the most brightly colored part of the peel, which contains all the flavor. Do not grate the pith or white portion of the peel, which can be bitter.

- Lemon juice is best freshly squeezed. If necessary, as a substitute, use Minute Maid "100% fresh lemon juice from concentrate," available in supermarket freezer sections—never an artificial juice.

- Nutmeg has a more pungent flavor when freshly grated, but bottled ground nutmeg can be substituted.

- Room temperature means 68° to 72°F. All baking ingredients except fats and water for pastry making should be at room temperature before beginning so they will blend properly.

- Oven temperatures vary considerably and are the greatest cause of baking failures. To prevent problems, purchase an oven thermometer in a cookware or hardware store and keep it on the middle shelf inside your oven. Adjust the external oven control indicator as needed to keep the correct internal temperature.

- To double-wrap a baked good for freezing, completely cool it, then wrap it airtight in plastic wrap or foil and place it inside a heavy-duty plastic bag or a crush-proof plastic freezer container marked with a label and date.

- When a range is given for doneness, always check the oven at the first time, then watch closely until the second: Your oven and mine may differ, and the only thing that really matters is how the baked product looks. Observe the signs for doneness given in the recipe as well as the time indicators.

- For information on sifted versus unsifted flour, see page 26.

- When a recipe calls for ½ cup chopped nuts, the nuts are chopped before measuring. If it calls for ½ cup nuts, chopped, they are chopped after measuring.

- A double boiler is simply a smaller pot that fits inside a larger one containing water. To improvise your own double boiler, you can use a metal bowl or small pot set into a larger pot or frying pan of water. The best arrangement, however, is to suspend the top pot so that its bottom is not actually touching the hot water below.

- In the ingredients lists for the recipes, the pastry recipe suggested first is the one I think most suitable. However, other ideas are also suggested—or you may prefer to select your own from the collection of Pastry Recipes (page 79).

MEASUREMENTS AND EQUIVALENTS

Note that all measurements used in this book are level. All eggs used in recipes in this book are U.S. Grade A large.

1 U.S. Grade A large egg	= 2 ounces = 3 tablespoons
1 large egg yolk	= 1 generous tablespoon
1 large egg white	= 2 tablespoons
2 large eggs	= scant ½ cup = 3 medium eggs
6 to 7 large egg yolks	= ½ cup
4 large egg whites	= ½ cup
3 large egg whites, beaten stiff	= 3 cups meringue, enough to top a 9-inch pie
4 large egg whites, beaten stiff	= 4 cups meringue, enough to top a 9- or 10-inch pie
1 cup heavy (36 to 40% butterfat) cream	= 2 cups whipped cream
1 pound butter	= 4 sticks = 2 cups = 16 ounces, 454 grams

¼ pound butter	= 1 stick = 8 tablespoons = ½ cup
	= 4 ounces, 110 grams
5 pounds unbleached all-purpose flour	= 20 cups
1 pound unbleached all-purpose flour	= 4 cups, sifted
1 cup unbleached all-purpose flour, unsifted	= 5 ounces, 140 grams
1 cup unbleached all-purpose flour, sifted	= 4¼ ounces, 120 grams
1 pound cake flour or pastry flour	= 4½ cups plus 2 tablespoons
1 cup cake flour, unsifted	= 4½ ounces, 120 grams
1 cup cake flour, sifted	= 3½ ounces, 100 grams
(*Note:* For flour substitutions, see page 24).	
5 pounds granulated sugar	= 10 cups
1 pound granulated sugar	= 2 cups
1 cup granulated sugar	= 7 ounces, 200 grams
1 pound brown sugar	= 2¼ packed cups
1 cup packed dark brown sugar	= 9 ounces, 254 grams
1 pound confectioners' sugar, unsifted	= 4 to 4½ cups
1 cup confectioners' sugar, unsifted	= 4½ ounces, 130 grams
1 cup confectioners' sugar, sifted	= 3½ ounces, 100 grams
1 pound whole almonds, shelled	= 3 to 3¼ cups, 454 grams
1 pound almonds, ground	= 2⅔ cups
1 cup blanched whole almonds	= 5 ounces, 140 grams
1 cup chopped almonds	= 4 ounces, 110 grams
1 pound whole walnuts, shelled	= 4 cups, 454 grams
10-ounce package walnut pieces	= 2½ cups
1 cup walnut pieces	= 4 ounces, 110 grams
1 pound whole pecans, shelled	= 4½ cups, 454 grams
1 cup pecan halves	= 4 ounces, 110 grams
1 pound whole hazelnuts (filberts), shelled	= 3¼ cups, 454 grams
1 cup whole hazelnuts (filberts), shelled	= 5 ounces, 140 grams
6 ounces semisweet chocolate chips	= 1 cup
1 ounce regular-sized chocolate chips	= ⅛ cup = 2 tablespoons

1 ounce chocolate	= 1 square solid baking chocolate
1 pound seedless raisins	= 3½ cups, 454 grams
12 ounces dried apricots	= 2 packed cups
1 average-sized coconut (4-inch diameter)	= 3½ cups grated coconut
4 ounces coconut, dried and flaked or shredded	= 1 scant cup
1 envelope unflavored gelatin	= scant 2¼ teaspoons, 7 grams, enough to hard-set 2 cups liquid
1 lemon	= 2 to 3 tablespoons juice, plus 2 to 3 teaspoons grated zest
1 orange	= 6 to 8 tablespoons juice, plus 2 to 3 tablespoons grated zest
1 large apple (6 ounces), peeled, or 1 large unpeeled pear (5 ounces)	= 1 generous (4 ounces) cup, sliced
3 large apples or 3 large pears	= 1 pound = 3 cups sliced ⅛ inch thick = enough to top one 11-inch tart with overlapping slices
5 to 6 medium-large peeled apples or pears	= 5 cups sliced = enough to fill one 9-inch pie
1 medium peach, nectarine, apricot, or plum (3 to 4 ounces)	= ½ cup, pitted and sliced
4 to 5 peaches, nectarines, or plums or 6 apricots	= 1 pound = 2 to ½ cups fruit, pitted and sliced ¼ inch thick
6 to 7 peaches, nectarines, or plums or 7 to 8 apricots	1½ pounds = 3 to 3½ cups sliced ¼ inch thick = enough to top one 11-inch tart with overlapping slices
2¼ pounds peaches or nectarines	= 5 cups sliced = enough to fill one 9-inch pie
1¾ pounds plums	= 4 to 5 cups = enough to fill one 9-inch pie
1½ pounds to 2 pounds apricots	= 4 cups = enough to fill one 9-inch pie
5 to 6 kiwis (about 3 ounces each)	= 1 pound = 2½ to 3 cups peeled and sliced ⅛ inch thick (6 to 7 kiwis, peeled and sliced are enough to top one 11-inch tart with overlapping slices)

1 quart fresh berries	= 4 cups
4 to 5 cups small fresh berries (blueberries or raspberries) or 4 cups large fresh berries (such as strawberries)	= enough to top one 11-inch tart or fill one 9-inch pie
	= enough to top one 11-inch tart or fill one 9-inch pie

PIE AND TART SERVING GUIDELINES

8-inch pie	= 4 to 6 slices
9-inch pie	= 6 to 8 slices
10-inch pie	= 8 to 10 slices
11-inch tart	= 10 to 12 slices

10

In general, tips on the different phases of pastry making will be found within the particular chapter describing each process. However, here are a few common problems and solutions that will guarantee successful pies.

1. *To keep bottom piecrusts from becoming soggy:* Be sure the oven is preheated and the temperature is hot enough (check by placing an oven thermometer inside your oven). Begin baking pies in the lower third of the oven so the greater heat in this area will quickly set the lower crust. Do not underbake piecrusts.

Do not add moist filling to a pie shell until just before baking. Do not set a filled pie plate on a cold baking sheet in the oven; if you are using a baking sheet underneath the pie plate, preheat it in the oven before use unless otherwise directed in the recipe.

With moist pie fillings, it is best to partially prebake the pie shell before adding the filling, or you can glaze the lower crust with a moisture-proof coating such as beaten egg glaze or brushed-on fruit preserves. For extra-moist fruit fillings, sprinkle cracker or cereal crumbs over the crust before filling; crumbs absorb excess moisture.

Cool all pies on a wire rack to prevent moisture condensation on the lower crust as the pie cools.

It is not essential to butter pie pans, but buttering the pan helps the lower crust to brown quickly.

Use pie plates of heat-proof glass, such as Pyrex, or sturdy anodized aluminum with a dull finish. Shiny metal deflects heat and extra-thick pans take longer to absorb heat, causing slow baking.

2. *To prevent piecrusts from shrinking:* Roll the dough large enough to fit comfortably into the pan. Never pull or stretch the dough to fit, or it will shrink back during baking.

Chill formed pie or tart shells until firm to relax the gluten before baking in a preheated hot oven. Use an oven thermometer to monitor temperature.

Do not add excess liquid when mixing dough.

Do not bake in too cool an oven.

3. *To prevent too-fast browning of pastries or top piecrusts:* Cover the pastry edges with a foil frame (page 22), shiny side up to deflect heat, after the pie has begun to brown; for oddly shaped pastries, make a foil tent to set atop the browned area.

The more sugar in the dough, the more quickly it will tend to darken and burn. Therefore, roll very sweet dough slightly thicker than normal and protect it from overbrowning with a foil frame.

4. *For ease in handling a removable-bottom tart pan:* Bake the tart on a flat cookie sheet that has been preheated in the oven; a cold sheet will retard the browning of the lower crust.

5. *Always use the pan size called for in the recipe:* Measure pans across the top inside diameter.

6. *To form a piecrust from a dough that is either too sticky or too crumbly to roll out:* Simply pat the dough into the pie plate with your fingers, or cover the dough with plastic wrap and press out under the plastic. Keep the thickness even and avoid overdense corners. Pinch or pat up a lip around the edge. Remove any plastic wrap used and chill the dough before baking.

7. *To have a handy supply of quickly made pie dough:* Make your own dry mix (page 96) and just add water and flavoring when needed.

8. *To have a handy supply of ready-made piecrusts and fillings:* Make a double or triple batch of pastry while you are at it. Roll out this extra dough into rounds that fit into your pie plates, then stack the rounds between layers of *lightly* floured foil and set on a piece of stiff cardboard. Wrap the package airtight in foil, put into a heavy-duty resealable plastic

bag, label it, and freeze. It takes only a few minutes to defrost one of these sheets of rolled dough and then slip it into a pie plate to fill and bake. Or you can prebake pie shells, then cool, wrap, and freeze them until needed. Fruit fillings can also be prepared and formed into appropriate pie-plate shapes, wrapped, and frozen (page 72). When ready to use, simply unwrap a pack of filling and bake it in an unbaked pie shell.

9. *To cut meringue-topped pies with ease:* Butter or oil your knife blade.

10. *If your pastries are not baking in the stated times or are giving unreliable results:* Check the oven temperature: Put an auxiliary oven thermometer inside the oven and adjust the exterior oven control until the *inside* reading is correct.

11. *To prevent pie juices spilled on the oven floor from smoking:* Sprinkle salt on the spilled juices. Or spread a sheet of foil (shiny side up with edges folded up) on the oven floor before baking. Do not place the foil on shelf under pie, or it may deflect heat and impede proper baking.

12. *To prevent fruit pie juices from leaking:* For a single-crust pie, be sure the fluting is high enough to contain all the filling; for a two-crust pie, be sure the top crust edge is folded over the bottom crust edge and that both are pinched together well and sealed before being fluted.

    Do not overfill a pie and then stretch the top crust over it; the stretched crust will surely shrink during baking, and juices will escape.

    Cut several steam vents in the tops of all 2-crust pies.

13. *To prevent piecrust from toughening:* Do not overhandle pastry dough. Do not use too much flour or liquid or too little fat; follow the recipe proportions carefully. Add a little acidity to the dough (lemon juice, vinegar, sour cream, etc.).

14. *To patch tears or holes in piecrust:* For a torn unbaked crust, brush water or beaten egg over the edges of the tear and press on leftover scraps of rolled dough before baking.

    For a partially prebaked shell, brush beaten egg or egg white over the cracked area and press on scraps of rolled raw dough; the patches will bake along with the filling.

    For a completely prebaked shell, remove the shell from the oven as soon as a crack is visible, brush the crack with beaten egg, and patch with scraps of rolled dough or a little quickly mixed flour-water paste. Return the shell to the oven and complete baking.

EQUIPMENT

· · · · · · · · · ·

Thirty seconds in any cookware shop may convince you that you cannot blend flour and water without an astonishing array of sophisticated gadgetry. Not so. Stripped to basics, pastry making requires little special equipment other than your hands, a countertop, a rolling pin (sometimes), a baking sheet or pie plate, and an oven. But, to be fair, you may want to add a few helpful tools to your list of essentials.

Measuring Cups and Spoons

Dry ingredients such as flour and sugar are always measured in dry measuring cups designed to contain a specific amount and no more (see liquid measuring cups, below). Spoon the ingredient into the cup, then pass a straightedge over the top to level it. Dry measuring cups are available in nested sets graduated in size from ⅛ cup to 2 cups. They vary widely in quality; inexpensive plastic or flimsy metal can dent, bend, hold unpredictable quantities, and become inaccurate. The best, available from specialty cookware shop and mail-order sources (page 363), are stainless steel and precisely calibrated.

Liquid measuring cups are designed differently from those for dry ingredients and have pouring spouts. To use, fill the cup to the desired mark, set the cup on the counter, and bend down to check the quantity at eye level. The extra space at the top of the cup is there so the cup can be moved and poured without spilling; if you fill the cup to the brim, you will have too much. Liquid cups are commonly available in 1- 2-, and 4-cup sizes. The best are made of heat-tempered glass and are microwave-safe.

Measuring spoons come in sets graduated in size from 1/8 teaspoon to 1 tablespoon. Metal spoons are much more accurate than plastic; my favorites are stainless steel.

Work Surfaces

Marble is the oldest, most luxurious, and best work surface for pastry because it retains and transmits cold, chilling the dough and preventing the fat from melting. If you do not have a marble counter, a portable marble slab is a handy luxury and can even be stored on a refrigerator shelf until needed. Stainless steel and Formica work well and clean easily. Care should be taken, however, as they can easily be scored or scratched by knives. In warm weather, you can chill these countertops by setting a roasting pan filled with ice water on them. Wood (or butcher's block) is a fine surface for rolling out dough. A looped plastic scrubbing ball is helpful for lifting off dough bits stuck to wood.

If you plan to do a lot of pastry making, you will save yourself countless backaches if you build your countertop height to fit your own stature. Extend your arms full length, then flex your palms at the height at which you are most comfortable pressing down on the counter, as if flattening dough.

Dough-Working Tools

For general handling of dough, there is one tool I could not work without: a dough scraper, also called a *coupe-pâte* or bench or dough knife. This is simply a rectangular metal scraper with a handle along one edge. Similar tools are made in both stiff and flexible plastic, good for scraping dough out of bowls. In general, this is the tool for cutting, kneading, lifting, and scraping dough as well as for cleaning dough off countertops. Substitute a broad pancake turner or a 3- or 4-inch-wide putty knife purchased in the hardware store.

To combine flour and fat to make pie dough, use your fingertips, two cross-cutting table knives, a wire pastry blender, an electric mixer, or a food processor. Procedures for each of these are given following the basic recipe for All-Purpose Flaky Pastry (page 45).

15

The food processor *used correctly* gets my vote for best pastry-making machine. It consistently produces a fine product quickly and effortlessly. The speed of the machine not only keeps the dough cold enough so it can be rolled out without chilling, but forms the dough so quickly that toughening gluten has no time to over-develop.

Sifters

For the recipes in this book, it is necessary to sift flour only when specified. Pastry and cake flours are more finely milled than all-purpose and tend to clump more. Thus, it is best to sift these flours, to aerate and lighten them. I prefer to use a single-screen sifter with medium-fine mesh, available in hardware and cooking supply shops. Although many types of flour are labeled presifted, assume the label is meaningless and sift whenever directed by the recipe. For further details on flour, see pages 24–26. Sift granulated sugar if it looks lumpy, and always sift confectioners' sugar.

Dough-Rolling Tools

While you can certainly roll out dough with a smooth-sided peanut butter jar or a wine bottle, there is a definite ease, elegance, and efficiency to be found in a good rolling pin. It should be made of hardwood with a smooth, nonabsorbent finish, be well balanced, and be heavy enough to contribute its weight to the rolling and flattening of dough. I use a 3½-inch-diameter 18-inch hardwood pin with a smooth finish with ball-bearing handles. I do not recommend either porcelain pins, which are too fragile, or glass pins, which hold ice cubes and can cause moisture to condense on the outside, making the dough damp. Most American rolling pins have a central wooden cylinder with handles. I prefer handles that turn on ball bearings, a feature that helps in rolling dough to an even thickness. French or Italian rolling pins are generally longer than American pins and have either straight or tapered ends, without handles. Some people feel they have more control with these pins than with the American type.

If you are feeling creative, you can make your own rolling pin. Cut a 1½-inch-thick smooth-grained hardwood dowel (available in a building supply store) into any length you prefer. Sand the dowel ends. To clean a wooden rolling pin, simply wipe it with a damp cloth or looped-plastic scrubbing ball and dry it immediately; never soak it in water.

You can roll dough out directly on a lightly floured countertop or between two sheets of floured wax paper, or you can use a rolling pin covered with a tubular cotton sock or stocking (sold in bakeware shops) and a pastry cloth or canvas. Special cloths are marked with circles to help in measuring the diameters of piecrusts. Rub these pastry cloths and socks with flour, then shake off the excess before using. After use, shake out the cloths and socks, then store them in a plastic bag; reuse without washing. Rinse them occasionally in mildly soapy hot water and let dry thoroughly.

Measuring Tools

When cutting rolled-out pastries to measure, I use a seamstress's tape measure, which I hang around my neck for convenience. A stiff ruler 12 to 18 inches long is handy for measuring the dimensions of rolled dough. A neat trick for measuring the thickness of rolled dough is to mark the desired thickness on a wooden toothpick. Then stick the toothpick into the dough to gauge the depth.

Dough-Cutting Tools

Tools for cutting dough can be plain or fancy. To cut strips of rolled dough for a lattice-topped pie, a sharp paring knife held against a ruler or a plain-edged pizza wheel will do a fine, straight-edged job, but a wavy-edged stainless steel pie jagger, or pastry wheel, will do the same job decoratively. To crimp or flute the edges of a pie, you can use your fingers or a fork. Or you can indulge your fantasy and fortune with any number of elaborate crimpers on the market; all are basically grooved wheels mounted on a handle. Professional bakers use stainless steel crimpers to guarantee the dough seal of turnovers and filled pastries.

Pie Weights

A blind-baked pastry shell is one that is baked empty, before the filling is added (page 66–67). When this is done, the oven heat often causes steam in the dough to push up large bubbles in the crust. To prevent this, and also to help prevent shrinking, it is best to cover the dough with foil or baking parchment and weight it down during baking. Bakeware shops sell a variety of pie weights, from a heavy unglazed 9-inch pottery disk to bean-shaped individual pieces of metal or beads on a wire. Raw rice, cherry pits, or dry beans do the same job and cost much less. If you use them, keep them in a labeled jar and reuse them only for this purpose. Marble chips sold in nursery or garden supply stores also work well as pie weights; their weight is greater than rice or beans and thus they are more effective in pressing the dough down firmly.

Pastry Brushes

A pastry brush is nearly essential for applying egg washes and jelly glazes to piecrusts and fruit tarts. Although you can do the job with your fingertips, a good brush greatly simplifies the task. When selecting a brush, note that the finer the bristles, the more delicate the job it can do. A flat square-ended 1- or 2-inch-wide brush made of sterilized hog's hair or nylon bristles is a useful all-purpose tool. Nylon, however, tends to be too coarse for glazing the tops of delicate pastries, making hog's hair the better choice of the two. Select a brush with dark hairs so they will be visible and can be extricated if they fall into the filling or stick to the dough.

For the very lightest touch when applying an egg glaze to delicate pastries, I prefer to use an imported European goose-feather pastry brush with a pretty braided quill handle. It is lovely to look at as well as to use, inexpensive, and available in specialty bakeware shops and from mail-order sources (page 363). The brush washes easily in mild soap and warm water, air-dries, and lasts for years.

Pastry Bags
and Decorating Tubes

For piping whipped cream or meringue topping onto tarts or pies, a pastry bag with a set of assorted tips is the answer. Select a bag lined with plastic or made of nylon, as both types are flexible and neither absorbs fat. Wash bags in hot water and dry after each use. Bags are available in a range of sizes, from 7 or 8 inches to nearly 24 inches in length; choose one larger than you think you need, as small bags are harder to handle.

As a substitute, use a heavy-duty plastic bag with a small hole cut in one corner or make your own disposable bag out of waxed or parchment paper folded into a cone, with a

18

hole cut out of the tip (see diagrams). Bakeware shops also sell precut paper triangles for folding into disposable cones. Metal tips can be dropped into these paper cones to pipe decorative designs.

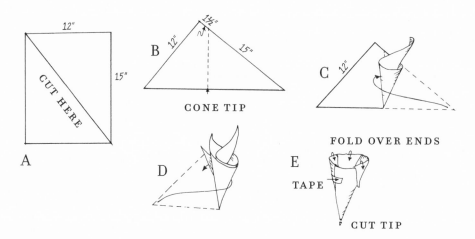

Pie Plates and Baking Pans

P ie plates are available in infinite variety, but some clearly produce superior results. For old-fashioned American pies, my first choice is always heat-proof glass, such as Pyrex. A good second choice is a dull-finished metal pan. Select pans with sloping sides and 8, 9, or 10 inches in diameter. For deep-dish pies, use pans at least 1½ to 2 inches deep. Avoid those earthenware pie plates that must be placed in a cold oven because extreme heat would cause cracks in the clay. To avoid disappointment, read directions and cautionary notes with care before buying baking utensils.

Be aware that glass pans absorb heat quickly and thus bake slightly faster than pottery or *heavy* metal pans. Pies baked in heavy pottery or metal pans with a textured or dark dull finish may take slightly longer than glass, but these pans absorb heat well, causing pastry to brown nicely. By contrast, highly polished metal tends to deflect heat, thus baking more slowly and endangering the quick setting of your piecrust—a bad idea. Some professional bakers use medium-heavy aluminum pans (*not* the foil type) with a dull finish. Aluminum pans absorb heat and conduct it very quickly, thus setting the crust quickly.

Pies and quiches are generally served from the pans in which they were baked. Tarts, however, are presented freestanding, removed from the straight-sided pans in which they were baked. There are many varieties of tart pans. The flan form is a bottomless metal ring or rectangle shape that creates an edge when set upon a flat baking sheet. The dough is fitted into the form and then shrinks away during baking, so the form can be lifted off and the tart slid onto a serving platter. Beginners find it easier to use a fluted French tart pan with a removable bottom. These are available in a variety of sizes, in round, rectangular, or decorative shapes (flowers, hearts, long narrow strips, etc.); for home baking, try the 7- to 11-inch rounds made of tin or black steel. Identical tartlet pans are available in various small sizes, typically 3 to 4½ inches. To unmold a tart from this type of pan, see page 55. (Be sure to butter all tart and tartlet pans very well before lining them with pastry; if the sides of the pans are fluted, press a buttered finger or brush into each indentation to be sure the job is done thoroughly. This facilitates removal of baked pastry.) As a substitute for the French tart pan, you can use a false-bottomed straight-sided metal American cake pan, widely available in 8-, 9-, and 10-inch sizes.

Pie plates and small tartlet pans made of inexpensive pressed aluminum are available in supermarkets. The pan surfaces are shiny, deflecting heat, and they are extremely thin. To compensate, you can double up the plates beneath your pie; this also helps with ease in handling after pies are baked. The chief virtue of these plates is that they are disposable and thus perfect when you are donating pies to a school bake sale or church bazaar.

Baking sheets, like pie plates, are best when made of heavy metal with a dull finish that absorbs heat instead of deflecting it. Cookie sheets generally have only one narrow rim, while so-called jelly-roll pans have a rim approximately ½ to 1 inch high all around. The latter are best for baking puff pastry, which may drip melted butter into the oven. If you have only thin sheets, or they tend to bake too quickly, try using two pans, one beneath the other, for baking.

To allow for even circulation of your oven heat, be sure your baking sheets are of a size that permits between 1 and 2 inches of clear air space between them and the oven walls.

Ovens and Oven Thermometers

Ovens vary beyond belief in their inability to hold heat calibration. While I have my ovens adjusted periodically, they eventually lose their exact calibration. I am finally resigned and have learned to always have *two* oven thermometers hanging inside the oven: one in front, the other in the rear, to check variations within the oven itself. Mercury-type glass thermometers mounted on metal stands are the most accurate for this purpose (see Sources, page 363). However, I often carry modestly priced hardware-store thermometers (replaced every year) when I travel and demonstrate pastry making. More recipes are spoiled by inaccurate oven temperatures than by any other cause. In fact, this is probably the most important tip in this book: *Get an oven thermometer and use it, adjusting your exterior oven thermostat so the internal oven temperature is correct at all times.*

Convection and Microwave Ovens

Convection ovens contain an interior fan to blow the heat around. The constant circulation causes them to cook foods about 25 percent faster than regular ovens, producing a nicely browned crust on pies and pie shells. However, the rush of air produced by the fan is too gusty for fragile meringue toppings and meringue shells. When converting ordinary recipes for use in a convection oven, lower the baking temperature by about 25 to 50 degrees. If your home oven has a convection fan on/off button, shut it off when baking meringues of any type. In fact, I never use it for baking pastries.

I use my microwave for melting butter and chocolate, defrosting, and warming baked goods. For actual baking, a conventional oven gives more control and produces a better texture.

Timers

A good timer is absolutely necessary if you expect predictable results in baking. Many good ones are on the market, available in hardware or cookware shops: No need to invest in an LCD multichannel timer—a simple ticker with a bell is adequate. A timer that hangs on a cord around your neck is great if you are either absentminded or often called to the telephone, or both, as I am; see Sources, page 363.

Gadgets

Baking gadgets can be fun, and some will even provide dinner party conversation, (though your pastry will surely steal the show on that count). Take the pie bird, for instance: a British invention, it's a small hollow pottery bird that sits in the center of your pie. He not only helps support the top crust, but allows the steam to escape through his wide-open beak, replacing the steam vent normally cut into the crust. The bird is sometimes used with fruit pies but actually is the modern replacement for the "four and twenty blackbirds baked in a pie." The most widely available pie bird is, in fact, a ceramic blackbird. Pie birds are available by mail-order (see Sources, page 363) and in many bakeware shops.

If you have ever struggled to retain your dignity while removing the first piece of a crumbling pie in front of your dinner guests, you will appreciate the pie lifter, a stainless steel wedge with a lip that fits the rim of a pie plate. However, not all lifters fit all pie plates; test for fit before using.) This gadget is baked right into the pie and after you slice the pie along its sides, you simply lift the first piece out on the metal wedge. These are available from the same sources as pie birds.

A pastry pincher, sometimes called a crimper, is a handy device used to give a finished edging to tarts. It is a small hinged pair of metal arms with grooves or teeth on the ends. When these teeth are applied to the top edge of a pastry shell at regular intervals, they produce a decorative marking.

Foil and Baking Parchment

Baking parchment is a specially formulated nonstick paper designed for lining baking pans. It is sold in rolls like wax paper, as well as in sheets of different sizes. Parchment does not usually have to be greased. It is more durable than wax paper and thus ideal for making decorating cones (page 18) and lining pastry shells before adding weights for prebaking.

Aluminum foil has many uses in pastry making. To prevent pastry from overbrowning in the oven, you can mold foil over a crust to deflect the heat. For one- or two-crust pies, you can use several 3-inch-wide strips of foil for this purpose, or you can easily make the handy device called a foil frame: For a 9-inch pie or tart, cut roughly a 10-inch square piece of foil, fold it in quarters, and tear out the center, leaving about a 2-inch edging. Un-

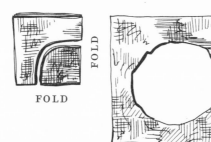

FOLD

FOLD

UNFOLDED FOIL FRAME

fold and set the opened frame shiny side down over the pie or tart. Gently bend the edges under the pan rim. When baking small dough decorations on top of pies or puff pastry cases, you can use the center torn from the foil frame to make a small foil tent to set over the highest pastry pieces, which may otherwise brown too quickly.

Foil can be cut into a 12-inch (or larger) square and used as a liner for pie weights when prebaking an empty pastry shell. The shiny surface of the foil deflects heat; therefore, place the foil *shiny side down* before filling with weights so the heat will reach the pastry.

23

Stainless Steel Knives and Nonreactive Saucepans

Because certain types of metal utensils (particularly aluminum and iron) react chemically to darken or discolor egg or wine preparations such as custards and sauces, I recommend that these items be cooked in enamel, heat-proof glass, ceramic, or stainless steel pans. Custards should be tested for doneness with a stainless steel or silver knife.

INGREDIENTS

· · · · · · · · · ·

A well-made pie pastry should be tender and flaky and have a delicious flavor appropriate to its filling. To define our terms, a "flaky" crust will, when broken, have clearly visible layers or flakes; it may cut unevenly. A "short" crust may be flaky or of finer crumb, more sandy than layered but still tender; this type will easily cut in a neat line. (A "crumb" crust, is not really a pastry in the literal sense, since it is made from crumbs rather than a flour paste.) While any one of several pastry recipes will produce good results, an understanding of what ingredients do and why will guarantee you fear-free, carefree pastry making with consistently professional results.

Flour

Different types of flour have different characteristics, depending upon the type of wheat from which they were milled and the geographic and climatic conditions under which the wheat was grown. Bakers are most concerned with the amount of gluten-forming proteins in the flour. Gluten is a stretchy elastic substance that develops when two of wheat's proteins blend with liquid. The flour with the highest protein content will absorb the most water—a factor that is useful in stretchy, elastic bread doughs but leads to toughness in piecrusts and pastries. A tender, flaky piecrust requires a lo protein, low-gluten flour. In piecrust we don't want to eliminate gluten, but rather keep its development to a minimum.

When selecting flour, read the package labels carefully. The labels on most commercial flour packages show protein content (an indicator of gluten content) under Nutritional Information. You will see, for example, that 1 cup of all-purpose flour has between 11 and 12 grams protein, while a cup of pastry flour has 8 grams and one of bread flour has 14 grams protein.

Unbleached all-purpose flour, milled from either a single type of wheat or from a blend, contains roughly 10 to 13 percent gluten (11 percent is the average); it gives excellent results in most piecrust and pastry recipes and is usually my first choice.

Pastry flour, milled exclusively from soft wheat, contains less gluten, about 8 grams per cup. It is a little too soft for ideal results in some piecrust recipes. Pastry flour is usually sold in 1-pound bags in gourmet or natural foods shops. Cake flour, also milled from 100 percent soft wheat, contains 6.5 to 10 percent protein, with 8 percent the average, and is usually sold in 2-pound boxes in the supermarket. (Self-rising cake flour contains added leaveners or baking powder and salt. Do not substitute self-rising for regular cake flour.)

Often a good choice for pastry and piecrusts, cake flour can be substituted for pastry flour. I find, however, that ideal qualities result when cake or pastry flour is blended with all-purpose flour. I often combine unbleached all-purpose flour with cake flour, using a combination of two thirds all-purpose flour and one third cake flour. To transform all-purpose flour into pastry flour, substitute 1 tablespoon cornstarch for 1 tablespoon of the flour in every cup. To make cake flour from all-purpose, replace 2 tablespoons of the all-purpose flour in every cup with 2 tablespoons cornstarch. Cake flour actually weighs a little less than all-purpose flour; to substitute cake flour for all-purpose flour, use 1 cup plus 2 tablespoons cake flour for each cup of all-purpose.

Whole wheat flour (15 to 16 percent gluten) contains the vitamin-and-fiber-rich wheat germ and bran, which increase its nutritional value but cause a heavy crumb. White whole wheat flour, made from a special strain of high-protein wheat, has less gluten than ordinary whole wheat (about 13 percent), but still too much for piecrusts. Whole wheat flour is sold in 5-pound bags in most supermarkets and is also available from specialty mills and natural foods stores. To make a whole wheat piecrust with a sufficiently light texture, blend whole wheat flour half-and-half with cake or pastry flour.

Instant-blending flour is processed to be granular so it will mix easily with water without lumping. This is useful for making gravy and some biscuits, but I have not found it successful in piecrusts.

Many types of flour are labeled "bleached," or whitened through a dual chemical and natural process. When flour is exposed to air, oxygen combines with any yellowish pigments and whitens them; traditionally, air-drying was the only bleaching method used. Today, air may still be used as a bleaching agent, but chemical bleaches and oxidants speed up the natural oxidizing process. Oxidation improves baking quality for certain types of cakes by strengthening the stretching and bonding characteristics of the gluten.

Many bakers believe unbleached flour is less processed and thus more healthful. However, some so-called unbleached flours have been oxidized or contain added dough conditioners; nevertheless, they probably have not been treated to remove the yellowing pigments. Unbleached flour may also be a little higher in protein than bleached flour, giving a slightly less tender result in baking. Unbleached flour is generally my choice for piecrusts and cookies, but I prefer to use bleached all-purpose flour for delicate pastry and cakes. The recipes in this book call for either regular all-purpose or cake flour but do not specify bleached or unbleached. Either one will work; the choice is yours.

Flour should be stored in a well-ventilated cool place, off the floor and away from dampness. It can absorb strong off odors as well as moisture. Flour stored for any length of time in hot weather or a warm location can become a haven for insects. It is best to store flour in the freezer or refrigerator. Flour will keep for about 1 year at 0°F.

How to Sift and Measure Dry Ingredients

Ignore the "presifted" label on store-bought flour. You can be sure the flour bags have been stacked and stored and the contents certainly will have settled. When you open a bag of flour, pour it into a wide-mouth canister with an airtight lid. Before measuring flour from the canister, stir it gently to lighten and aerate the contents.

It is important to remember that too much flour can toughen baked goods; use only as much as a recipe calls for. For the most precise results, measure flour by weight, on a scale; since that is not commonly done in this country, however, when measuring by volume, in cups, take great care. Generally, sifting flour for piecrust is not necessary if you follow my "stir and spoon" technique:

When a recipe in this book calls for "½ cup unsifted flour," stir the flour in the canister to aerate it, then lightly spoon the flour into a dry-measuring cup (page 14) and level the top with the back of a knife or other straightedge. Take care not to knock or tap the filled cup, or the flour will compact and require as much as 2 extra tablespoons to fill the cup to the top.

When a recipe calls for "½ cup sifted flour," pass the flour through a medium-fine-mesh strainer onto a piece of wax paper or into a bowl. Spoon this sifted flour into the measuring cup, heaping it slightly and taking care not to tap the cup. Finally, take the back of a knife and sweep off the excess, leveling the top.

Fats for Baking

Baking fats used in this book include butter, margarine, vegetable shortening, oil, and lard. In my opinion, the combination of butter, for good taste, plus a high-fat shortening such as lard or Crisco, for flakiness, produces the ideal pastry.

In baked goods, fats tenderize, moisturize, carry flavors and aromas, add nutrients, and contribute to aeration and flakiness and/or smoothness of texture. Because fats have different melting points and contain different percentages of water, successful baking depends upon choosing the appropriate type of fat and correctly blending it into the dough or batter.

When fat is combined with flour, it coats the elastic strands of gluten, making them slippery, separated, and tenderized, or short (hence the term *short pastry dough*). For flaky pastry, a cold solid fat is most desirable. The colder the fat, the less it soaks into the flour starch and the more separate it stays, creating little flakes or layers as it is pinched into the flour. In a hot oven, the liquid in the pastry dough makes steam that pushes up the layers while the heat sets them firmly; this action creates the quality of flakiness in a piecrust. In contrast, oil, or any melted fat, coats the gluten strands, preventing toughness, but because it is absorbed into the flour starch, it makes a crust with a sandy crumb, never a flaky one.

The amount of water released by the fat contributes to the total liquid of a recipe. A fat that contains a lot of water can require more flour and thus result in a tough product. Whipped butter, tub margarine, and margarine spreads (as opposed to solid stick margarine) contain so much water and/or air that they should never be used in baking.

BUTTER

Butter has the best flavor of all baking fats. It melts in the mouth because it has a melting point near body temperature (approximately 92°F). I prefer to use unsalted butter because it is (or should be) dated or sold frozen, so it will be fresher than salted. Butter, an animal fat, contains cholesterol as well as enzymes that can affect and accelerate rancidity. Producers add salt to butter not only to enhance its flavor, but also to mask off flavors and to prolong shelf life; different brands of butter contain different quantities of salt. The best butter tastes sweet and very fresh. When you add all the salt yourself, you can control the amount of salt in the recipe.

Margarine

Margarine was created to simulate butter, but it never duplicates the real thing. It is made from a variety of oils and solid fats that are blended, heated, and combined with water, milk, and/or milk solids; emulsifying agents; flavorings; preservatives; coloring; and vitamins. Margarine is made from oil that is partially hydrogenated (see below) to make it solid and it has a slightly higher melting point than butter, so it doesn't melt as quickly in the mouth. When piecrust is made solely with margarine, the margarine should be well chilled or frozen before using; the dough is usually best rolled out between sheets of wax paper. The resulting crust will still tend to taste a little oily.

While stick margarine lacks the good taste and texture of butter, it has roughly the same fat content, around 80 percent, but it is much lower in cholesterol. Many (but not all) brands contain no cholesterol. If you wish to follow kosher dietary laws, select a solid stick margarine with a high percentage of oil (70 to 80 percent), without milk solids or animal fats; read labels carefully. I have good luck with Fleischmann's Unsalted Stick Margarine.

Soft margarine spreads, tub margarine, and low-fat margarines can contain as little as 30 to 40 percent oil plus unspecified quantities of water, air, flavoring, and other additives, making them absolutely unreliable in baking.

Solid Shortening and Hydrogenation

To transform liquid vegetable oil into solid or spreadable form (margarine or solid shortening), the oil must be hydrogenated. This is a commercial process by which hydrogen molecules under pressure are forced through the oil. In addition to hardening the fat, hydrogenation increases its stability and prolongs its shelf life. During this process, the molecular structure of the oil is changed; the more an oil is hydrogenated, the greater the change and the more solid the product; squeeze-bottle or soft tub margarines have been changed less than hard stick margarine.

Unlike margarine, solid shortening is designed to go in, not on, food. It does not have to taste or feel good in the mouth, so it can contain a generous quantity of emulsifiers to preserve the suspension of the fat in liquid, to hold more air, and to stabilize the moisture content of a dough or batter. Hydrogenized vegetable shortening (Crisco) has the highest melting point of all baking fats, 110° to 120°F. Piecrust made solely with vegetable shortening is very flaky but nearly tasteless.

Hydrogenated shortenings and margarine—once considered the perfect alternative to butter—are now being scrutinized by scientists because, as oil hardens during the hydrogenation process, new structures are formed called trans fatty acids (tfa's). The trans fatty acids help prevent rancidity in the hydrogenated fat, but because tfa's act like other unhealthy saturated fats in the body, many studies have recommended that human tfa consumption be reduced. While tfa's occur naturally in small amounts in such common foods as meat, butter, and milk, researchers now suggest that tfa levels in hydrogenated fats such as hard stick margarines, partially hydrogenated vegetable oil, and commercial shortenings and frying oils may be excessive.

When selecting a fat for baking, consider that butter, although a saturated fat, has the best taste and is usually the best choice. Solid stick margarine is not an ideal substitute—it lacks butter's flavor and contains some saturated fat and trans fatty acids. Its advantage is that it does not (usually) contain cholesterol, and it is available in a kosher form. You can certainly bake with margarine, but the recipes in this book were developed for butter (unless another fat is specifically noted in the ingredients list).

LARD

Lard is almost 100 percent animal fat, with a small percentage of water. It has the best shortening power and produces the most tender and flaky piecrust of all fats. The best type is leaf lard, rendered from pork kidney fat. Some lard is rendered from fat from other parts of the pig and may have a stronger pork flavor than leaf lard. Lard is most often sold in 1-pound blocks in the meat section of the supermarket.

For storage, lard must be refrigerated unless it is hydrogenated; check the label carefully. Regular lard stored at room temperature can turn rancid; never use lard that has an off scent or flavor.

While lard contains cholesterol and saturated fat (as does butter), it has high levels of mono-unsaturated fat and therefore eating it in a piecrust is not a significant factor in raising blood serum cholesterol levels in most people.

OILS

When selecting an oil for baking, choose one with a light neutral flavor and a light fresh scent (smell the oil before using it), such as canola, safflower, sunflower, peanut, or corn. Vegetable oils contain no cholesterol.

HOW TO STORE SOLID FATS AND OILS:

Fats have the tendency to absorb strong odors; all fats should be stored covered, away from strong-smelling ingredients. Butter and margarine should be refrigerated and/or frozen for short-term use; for long-term storage, they should be frozen. Oils should be stored in opaque containers in a cool dark location or refrigerated. Chilling sometimes turns oil cloudy; this is not harmful and clarity returns as the oil returns to room temperature. Dark-colored specialty oils, such as walnut and hazelnut, are the least stable, with a shelf life of only 4 to 6 months. Refined vegetable oils (such as canola, safflower, and corn) generally stay fresh 6 to 10 months. Many vegetable oils naturally contain vitamin E or similar antioxidants that protect them from rancidity; safflower oil, an exception, does not, and must always be refrigerated.

HOW TO MEASURE FATS

Oil, a liquid fat, is measured in a liquid measuring cup. Butter, margarine, and Crisco are conveniently sold in quarter-pound sticks, marked on the wrapper to indicate tablespoon and cup divisions. Commercial lard is generally sold in 1-pound blocks; to measure easily, divide lengthwise into 4 quarter-pound sticks, then mark off 8 tablespoons per stick as for a stick of butter.

SOLID FAT MEASURING GUIDE:

1 stick = 8 tablespoons = ½ cup
5⅓ tablespoons = ⅓ cup
4 tablespoons = ¼ cup

To measure solid fat using measuring spoons or cups, pack it into dry (not liquid) measuring spoons or measuring cups, taking care not to trap any air pockets. Level the top with a straightedge. I prefer not to use the water displacement method—in which solid fat is added in increments to a specific amount of water in a measuring cup until the water reaches the desired level—because water left clinging to the fat may disrupt the balance of liquid in a recipe.

Liquid

Liquid is added to dough to dissolve the salt and any sugar, to work the flour, and—along with the moisture in the melting fat—to create the steam that pushes apart the dough flakes in the oven's heat. Liquid should be used sparingly, as too much overactivates the gluten, toughening the pastry. Liquid should be ice-cold when added to dough. You can use water, eggs, milk, fruit juice, or even alcohol for the liquid in pastry dough. (*Note:* Alcohol adds flavor but evaporates fast in the oven and can create a rather tough crust.)

A little lemon juice or vinegar can be added as part of the measured liquid without noticeably altering the pastry's flavor. The addition of the acid these liquids contain softens the gluten, tenderizing the crust. Yogurt and sour cream used in place of liquid, as is the practice in Eastern European baking, similarly contribute the benefits of acidity, as well as adding flavor.

About Eggs

Eggs help with leavening; add richness, proteins, vitamins, and minerals; and contribute to the structure, texture, color, and flavor of baked goods. Eggs also help bind a dough or a batter together.

Whole eggs and egg yolks tenderize baked goods because the fat they contain helps to inhibit the development of potentially toughening gluten in the flour. In addition to fat, yolks also contain natural lecithin, an emulsifier that helps make piecrusts pliable and helps eggs whip into a stabilized foam.

To the cook, there is no difference between brown and white eggs, but eggs do vary in freshness, size, and whipping qualities. For baking, eggs should be at room temperature. If they are very cold, set them, in the shell, in a bowl of warm water for about 10 minutes.

How to Store and Freeze Eggs

Separated egg whites or yolks can be refrigerated in a covered jar for 2 or 3 days. (I like to put a drop or two of water on the yolks to prevent a skin from forming.) The best way to store eggs is in the freezer; add a pinch of sugar to yolks to prevent stickiness when thawed. Lightly beaten whole eggs can be blended with a few grains of salt or sugar and then frozen in ice cube trays (1 cube then equals 1 whole egg). Frozen eggs, whole or separated, should be thawed overnight in the refrigerator before use. Never refreeze thawed frozen eggs.

Egg size is very important in baking. In this book, all eggs are US Grade A large, weighing 2 ounces in the shell.

. . . .

MEASURING EGGS:

4 to 4½ whole eggs = 1 cup
1 large egg yolk = 1 tablespoon
1 large egg white = 2 tablespoons
4 large whites = 8 tablespoons = ½ cup
4 large whites, beaten until stiff = approximately 4 cups meringue

. . . .

How to Whip Egg Whites

When egg whites are mixed with sugar and whipped into a stiff foam, they form a meringue. When meringue is exposed to heat in the oven, the molecules of air in the foam cells get warm, expand and enlarge, and then set. For the correct procedure for whipping egg whites into a meringue, read About Meringue (page 106).

About the Safety of Eggs and Meringues

Egg safety and the possible health hazards of eating uncooked eggs and meringues are significant issues for cooks. Some incidents of bacterial contamination, from the bacterial organism *Salmonella enteritidis*, have been attributed to raw, improperly cooked, or undercooked eggs. Until the hazard is eliminated, it is prudent to be cautious in baking, although the likelihood of a problem is slim. According to the American Egg Board, studies have indicated that the chances of a home cook finding an infected egg are about 0.005 percent. *Here are a few simple guidelines:*

When shopping, buy only from a store that has well-refrigerated egg cases. Open the carton and look at the eggs; avoid eggs that are cracked or unclean. At home, refrigerate eggs promptly, storing them inside the refrigerator, where it is colder, rather than on the door. Wash any container, utensil, or food preparation surface that has come in contact with raw eggs before reusing it. Avoid eating raw eggs.

Refrigerate all baked goods containing custards or meringues. Keep cold foods cold (at or below 40°F) and hot foods hot (above 140°F) to prevent growth of Salmonella bacteria.

While the bacteria causing the common food poisoning, Salmonellosis, is sometimes present in egg whites or yolks, it has also been found on the skins of fruits grown in contaminated soil. Washing produce carefully helps, and there is no question that the bacteria cannot survive high temperatures. Commercial food handlers and many restaurants avoid the possibility of this problem by routinely cooking with pasteurized liquid eggs instead of fresh eggs.

For the baker, egg white caution means following instructions carefully when preparing meringues or other preparations such as mousses. While it is highly unlikely that eating a small amount of egg glaze or uncooked meringue in a chiffon pie will make you sick, at least you should be informed. According to the American Egg Board, to destroy the bacteria, egg whites must be held at a temperature of 140°F for 3½ minutes or at some point reach 160°F.

HOW TO COOK RAW YOLKS FOR USE IN UNCOOKED RECIPES

If a recipe for an unbaked soufflé, sauce, or pudding calls for raw egg yolks, they can be prepared as follows to remove any danger of bacteria: Blend the yolks with at least 2 tablespoons of water or other liquid per yolk in a heavy saucepan and cook over very low heat, stirring constantly, until the mixture coats a metal spoon or reaches 160°F. Cool quickly (over an ice water bath if desired), and proceed with the recipe.

POWDERED EGG WHITES

To avoid any danger of salmonella contamination in egg whites, many home bakers, like commercial bakeries, are substituting pasteurized powdered dried egg whites. There are several products on the market, some available in specialty gourmet shops or baker's catalogues (see mail-order sources, page 363), others in supermarkets. One that I use is Wilton Meringue Powder, sold wherever cake baking supplies are. With this product, Wilton recommends using 2 teaspoons of meringue powder plus 2 tablespoons water to make the equivalent of 1 large egg white; sugar can be added as indicated in your recipe.

How to Separate Eggs

There are several easy techniques for separating eggs: The first and most common is to crack open the egg by sharply tapping its center against the edge of a bowl. Hold the half-shell containing the yolk upright in one hand while you pour the egg white from the other half-shell into a cup. Then tip the yolk out into the empty half-shell over the cup while the white that surrounds it falls into the cup. Go back and forth once more if necessary, then place the yolk, minus all the white, in another cup. The second method is fun, especially for children, who don't mind getting their hands sticky. Crack the egg, then hold it over a bowl and pull the halves apart, simultaneously turning one half-shell upright so it contains the entire egg. Holding this full half-shell with one hand, discard the empty half-shell, then turn your empty hand palm up and dump the whole egg into it. Spread your fingers slightly and let the white slip through them into a bowl below while the yolk remains cradled in your palm; put the yolk into another cup. The third method is to use a separating gadget: a metal or plastic disk with a ring-shaped slot surrounding a central depression. Break the egg onto the disk so that the yolk is trapped on the center pad and hold it upright while the white slides through the slot into a cup below. Place the yolk in another cup.

Salt

Common table salt, or sodium chloride, is the type used in baking. It enhances flavors and improves taste, aids digestibility, and strengthens gluten in yeast products. When salt is omitted in baked goods, they taste flat; keeping in mind today's health concerns, I have reduced the salt slightly in some of the recipes, but retained the amount necessary for good taste. Always bake with unsalted butter so you can be in control of the amount of salt added to your baked goods; different brands of butter contain varying amounts of salt.

Sugar and Other Sweeteners

In baking, sugar provides sweetness, helps the creaming and whipping of air into batters, and contributes tenderness, texture, and color. When it is cooked, sugar caramelizes, adds a special flavor, and aids in browning. Sugar, sugar syrups, molasses, and honey attract and absorb moisture, which helps keep baked goods moist and fresh.

Sugar has the potential to slow down the development of gluten, the elastic portion of the protein in wheat flour. When there is a lot of sugar in a dough, the gluten-forming proteins cling to the sugar rather than to each other, preventing the development of the stretchy network that holds gases produced by leavening agents. Cookies and pastries contain a relatively high proportion of sugar compared to bread dough, so there is very little gluten development and very tender texture.

A small amount of sugar can be added to pie pastry without changing its texture. However, be aware that the more sugar you add, the more fragile and crumbly the dough becomes. Pastry with as much as ⅓ to ½ cup sugar tastes like a sugar cookie and is perfect for a rich tart crust, but you may have to pat the dough into the pie plate or tart pan with your fingers because it will be quite crumbly.

Granulated and superfine sugars should be sifted only if they have become lumpy or caked. Confectioners' sugar should always be sifted before use.

White Sugar

The most common sugar used in baking is sucrose, a natural sugar found in plants. Sucrose is available to the baker as white or brown sugar or molasses. Each type comes from a different stage in the refining process. White sugar is available in crystal sizes ranging from regular granulated to superfine (also called ultrafine or bar sugar) to 10X confectioners'. Crystal size determines how fast the sugar will dissolve; superfine dissolves very quickly and is thus good for meringues. You can make your own superfine sugar by whirling regular granulated sugar in a food processor. British castor sugar is an extra-fine granulated type; British icing sugar is the same as confectioners' sugar.

Confectioners' Sugar

Confectioners' sugar is granulated sugar ground to a specific degree of fineness. 10X is generally the grade for home baking use; 4X and 6X are used commercially. In France, it is common to use confectioners' sugar interchangeably with granulated sugar in pastry dough; in fact, confectioners' sugar is often preferred because of its softer quality. Each 1-pound box of confectioners' sugar contains approximately 3 percent cornstarch, added to prevent lumping and crystallization. It is the cornstarch that gives powdered sugar a raw taste that is best masked with flavorings or through cooking. Since it dissolves so quickly, confectioners' sugar is used for meringues, icings, and confections.

Brown Sugar

The darker brown the sugar, the more molasses and moisture it contains, and the more intense the flavor; light brown sugar has a honey-like taste. Turbinado sugar, sold in natural foods shops and supermarkets, has a coarse granulation and a variable moisture content; it is unpredictable as a baking ingredient but can be used as topping. Both light and dark brown sugar have the same sweetening power as an equal *weight* of white sugar, although the white sugar is more dense; to achieve equal sweetness, brown sugars must be firmly packed before measuring by volume. Brown sugar is added to baked goods, streusel or crumb toppings, and icings for color, flavor, and moisture. Brown sugar can dry out and become lumpy or hard when exposed to air. To prevent this, store it in a covered glass jar or heavy-duty zip-lock plastic bag. If the sugar hardens despite your efforts, add a slice of apple to the storage container for a few days, or sprinkle on a few drops of water. To make 1 cup of your own dark brown sugar if you only have white on hand, add 4 tablespoons unsulfured molasses to 1 cup granulated sugar.

Molasses

Molasses is the liquid separated from sugar during the first stages of refining. The color and strength of the molasses depends upon the stage at which it is produced. "First" molasses is drawn off in the first centrifuging process and is the finest quality. "Second" molasses has more impurities, and the third stage, called "blackstrap," is the blackest and has the strongest flavor. Most cooking molasses is the first type, blended with cane syrup to standardize quality. The best type of molasses for baking (and the one I recommend in this book) is called "unsulfured" because it is made from sugarcane that has not been treated with sulfur dioxide, a procedure used to clarify and lighten the color of cane juice but that also produces a sulfur taste many find disagreeable. To measure molasses easily, first oil the measuring cup so the sticky molasses will slide out.

HONEY

Honey contributes moistness, softness, chewiness, and sweetness to cakes and pastries. The flavor of honey varies depending upon the type of flowers visited by the bees and the area in which it was produced. While honey is not a sugar, it does have the same sweetening power. However, it cannot replace sugar entirely because it is a liquid and thus does not have the same function in a batter. Honey caramelizes quickly at a low temperature, giving a dark color to baked goods. Its degree of natural acidity varies, and baking soda is almost always used with it as a neutralizer.

For cake baking, use clear liquefied honey rather than a solid or comb form. To liquefy granular or hardened honey, place the opened jar on a rack in a pot of gently simmering water until the honey clarifies completely; flavor will not be altered.

To substitute honey for granulated sugar, use about ⅞ of the quantity of sugar called for and decrease the liquid in the recipe by 3 tablespoons per each cup of honey. One cup granulated sugar equals ⅞ cup (¾ cup plus 2 tablespoons) honey.

MAPLE SYRUP

Pure maple syrup comes from the sap of the sugar maple tree, which is boiled down until evaporated and thickened. It takes about 30 gallons of sap to produce 1 gallon of syrup. Grade A, or Fancy, syrup is light amber in color, delicate in flavor, and the most expensive. Grade B is darker brown and richer in flavor, but harder to find. Store opened syrup in the refrigerator. If you find mold forming on top, pour the syrup into a saucepan, heat just to boiling, and skim off the mold. Bring back to a quick boil, then cool and pour into a clean container.

Corn Syrup

Sweet corn syrup is made when the starch in corn kernels is broken down with acid or various enzymes. Corn syrup, made up of glucose from the natural sugar in the corn plus some added fructose and water, is useful in baking because of its sweetness as well as its other physical properties. Its viscosity enables it to help trap air bubbles in a whipped batter, aiding a cake's aeration. Corn syrup adds flavor, and because glucose browns at a lower temperature than other sugars, its presence can cause baked goods to brown quickly. Corn syrup imparts a chewy texture to baked goods and helps them remain moist, increasing their shelf life.

Chocolate and Cocoa

Chocolate really does grow on trees—the *Theobroma cacao* tree, to be exact, a native of South and Central America, and cultivated in Africa and Southeast Asia. Inside the pods of this tree are beans and pulp, which are scooped out, dried, fermented, and cured. The beans are roasted, then hulled, and the inner nibs, which contain about half cocoa butter, are crushed and ground in order to liquefy and draw off most of the cocoa butter. What remains is chocolate liquor, a dark brown paste that is further refined, churned, mellowed, and molded before it is solidified and sold as unsweetened or bitter chocolate. Varying proportions of sugar and cocoa butter are combined with this liquor to make the blends known as bittersweet, semisweet, and sweet chocolate. When dry milk solids are added, the result is milk chocolate.

Store all chocolate in a cool dry location at about 60°F. When chocolate is kept at a warmer temperature, you may see a gray or whitish surface coloring, called bloom, which is the cocoa butter rising to the surface. Bloom does not affect flavor and will disappear when the chocolate is melted. If chocolate is stored at excessively cold temperatures, it may sweat when brought to room temperature, introducing dreaded moisture droplets that will interfere with melting; therefore, do not store baking chocolate in the refrigerator or freezer.

Since the quality of chocolate is vital to the quality of the dessert, always use pure chocolate, not imitation. Read labels carefully. To mail-order fine chocolate, see Sources, page 363. Among my favorite brands are: unsweetened chocolate—Baker's, Nestle, and Guittard; semisweet—Baker's, Guittard, Callebaut, and Ghirardelli (Dark Sweet); bittersweet—Callebaut, Lindt (Excellence or Courante), Guittard, and Tobler Extra Bittersweet.

....

CHOCOLATE MEASURING GUIDE

2 tablespoons regular-size chocolate chips = 1 ounce solid chocolate, chopped
1 cup regular-size chocolate chips = 6 ounces
¼ cup unsweetened cocoa = 1 ounce

....

WHITE CHOCOLATE

White chocolate is not a true chocolate because it does not contain any chocolate liquor. It is actually a blend of whole milk and sugar, cooked, condensed, and solidified. In the best brands, some cocoa butter has been added to enhance the flavor. Other additives include whey powder, lecithin, vanilla, and egg whites. The finest quality white chocolate contains the highest proportion of cocoa butter and will list that ingredient first on the label. Brands with excellent flavor and smooth melting quality include Ghirardelli Classic White Confection, Ghirardelli Classic White Chips, and Baker's Premium White Chocolate Baking Squares (all available in supermarkets), as well as Guittard Vanilla Milk Chips, Lindt's Swiss White Confectionery Bar, Callebaut White Chocolate, and Tobler Narcisse.

HOW TO MELT DARK OR WHITE CHOCOLATE:

Unless handled carefully and melted over very low heat, chocolate can separate into cocoa butter and solids; it can also take on a cooked or scorched flavor. It is best to melt chocolate (which should be finely chopped) in the top of a double boiler set over hot (125°F; not boiling) water. Ideally, melt half or two thirds of the chocolate, then remove it from the heat and stir in the remaining chocolate until it melts. Dark chocolate should not be heated above 120°F, or it may turn grainy. White chocolate is even more fragile. It must be melted, stirring, over warm to medium-hot water so it does not get above 110° to 115°F, or it will crystallize and look lumpy, grainy, and dry.

Be careful not to get a drop of water or other liquid in any chocolate as it melts, or the chocolate will seize and harden. If this happens, the chocolate is not always salvageable,

39

but sometimes you can smooth it out by stirring in 1 teaspoon Crisco or cocoa butter per each ounce of chocolate. (To combine liquid and chocolate without seizing, you must add a *minimum* of one tablespoon water per two ounces chocolate). To avoid the moisture problem entirely, you can melt chopped dark chocolate in a microwave-safe bowl on medium-low (50%) power for 20- to 30-second intervals (for milk or white chocolate, use 30% power); check and repeat until melted, then stir well until smooth. Pay attention, because chocolate will not always lose its shape as it melts in the microwave; you must stir it to check the consistency. It can also burn easily.

Cocoa

To make cocoa, chocolate liquor is pressed a second time to remove more than half of the remaining cocoa butter. The result is a dry cake of residue that is pulverized and sifted to make fine unsweetened cocoa powder. This natural processed cocoa, like chocolate, is acidic and has the fruity flavor of the cocoa bean. To neutralize some of the acid, and to darken and redden the color and give a somewhat richer flavor, cocoa may be Dutch-processed, or factory-treated with alkali. This name comes from the fact that a Dutchman, Coenraad van Houten, invented the process. Popular brands using this method are Droste, Van Houten, Fedora, and Hershey European (in a silver-colored container). The most widely available American brands, Hershey's (in a dark brown container) and Baker's, are "natural," not alkali-treated, so have a higher acidity. Both types can be used in recipes calling for baking soda, which interacts and neutralizes the acidity of the cocoa, but Dutch-processed cocoa requires less baking soda to neutralize it because it contains less acidity. Both types are good, but they are slightly different. It is important to use the specific type of cocoa called for in a recipe.

To substitute cocoa powder for solid unsweetened chocolate, use 3 level tablespoons natural (not Dutch-processed) cocoa plus 1 tablespoon solid vegetable shortening or unsalted butter for each 1 ounce unsweetened chocolate. (*Note:* Powdered or granulated instant cocoa drink mixes contain dry milk solids, sugars, and sometimes other additives and should never be substituted for unsweetened baking cocoa.)

Nuts

Many pie fillings and toppings call for toasted nuts. Toasting dries out the nuts, making them easier to grate or grind. It also intensifies their flavor. To toast, spread nuts in a shallow pan and bake in a preheated 325°F oven for 10 to 15 minutes, or until aromatic and a slightly darker color. Toss or stir once or twice for even coloring. You can also toast nuts until aromatic and golden in a frying pan set over medium-low heat.

To remove skins from hazelnuts, wrap the toasted nuts in a textured towel for several minutes to steam, then rub off the skins.

To remove skins from whole almonds, cover them with water in a small saucepan and boil for 2 or 3 minutes. Drain. Cool the nuts in cold water, then pinch off their skins.

Gelatin

In the United States, unflavored gelatin is most commonly used in dry granulated form, sold to the home baker in envelopes, containing a scant 2¼ teaspoons (¼ ounce, 7 grams), which will set 2 cups liquid (1⅛ teaspoons gelatin per cup). For ease in measuring and storing, I like to empty several envelopes into a screw-top jar. The actual amount of gelatin needed depends upon the particular recipe; as a general rule, I use a little less than average, about 1 teaspoon per cup of liquid, for a more tender set. Always use level measures and follow amounts carefully. Ideally, a pie made with gelatin should be melt-in-your-mouth creamy but still hold an edge when sliced.

Envelopes of gelatin are not freshness-dated, and in my experience, the product seems to lose strength after about 2 years on the shelf; if you are not sure about the age of your gelatin, throw it away and replace it.

To dissolve dry granulated gelatin, sprinkle it on top of a small amount of cool or warm liquid (water, fruit juice, coffee, or wine) in a small saucepan. Let it sit for 2 to 3 minutes so the granules can soften and swell. Then set over low heat and stir for about 2 or 3 minutes, or until the granules dissolve completely. Do not let the mixture boil, or it will lose some of its setting power. In a clear liquid, any undissolved granules will be visible, but to be sure the gelatin is totally dissolved, pinch a drop of the mixture between your fingers—it should feel smooth. Soaked and swollen granules can also be stirred into a very hot liquid or custard and stirred until dissolved. To dissolve gelatin in a microwave, sprinkle the granules over cold water in a glass measuring cup and let stand for 2 minutes to soften. Microwave at 100% power (high) for 40 seconds, stir, and let stand for 2 minutes longer, or until completely dissolved. If some granules remain, microwave for 5-second intervals. Desserts set with gelatin require 3 to 4 hours of refrigeration to set enough to serve.

In Europe, gelatin is most commonly used in leaves or sheets (about $2\frac{7}{8} \times 8\frac{1}{2}$ inches each, but sizes vary). To reconstitute the sheets, available in bakers' supply shops in the United States (see Sources, page 363), cover them with cold water and soak for 10 to 30 minutes (follow package directions). Then squeeze them to release the soft gelatin, and stir the gelatin into a warm mixture or liquid. The exact ratio of conversion from sheets to granulated gelatin depends upon the size of the gelatin sheets, but the average is 4 to 5 sheets per 1 envelope (scant $2\frac{1}{4}$ teaspoons) dry granulated gelatin.

Gelatin cannot be used with certain tropical fruits because they contain enzymes that soften and dissolve protein molecules, preventing the gelatin from setting. These fruits include fresh figs, kiwis, papayas, pineapples, honeydew melons, fresh ginger, and prickly pears. However, all except kiwis can be used with gelatin if they are first cut up and boiled for about 5 minutes to break down the offending enzymes. Highly acidic fruits may also weaken gelatin's setting power and require slightly more gelatin to hold a set.

Gelatin is a natural animal by-product derived from collagen, the protein found in bones and connective tissue. Vegetarian substitutes, available in natural foods stores, include agar-agar, a jelling product from Japan made from seaweed, available in crystallized powder or gel, and pectins such as Pomona's Universal Pectin, made from natural pectins without sugar. To use, follow package directions. Kosher gelatin, formulated with vegetable gums, is available from Kojel Food Company, Inc. (see Sources, page 363).

HIGH-ALTITUDE BAKING

When I teach baking at altitudes above 3000 feet, I am always concerned about whether my New England recipes will perform properly. If you live and bake at high altitudes, you won't be surprised to hear that when I bake in Denver, for example, some of my recipes require no changes at all but others need a variety of adjustments. There are no all-purpose hard-and-fast rules. It is best to try your favorite baked recipes at high altitude once exactly as written to see how they behave before tinkering with them. Most piecrusts and cookies may work perfectly or need just a few more drops of liquid; cake recipes usually need more help.

At 3000 feet above sea level, adjustments must usually be made in baking techniques because of the low humidity in the atmosphere and the decrease in air pressure. The higher the altitude, the more adjustments are needed. Low humidity causes flour to be drier; thus it will absorb more liquid. A recipe may need less flour, or more liquid, to maintain proper consistency. Storing flour in moisture-proof containers does not solve the problem.

Decreasing atmospheric pressure causes gases to expand more easily. In cake baking, decreased atmospheric pressure can have a dramatic effect: The leavening powers of baking powder and soda are infused with such enthusiasm they can cause a cake to rise until it literally bursts—and then collapses. To prevent this, try decreasing the amount of leavening slightly. Meringue toppings and meringue (angel) pie shells as well as angel and sponge cakes depend for leavening upon whipped air, which, like leavening, tends to go too far too fast. The remedy: Whip whites to medium-soft peaks instead of stiff peaks. You can also add strength with a bit more flour and a bit less sugar. And if you increase the baking temperature by 15 to 25 degrees, the batter may be able to set before the air bubbles or leavening gases become too expansive.

As altitude increases, both air pressure and the boiling point of water decrease. At sea level, water boils at 212°F; at 3000 feet above sea level, at 207°F; and at 5000 feet, at 203°F. The result is that more water evaporates during the baking process so baked goods tend to dry out. In a piecrust or cake, this can mean little moisture and comparatively too much sugar, which can weaken cell structure; in extreme cases, this alone can cause a cake to fall. Cutting back sugar and/or adding a little liquid usually helps. If your pastry recipes are disappointing, try cutting back slightly on leavening and sugar and/or add a bit of liquid and a pinch of flour.

For specific recommendations for your altitude, consult the Agricultural Extension Service of a nearby university. Your local library, bookstore, or cookware shop probably stocks hometown cookbooks and surely will be a resource for finding cooks and bakers willing to share practical advice.

GENERAL TIPS FOR ADAPTING SEA LEVEL PASTRY RECIPES TO ALTITUDES ABOVE 3000 FEET:

· Reduce the sugar in your recipe 1 to 3 tablespoons per each cup of sugar used
· Increase the liquid by 1 to 4 tablespoons
· Reduce each teaspoon of baking powder by $\frac{1}{8}$ to $\frac{1}{4}$ teaspoon
· Increase oven temperature by about 25°F

THE BASICS OF PASTRY MAKING

Promises and pie-crust are made to be broken.

JONATHAN SWIFT,
Polite Conversation

All-Purpose Flaky Pastry

Unlike a broken promise, the breaking of this crust is a cause for celebration; it is delicious, tender, and flaky. The recipe is foolproof; the equivalent of the French *pâte brisée*, or "short paste," it is the best recipe for beginning bakers, but it will also satisfy the experienced pastry chef. When sugar is added, it becomes *pâte brisée sucrée*. With the addition of sugar and egg yolk, it is known as *pâte sablée*, "sandy paste," or *Mürbeteig* in German.

All-Purpose Flaky Pastry
for
Two-Crust 9-Inch Pie

. . . .

This recipe makes enough dough to comfortably fit a two-crust 9-inch pie with a generous edge to flute. If, however, you wish to have extra dough for cutout pastry decorations, use the larger recipe that follows (3 cups flour). When measuring flour, be sure to spoon it lightly into the cup, then level it off with a straightedge.

For extra-flaky texture plus great taste, I always use a combination of butter and chilled Crisco, but you can use all butter (the taste will still be excellent, the degree of flakiness slightly reduced). If you're making the pastry in the food processor, freeze the butter and shortening. The egg yolk contains natural lecithin, which helps make the dough easy to handle, and the lemon juice or vinegar slows development of the gluten, to insure a tender crust. For fruit and berry pies, I like to add a little granulated sugar (about ¾ to 1 tablespoon per cup of flour); sifted confectioners' sugar can be substituted.

Flavor variations and the preparation techniques for hand, electric mixer, and food processor follow these ingredients lists.

YIELD: For one two-crust 9-inch pie, one 11- or 12-inch pie or tart shell, or nine to ten 4-inch tartlets

> 2½ cups unsifted all-purpose flour
> 2 to 2½ tablespoons granulated sugar, optional
> ¾ teaspoon salt
> 10 tablespoons (1¼ sticks) cold or frozen unsalted butter, cut up
> 3 tablespoons cold or frozen shortening (Crisco or solid stick
>   margarine)
> 1 large egg yolk
> 1 tablespoon fresh lemon juice or white vinegar
> 3 to 4 tablespoons ice water, or as needed

All-Purpose Flaky Pastry

for

Two-Crust 10-Inch Pie or Two-Crust 9-Inch Pie Plus Pastry Decorations

. . . .

YIELD: For one two-crust 9-inch pie plus pastry decorations, one two-crust 10-inch pie, three 8-inch pie shells, or twelve to thirteen 4-inch tartlets

- 3 cups unsifted all-purpose flour
- 2 to 3 tablespoons granulated sugar, optional
- 1 teaspoon salt
- 12 tablespoons (1½ sticks) cold or frozen unsalted butter, cut up
- 6 tablespoons (¾ stick) cold or frozen shortening (Crisco or solid stick margarine)
- 1 large egg yolk
- 2 tablespoons fresh lemon juice or white vinegar
- 3 to 5 tablespoons ice water, or as needed

All-Purpose Flaky Pastry
for
Single-Crust Pie or Tart Shell
. . . .

YIELD: For one 9-, 10-, or 11-inch pie or tart shell or eight 3-inch tartlets

> 1½ cups unsifted all-purpose flour
> 1 to 1½ tablespoons granulated sugar, optional
> ½ teaspoon salt
> 6 tablespoons (¾ stick) cold or frozen unsalted butter, cut up
> 3 tablespoons cold or frozen shortening (Crisco or solid stick margarine)
> 1 large egg yolk
> 2 teaspoons fresh lemon juice or white vinegar
> 3 to 4 tablespoons ice water, or as needed

Basic Flaky Pastry Variations:

The quantities given below are for All-Purpose Flaky Pastry made with 2½ cups flour. If you are changing the amount of flour in your recipe, change these variations proportionately: i.e., increase them slightly for the 3-cup recipe; halve the amounts for 1 cup flour; reduce them only slightly for 1½ cups.

Nut Pastry.
Add ½ cup finely chopped or ground nuts (almonds, peanuts, hazelnuts, pecans, Brazil nuts) as part of the dry ingredients.

Sesame Seed Pastry.
Toast ⅓ cup hulled sesame seeds in a frying pan, stirring constantly, over medium heat *just* until the seeds are fragrant and golden. Add as part of the dry ingredients.

Coconut Pastry. Add ½ cup sweetened flaked coconut along with the dry ingredients.

Orange or Lemon Pastry. Use 3 tablespoons fresh orange or lemon juice as part of the liquid and add 1 tablespoon grated orange or lemon zest along with the dry ingredients.

Chocolate Pastry. Add 4½ tablespoons unsweetened cocoa, sifted, plus ¼ cup packed light brown sugar along with the dry ingredients.

Cheddar Cheese Pastry. Add ½ cup grated sharp natural Cheddar cheese just after the shortening is cut into the dough.

Herb Pastry. Add 2 teaspoons celery seeds or 1 tablespoon mixed dried herbs (e.g., thyme, marjoram, dill, parsley, celery seeds) along with the dry ingredients.

Sherry Pastry. Substitute dry sherry for all the liquid in the recipe.

Wheat Germ Pastry. Add 3 tablespoons toasted wheat germ to the dry ingredients.

Basic Pastry Preparation Technique

BASIC HAND PREPARATION TECHNIQUE

Combine the dry ingredients (flour, salt, optional sugar) in a large bowl and whisk to blend. Add the cut-up chilled fat (butter, Crisco, or solid stick margarine). Working quickly and lightly, pinch and slide lumps of dough between your fingertips until the mixture resembles dry rice. This process layers the shortening and flour together, creating "leaves" that will form flakes when baked. Cool fingertips are used instead of the warmer palms of your hands because warmth would melt the shortening, which could then be absorbed by the flour, causing the dough to toughen. The rule: Keep everything as cold as possible. Instead of fingertips, you can also use a wire pastry blender, a fork, or two cross-cutting table knives.

Add the yolk, lemon juice or vinegar, and the minimum amount of iced water. Take care not to overwork the dough, lest you develop its elasticity. Lightly toss the dough until it *just* begins to cling together in clumps but has not begun to form a ball. Sprinkle on a tiny bit more water if the dough looks too dry. The dough should cling together and feel pliable like clay, but not be sticky. If you catch the dough at this point, you will not have over-worked the pastry. At this stage, you can go directly to step 3, make a ball of dough, and chill it, or you can further layer together the fat and flour and increase flakiness by a technique known in French as *fraisage:* Break off a small lump of dough, put it under the heel of your hand on the counter, and push on the dough as you slide it forward about 4 inches. Scrape up and set aside that piece of dough and repeat with the remaining dough. Gather all the dough together.

Turn the dough out onto a sheet of wax paper. Lift the paper's opposite corners and press them together, squeezing the dough into a cohesive ball. Flatten the ball into a 6-inch disk for a single pie shell, or divide in half and make two disks for a 2-crust pie. Wrap dough and refrigerate before rolling for at least 30 minutes, but the longer the better—up to several hours or even overnight. (Or the wrapped dough can be refrigerated for 3 to 4 days or double-wrapped airtight and frozen for up to 6 months.) Chilling allows the glutinous, or elastic, properties of the flour to relax and helps prevent the dough from shrinking during baking. (*Note:* Allow the chilled dough to sit out at room temperature a few minutes to soften it slightly before rolling it out.) To roll out, form, and bake the dough, see pages 52–70.

Electric Mixer Method

Read the Basic Hand Preparation Technique, above. If your mixer is so equipped, fit it with the paddle attachment; otherwise, use regular beaters. Add the flour, salt, and the sugar, if you are using it, to the mixing bowl. Beat for 30 seconds to blend, then add the cut-up fat. Beat on low speed until the mixture forms rice-sized bits.

A little at a time, add the yolk, lemon juice or vinegar, and the minimum amount of ice water. Beat on low-medium speed only until the dough *begins* to pull away from the bowl sides and starts to clump together. Sprinkle on a tiny bit more water only if the dough looks too dry. Do not allow a ball of dough to form. Turn the dough out onto a piece of wax paper and form it into a ball, flatten it into a 6-inch disk, wrap it, and refrigerate for at least 30 minutes, or several hours or overnight. To roll out, form, and bake the dough, see pages 52–70.

Food Processor Method

Read the Basic Hand Preparation Technique, above. Freeze or hard-chill the butter and shortening, then cut it up into small pieces. Add the flour, salt, and the sugar, if you are using it, to the work bowl fitted with the steel blade. Cover the bowl and pulse quickly (short on-off spurts) 2 or 3 times, to lighten the dry ingredients.

Uncover the bowl and add the cut-up fat. Pulse for 5 to 10 seconds, until the dough has the texture of rough cornmeal.

Add the egg, lemon juice or vinegar, and the minimum amount of ice water through the feed tube and pulse 2 to 3 times. Add more liquid only if the dough seems powdery, following each addition by 2 quick pulses. Watch the dough carefully at this stage, and stop the machine the instant the dough starts to clump together. It will still look rough and lumpy, and you will see specks of yolk and butter. This is normal. Lift the cover and pinch the dough between your fingers. If the dough holds together, it is done. Do not allow a dough ball to form on the machine blade, or the pastry will be overworked and tough.

Turn the dough out onto a piece of wax paper. Lift the opposite corners of the paper and press on the dough, forming it into a ball, then press it into a 6-inch disk. Wrap the dough and refrigerate for at least 30 minutes, or several hours or overnight. To roll out, form, and bake the dough, see pages 52–70.

51

ROLLING, FITTING, SHAPING, AND BAKING PIE AND TART CRUSTS

. . . .

PREPARATION AND ROLLING OUT OR PRESSING DOUGH

After the dough has been chilled until firm, it is ready to be rolled out. Set the disk of dough in the center of a lightly floured work surface. Sprinkle the top of the dough with a little flour, and rub some flour onto the rolling pin. Remember that too much flour toughens dough; use only enough to prevent sticking.

Roll out the dough with short, even strokes, working from the center of the dough disk to the edges. Lift the rolling pin as you approach the dough edges; rolling over the edges thins the dough too much. To keep the dough from sticking and to make an even circle, lift and turn the dough disk after every few strokes, tossing a fine dusting of flour beneath the dough if needed. If the dough sticks to the work surface, use a dough scraper or spatula to ease it up. Roll the dough to a ⅛-inch thickness, or as specified in the recipe, and 2 to 3 inches larger across than the pie or tart baking pan—you can set the pan upside down over the dough to measure; the extra width insures enough dough to flute the pie edge. For example, a two-crust 9-inch pie needs 2 circles of dough roughly 12 inches in diameter, but a single-crust 9-inch pie shell should be about 12½ inches, to allow you to fold under an edge of dough sufficiently thick to hold a decorative flute (page 57).

If the pastry dough is oily, very soft, or crumbly, it can be most easily rolled out between two lightly floured sheets of wax paper or plastic wrap. If the paper wrinkles, lift and reposition it occasionally. To keep the paper from slipping, lightly dampen the work surface beneath it. Dough of any consistency, but particularly soft or problem doughs, can also be rolled out easily on a floured cotton pastry cloth with a flour-rubbed cloth sock, or stocking, on the rolling pin.

If the dough feels too soft to roll, you can chill it for an extra 30 minutes, or simply press it into the baking pan with your floured fingertips. Nut and high-sugar crusts are especially crumbly and best shaped in this way. If the dough sticks to your fingers, cover it with plastic wrap before pressing out.

A Note About Buttering Baking Pans

Tarts are served freestanding, out of their pans, and must be able to be easily unmolded. Thus, tart pans and flan rings set on flat baking sheets should be well buttered before they are lined with pastry. Pie plates do not have to be buttered; however, buttering aids in the quick browning of pastry, so it is optional.

53

Fitting Dough into Pie Plates or Tart Pans

If you have rolled the dough out on a floured countertop or a pastry cloth, use a dough scraper or spatula to help lift the edges of rolled dough. Once the dough is released from the counter, fold it in half onto itself, then into quarters. Pick up this folded dough triangle and position it over the baking pan so the center point of the triangle is in the center of the pan. Unfold the dough, allowing it to drape evenly across the pan. Alternatively, you can roll the dough up onto the rolling pin, lift it into place, and unroll it over the pan.

If you have rolled the dough between sheets of wax paper, peel off the top sheet, lift the dough on its backing paper, and center it upside down over the baking pan. Lower the dough into place and peel off the backing paper, which is now on top.

Once the dough is positioned over the pan, pick up one edge of the dough and ease it down so the dough fits flat along the bottom and up the sides of the pan. Go all around the pan, easing in the dough. Press out air pockets with your fingertips or a small dough ball dipped in flour. *Never* stretch dough to fit, or it will shrink during baking. If there are any holes or tears in the dough, dab water on the edges, then press on a scrap of rolled dough to make a patch. Leaving a ¾- to 1-inch dough overhang all around the edge, cut away excess dough

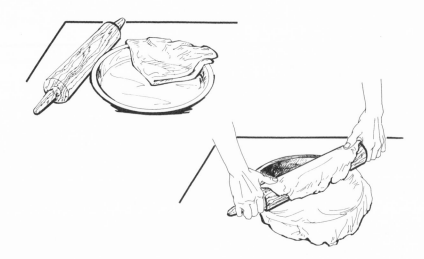

with a sharp knife or kitchen shears. Refrigerate or freeze dough scraps for tartlets, save
for trimming, or add to the top crust of a double-crust pie.

To Shape Dough for a Two-Crust Pie

Prepare the dough, following the recipe of your choice. For a two-crust pie, refrigerate
one half the dough while lining the pan with the other as described above.

Following the directions in your specific recipe, moisture-proof the lower crust with egg
glaze (egg beaten with 1 tablespoon water) if desired, then add the pie filling. For the top
crust, combine any dough scraps with the remaining chilled dough if desired and roll it
out into a circle as you did previously. For a fruit pie, you can cut steam vents in the top
piece of dough (page 59) now or after the top crust is in place. Moisten the rim of the lower
crust by brushing on water or egg glaze. Fold the rolled-out top crust in half or quarters,
lift it, and position it over the filled pie, or use a rolling pin to lift up and position the
crust. Trim a ¾-inch overhang on the top crust. Fold the top crust edge around and under
bottom crust edge and press them together to seal, then pinch the edges up into a raised
rim all around. Crimp or flute as desired (page 56). Cut steam vents now if you haven't already done so. (*Note*: If you are freezing the pie before baking, do not glaze or cut any
steam vents at this time.) To freeze the pie before or after baking, see page 71.

If you wish, glaze the top of the pie with brushed-on milk or egg glaze (page 65) and sprinkle with sugar, for a richly golden crisp crust. Follow the specific baking directions in your recipe, or see page 65.

To Shape Dough for a Single-Crust Pie or Tart Shell

Prepare the dough according to the recipe of your choice. Following the directions on pages 53–54, roll out the dough, position it in the pan, and trim a ¾-inch overhang.

For a Single-Crust Pie Shell. Fold under the dough overhang, making a double-layered edging even with the rim of the pie plate. Then pinch the edge up into a raised rim all around and crimp or flute as desired (page 56). At this point, the pastry-lined pan can be wrapped and frozen (page 71) or baked as explained below.

For a Tart Shell. Use a removable-bottom tart pan or a flan ring set on a baking sheet. Generously butter the inside of the pan or ring. After lining the pan with dough and trimming the ¾-inch overhang, fold it inward, and press the two edges together against the pan sides to compress and seal them. The double-thick edge gives the strength needed by a tart or flan because it is to be removed from the supporting pan before serving; since the filling presses outward, the pastry edging will be under stress and may crack if very thin. Then to cut off excess dough and to compress the edging, roll a rolling pin over the top of the pan. Lift off any dough bits caught on the pan's outer edge. Pinch up the dough edge into a straight-sided lip about ¼ inch high. Do not let this lip bend over. Crimp the top surface of the lip with a pastry pincher tool or score with slanted lines at ¼-inch intervals with the back of a paring knife. At this point, the pastry-lined pan should be chilled until the dough is firm, then it can be wrapped and frozen (page 71) or filled and baked.

To Unmold Tarts from Flan Pans and Tart Pans

To remove a flan ring after baking and cooling a tart, simply lift it directly up off the tart. The pastry will have shrunk during baking, separating it from the ring. Use a broad spatula to ease the tart off the baking sheet onto a flat serving platter. (*Note:* Single-crust pies are served directly from their baking pans.)

After baking and cooling a tart made in a removable-bottom pan, center the bottom over a wide-topped jar. The tart will remain on the metal bottom disk sitting on the jar, while the outer ring will fall down. Use a broad spatula to ease the tart off the bottom disk onto a flat serving platter, or simply serve the tart from the disk.

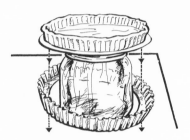

To Crimp or Flute Pastry Edges

This technique produces a decorative edging around a pie or tart. For two-crust pies, it also helps seal the layers of pastry together to prevent juices from escaping. There are a variety of styles.

Plain Fork Tines. This is the easiest edging to make. Form an even dough edge around the rim. Dip the tines of a table fork into flour, then press the tines into the dough at a right angle to the pan edge. Repeat all around.

Herringbone Fork Tines. Form an even dough edge around the rim. Press floured fork tines

into the dough rim on a diagonal. Then turn the fork 90 degrees and make the next depression beside the first. Continue so the lines alternate directions all around the rim.

Simple Flute. Form an even, raised dough edge around the rim. Place your left forefinger inside the pie rim and your right thumb and forefinger outside the rim. Press your fingers toward each other, forming the raised dough edge into a V. Repeat, making side-by-side Vs all around the rim. Turn the pie plate around after a series of Vs to get a better angle—it's easier than moving yourself. To make more pointed shapes, you can pinch together the tip of each V.

Deep Flutes. Form an even, raised dough edge around the rim. Make a 1-inch-wide U shape with the thumb and forefinger of one hand, pointing downward, and place them against the inside edge of the pastry-lined pie plate. Reach inside the U with the forefinger of your other hand and pull inward on the raised dough edge; simultaneously press the sides of the U to the outside, away from the pie center. Repeat, making another flute alongside the first. Continue around the plate. It may feel more comfortable to you to move the plate around after a few flutes rather than to reach across it to work.

Scallops. Form an even, raised dough edge around the rim. Make simple or deep flutes as above. Then press the floured tines of a fork into the flutes that rest on the plate rim. This is a good method for sealing juicy two-crust pies.

Rope. Make a neat, high-standing dough edge. Press your right thumb into the dough edge at an angle. Grip and squeeze the dough between your thumb and the knuckle of your forefinger. Repeat, keeping your thumb at an angle and making a ropelike edging all around.

Leaf Edging. With tiny hors d'oeuvre cutters or a sharp knife, cut out ¾- to 1-inch-long oval leaves from rolled dough scraps. Press veins into the leaves with the back edge of a floured table knife. Moisten the dough on the rim of the pie with brushed-on beaten egg glaze or water. Position the leaves in an overlapping pattern around the edge. Glaze the tops of the leaves with egg wash before baking.

STEAM VENTS AND SLITS

To allow steam to escape from juicy two-crust pies or any moist filling wrapped in a crust, steam vents or slits are cut into the top crust. The vents can be plain or fancy.

Snowflake Cut. After rolling out the top crust, fold it into quarters. With kitchen shears or a sharp knife, cut two parallel slits 1 inch apart and 1 inch long into each folded side. Unfold the crust and position it over the filling. The cut slits will make symmetrical double Vs in a square pattern.

FOLD

FOLD

Free-form Cuts. After rolling out the top crust, use the tip of a sharp paring knife to cut a freehand circle, heart, flower, or letter shape from the center of the dough. Or cut a shape with an hors d'oeuvre or aspic cutter. Then position the dough over the filling.

FREE-FORM CUT

Direct Cuts. After rolling out the top crust and positioning it over the filling, cut a round ³/₄-inch hole into the center of the top crust with the tip of a sharp paring knife. Then you can make diagonal slashes around the pie, halfway out from the center.

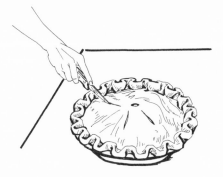

LATTICE TOPPING

Dough strips can be crisscrossed or woven into a lattice to make a decorative topping for fruit pies or tarts. Lattice tops require the same amount of dough as a plain two-crust pie.

Prepare pastry for two-crust pie. Roll out the bottom crust, fit it into the pan, trim lower edge, moisture-proof, if desired, and add the filling. Trim the lower dough edge to a ³/₄-inch overhang. Roll out the second crust to the same size as the first (2 to 3 inches bigger than the pan). (*Note:* Roll this top dough slightly thicker than usual, a generous ¹/₈ inch, for ease in handling.) If you have rolled the dough between sheets of wax paper, peel off the top sheet. With a plain or fluted pie jagger, by eye or using a ruler as a guide, cut ¹/₂-inch-wide (or wider, if you prefer) strips of dough. Following the instructions below, form the lattice. The longest strips, cut from the center, go across the center of the pie, the shorter strips go across the edges. After forming the lattice, glaze it as you would a regular crust by brushing it with egg glaze.

Simple Lattice. This is a shortcut method, where strips are crisscrossed instead of being woven. Dampen the edge of the lower crust by brushing on a coating of beaten egg glaze or water. Position a row of cut dough strips about ¾ inch apart across the baking pan. Press the strip ends in place on the dough rim and pinch off the excess. Place the remaining strips at similar intervals in the *opposite* direction, so they cross the first strips at right angles. Attach and cut off the strip ends as before. Or, make a diamond lattice by positioning the second strips at an angle to make diamond-shaped holes. To complete, lift up the overhang of the bottom crust and press it onto the lattice strip ends to seal. Pinch the dough edge up into a raised rim and flute as desired (page 56).

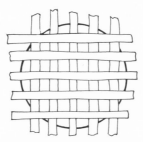

Curled Lattice. Cut dough strips slightly longer than for a plain lattice. Twist each strip four or five times as you set it in place on the pie.

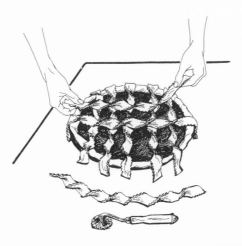

True Woven Lattice. The easiest method is to make this on a piece of lightly floured wax paper or foil, then position the woven strips directly over the pie and invert, setting the lattice in place and peeling off the backing paper. Alternatively, strips can be woven directly on the pie as follows.

Position dough strips evenly spaced across the top of the pie. Leave the strip ends over-hanging all around—these are called the side strips. Fold back in half side strips 2 and 4. To start the weave, select a long center strip from those still on the counter and place it across the center of the pie at a right angle to the side strips. Unfold the two side strips so they now overlap the central cross strip. Fold back side strips 1, 3, and 5 and add a second cross strip about ¾ inch from the first. Unfold the strips. Continue, folding back alternate side strips as you weave in the cross strips and working from the center of the pie out to each side. Trim the lattice ends to the edge of the pan.

Brush water or egg glaze on the rim of the lower crust, under the lattice ends, then fold the lower crust edge over the lattice ends and press to seal. Pinch the dough edge up into a raised rim and flute (page 56). Make a high fluted edge if needed to hold in the juices of a fruit pie.

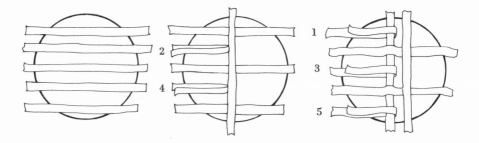

Free-form Lattice. Cut dough strips and arrange them in any pattern you like atop the pie. Try spelling out a name or initials, or make a spiral from the center out to the edge. Or make a series of wedges or Vs inside each other, pointing to the center of the pie.

QUICK MOCK LATTICE

Simple to prepare but fancy looking, a mock lattice topping is nothing more than over-lapped dough strips baked separately on foil. Before serving, this lattice is slid onto the top of the fruit pie that is baked with a flat (*not* fluted) pastry edge. If you love the look of a lattice but are intimidated by weaving dough strips on top of a pie filling, this never-fail trick is for you.

Prepare the pie pastry, line the pie plate with half the dough, fill, and bake the pie per the recipe. Make an egg glaze (1 whole egg beaten with a tablespoon of water) and set it aside. Roll out the remaining dough on a lightly floured surface, making a circle about 12 inches in diameter and ⅛ inch thick (just a tad thicker than for the bottom crust). With a pie jag-ger or a sharp knife held against a ruler, or by eye, cut the dough into 10 strips, each ap-proximately ¾ to 1 inch wide; start from the center of the rolled circle in order to cut long strips from the widest portion of the circle (a).

A

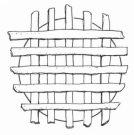

B

Spread Crisco or butter on the *dull* side of a 12- to 14-inch square of heavy-duty alu-minum foil or doubled regular foil. Invert a 9-inch pie plate onto the buttered foil and run a toothpick or your fingertip around the rim, marking its size.

Lift up one of the longest cut dough strips and place it in the center of the buttered foil circle. Then evenly space 2 strips to each side of the center. Brush the tops of each strip with egg glaze. Now place 5 more strips at right angles to the first strips, at similar inter-vals (b). Use your fingertips to press gently on the top strips to seal them to the ones below.

With a paring knife, cut around the edge of the marked foil circle and remove the excess dough strips. Brush the top strips with egg glaze.

To make an edging border around the lattice, cut the dough scraps into strips about ½ inch wide; reroll dough scraps if necessary. Press the strips onto the ends of the lattice following the marked circle (c), overlapping the ends of the strips. Press gently on this border to seal it to the strips below. Brush the border with egg glaze and sprinkle a little sugar over the entire lattice.

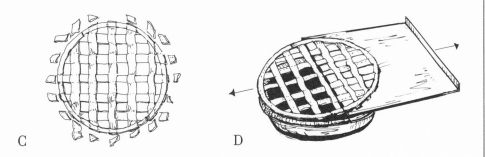

C   D

Slide the foil containing the lattice onto a cookie sheet and bake it in the center of a preheated 350°F oven for 13 to 15 minutes, or until the pastry is golden brown; it will bake much more quickly than a lattice on top of a pie, so keep peeking and remove it when the color is right. Slide the foil containing the lattice off the cookie sheet onto a wire rack or the counter to cool completely.

After the baked pie has cooled for at least 20 minutes, it is ready to receive the lattice topping. To do this, slide a flat edge of the cookie sheet beneath the lattice, working it free of the foil and lifting it up carefully. Hold the cookie sheet over the pie and gently slide the lattice off the sheet and into position on top of the pie (d).

Decorative Pastry Cutouts

Instead of topping a pie with a full upper crust or a lattice, try this creative and personal touch for any open-faced pie or tart, whether baked fruit or berries (blueberry, apple, cranberry) or unbaked chiffon (pumpkin chiffon): Use the dough for the top crust—or leftover dough—for shapes cut with cookie, aspic, or canapé cutters or drawn freehand with a paring knife. Use hearts, stars, flowers, letters of the alphabet, fruit shapes, leaves— any design appropriate to the pie filling, season, or special occasion.

For cutouts, roll out dough a generous ⅛ inch thick. Dip cookie cutters, or other cutters, in flour before using. To make freehand leaves, you can draw leaf shapes and cut them out of stiff paper; rub flour on the paper before placing it on the dough so it will not stick. Press veins into the dough leaves with the back of the knife blade. As you make the shapes, set them on a piece of buttered aluminum foil or baking parchment, then chill for a few minutes, until the dough is firm.

Before baking, brush the chilled cutouts with a light coating of egg glaze (1 whole egg or 1 egg white beaten with 1 tablespoon water), then sprinkle with a little granulated sugar.

Bake cutouts as if they were cookies, separately from the filled pie. Place the foil containing the cutouts on a cookie sheet and bake in a preheated 350°F oven for about 10 to 12 minutes, or until golden brown. If you've made them in advance, store them in a crush-proof airtight container. Shortly before serving, place the pastry cutouts on top of the pie or tart.

General Baking Notes

As a general rule, two-crust fruit pies are baked in the lower third of a preheated 425°F oven for about 12 to 15 minutes, then the heat is lowered to 350°F, the pie may be raised to a center shelf, and it is baked for 40 to 45 minutes longer, or until the filling is done. Be sure to check the pie when it is about half-baked and add a foil edging, or frame (page 22) if necessary, to protect the crust from overbrowning. Cool the pie on a wire rack.

Depending upon your specific recipe, a single-crust pastry shell can be either baked raw along with its filling or partially or completely baked in advance. To prevent the dreaded soggy bottoms or lower crusts that become soggy when a filling is moist, it is always best to partially prebake these shells. Before prebaking a tart shell, the prepared pastry can be pricked all over the bottom with the tines of a fork. Pricking holes permits steam to escape from unfilled baking dough and thus reduces its tendency to puff up. If filling will be very juicy, do not prick the shell or the filling will leak. All types of prepared shells and two-crust pies also benefit from being chilled for at least 30 minutes to firm the dough before baking. Cold relaxes the gluten, thereby helping to make the pastry tender, and prevent it from shrinking.

To Bake Empty Pastry Shells (Blind-Baking)

After being shaped and chilled, a pastry shell is ready to be baked. This is always done at first in the hottest part of the oven, the lower third, in order to set the pastry quickly and help make it flaky. The steam produced during the hot baking, however, sometimes causes the dough to puff up in spite of the pricked fork holes. To remedy this, you have several choices. You can simply peek in the oven from time to time, pierce any dough bubbles with a fork, and press down the dough with a pot holder, but the most effective and reliable method of preventing dough from puffing is to weight it down. To do this, cut a square of baking parchment or foil slightly larger than the baking pan and fit it into the unbaked pastry shell. Always use foil *shiny side down* so as not to deflect heat away from the pastry. Fill the liner about one-quarter full with pie weights (rice or beans or other weights used exclusively for this purpose, see page 17).

For a Partially Prebaked Shell. Bake the pricked and/or weighted shell in a preheated 425°F oven for about 12 minutes. Remove the liner and weights, if any. Brush the shell with moisture-proofing glaze if called for in your recipe. Replace the shell in the oven and continue baking for an additional 3 to 5 minutes, or until the dough is no longer translucent but not yet golden brown. Cool on a wire rack. This shell will be filled and baked again.

For a Completely Prebaked Shell. Bake the pricked and/or weighted shell in preheated 425°F oven for about 12 minutes. Remove the liner and weights, if used. Lower the heat to 350°F and continue baking for an additional 10 to 15 minutes, or until the pastry looks golden brown. Look in the oven occasionally to observe the color; do not overbake. Brush the hot shell with moisture-proofing glaze if called for in your recipe. Cool on a wire rack. This shell will not be baked again.

To Moisture-Proof Partially or Completely Baked Pastry Shells. When shells are to be filled with particularly juicy fruits or liquid mixtures, you can prevent them from becoming soggy by giving them a moisture-proof coating. According to the specific recipe, you will be instructed to brush the shell, before filling, with warm fruit preserves, Plain Fruit Glaze (page 153), or egg glaze (a whole egg beaten with 1 tablespoon water). Or you can lightly caramelize the inside of the shell by sprinkling it with a little granulated sugar mixed with grated lemon or orange zest and heating it in the oven just until sugar begins to melt. As another alternative, certain chiffon pie fillings are complemented by a thin undercoating layer of melted semisweet chocolate brushed over the shell.

TO SHAPE AND BAKE TARTLETS OR FREESTANDING PASTRY SHELLS

Tartlet shells are almost always prebaked before filling. Any pastry recipe can be used, but traditionally the preferred ones are All-Purpose Flaky Pastry (page 45), Cream Cheese Pastry (page 90), and Rich Tart Pastry (page 88). Try adding the grated zest of a lemon or orange to tartlet dough for a delicious flavor.

Preparation. Tartlet molds come in all sizes and shapes, from fluted round cups to oval boats. Any type can be used. Tartlet shells can also be made by shaping dough over the cups of an upside-down muffin pan.

Make and chill the dough. Set out the molds and butter them well. Be sure to run a buttered fingertip into each groove of a fluted tin.

Rolling. Set the flattened disk of dough on a lightly floured surface and roll out with a floured rolling pin. Or roll between two sheets of lightly floured wax paper or plastic wrap, or on a flour-rubbed pastry canvas with a cloth-covered pin (see page 53). (*Note:* Too much flour makes dough tough; use only enough to prevent sticking. You can also dust the surface with sifted confectioners' sugar instead of flour.) The more sugar in the dough, the more quickly it tends to darken and burn. To avoid this possibility, roll very sweet dough slightly thicker than normal. If the dough feels too crumbly to roll, it can be pressed into the pans with your fingers.

Fitting. Place 6 small buttered molds side by side. Lift up the dough on the rolling pin and drape it over the tops of the molds. With a small dough ball dipped in flour, press the dough down into each mold, fitting it to the sides. Roll your pin over the mold tops to cut off excess dough. Use your fingertips to press the dough firmly into each mold, raising the top edge slightly above the rim of the mold. Chill until the dough is firm before baking.

To fit dough into medium or large buttered tartlet molds, with a cookie cutter or the floured rim of a glass, cut rounds about 2 inches larger than the diameter of the molds. Prick the dough all over with a fork. Then lift each dough round and fit it into a mold. Press out the air with a small floured ball of dough or your fingertips. Use your fingertips to press the dough firmly into the mold, raising the top edge slightly above the mold rim. Chill the dough until firm before baking.

To fit dough over the back sides of muffin cups, use a cookie cutter or the floured rim of a glass to cut dough rounds about 2 inches larger in diameter than the muffin cups. For a 3-inch cup, use a 5-inch dough round. Prick the dough all over with a fork. Then lift each dough round and fit it over the buttered back of a muffin cup. Press the dough firmly and pleat the edges to fit. Chill until the dough is firm before baking.

Weighting Tartlets for Blind-Baking. To keep the dough from puffing up in the heat of the oven, you can line each tartlet pan with a square of foil (shiny side down) and fill it with pie weights or some raw rice or dry beans used only for this purpose. Or you can fit a second mold of the same shape, with its bottom buttered, into the mold, sandwiching the dough in the middle. Or, instead of weighting the dough, you can simply prick any bubbles that appear during baking with a fork, then press the dough down with a pot holder. If you choose to do this, check progress in the oven regularly.

Baking Tartlets. For ease in handling, set groups of pastry-lined small tartlet molds on a flat baking sheet. Set them in a preheated 400°F oven and bake for about 5 to 6 minutes. Remove the foil and weights from the tartlets. For *partially baked* tartlet shells, bake *only* until the pastry loses translucence. For *completely baked* tartlet shells, continue baking for an additional 5 to 8 minutes, or *just* until the pastry looks golden brown and is completely baked through. Timing depends upon the type and thickness of the dough; larger tartlets can take 20 minutes. *Check the oven from time to time and bake by color, not by recipe.* Cool the molds slightly, then remove fully baked pastry shells and cool them on a wire rack. Do not unmold partially baked shells, since they will be baked again.

For dough molded over upside-down muffin cups, bake at 400°F for 5 to 8 minutes in all. With this method, gravity helps prevent the dough from puffing up, eliminating the need for weights. However, if you notice a bubble in the baking dough, prick and deflate it with a fork. Cool these cups right side up on a wire rack.

To Shape and Bake Freestanding Pastry Shells. You can make your own freestanding pastry shells by molding the dough (rolled out a generous ⅛ inch thick) over the back side of any buttered pan whose shape appeals to you—a ring mold or oval baking dish, for example. Or model your own "pan" from a triple thickness of heavy-duty foil. Turn the pan upside down, butter the bottom, and press the dough over it. Trim the rough edges, but leave them fairly high, since they tend to shrink. Prick the dough all over (bottom and sides) with a fork; if you are using foil for a "pan," be careful not to puncture it. Before baking, chill the dough on the pan until firm.

To bake, set the pastry-covered pan directly on a shelf in the lower third of a preheated 425°F oven and bake for about 4 to 5 minutes. Gravity usually prevents the dough from puffing up; however, occasionally it happens. If the dough is beginning to bubble up in places, pierce the bubbles with a fork very gently to release steam and deflate. Or press the bubbles down gently with a pot holder. If the bubbles still persist—this only works on real rather than foil "pans"—you can weight the baking pan with another plate of the same size, buttered on the bottom and filled with beans to make it heavy. Remove the weighted pan a few minutes before the end of baking time.

For a *partially baked* shell to be filled and baked again later, bake for a total of 6 to 8 minutes. For a *completely baked* shell that will not be baked again, bake for a total of 12 to

15 minutes, or until golden—exact time depending upon the thickness and type of dough. (*Note:* Freestanding shells bake slightly faster than bean-weighted pastry-lined shells.) Finally, lift the pastry shells completely off their molds and cool them upright on a wire rack. To moisture-proof these shells, brush with egg glaze (page 156) or Plain Fruit Glaze (page 153) before filling.

MOLDED SHELL WEIGHTED

MOLDED SHELL

UNMOLDED SHELL

ABOUT FREEZING PASTRY

Absolutely no pastry tastes as good after freezing as it does freshly baked. That said, I must add that freezing baked goods can be a great time-saver as well as a convenience when you are entertaining. You *can* freeze baked and unbaked pies, pie fillings, and piecrusts. Fruit, berry, and mince pies and tarts are the most successful candidates, along with most individually shaped, pastry-wrapped hors d'oeuvre. Pumpkin, squash, and certain types of chiffon pies freeze successfully as well. Opinion is divided about cream and custard pies, since their fillings can separate on freezing; I prefer not to freeze them. When freezing pies to be baked or reheated in the oven, use a metal pie plate or one that can go from freezer to oven.

Your Freezer

To protect your health as well as the quality of your frozen products, it is important to use an auxiliary freezer thermometer to monitor temperature levels. Check the manufacturer's directions as to temperatures. For a guideline, note that a fast-freeze shelf or section may be as low as −10° to −20°F, while the main section should be a constant 0°F to no higher than 5°F.

Packaging and Labeling
for the Freezer

Pies and pie shells to be frozen should be wrapped airtight in heavy-duty aluminum foil or freezer-weight plastic or coated paper. Check package labels to be sure the material you are using is freezer-weight. You can also use heavy-duty freezer-weight bags—but not the type supermarket fruit is packaged in, which is too thin. To protect pies, pie shells, and individual pastries or bite-sized hors d'oeuvre from being poked or dented on a freezer shelf, wrap them airtight as above, then store in a protective stiff plastic or cardboard box (waxed is best).

Every item placed in the freezer should be labeled, with date and quantity noted. Oil-based felt-tipped pens will mark easily on foil or plastic or paper. Freezer tape is a special product that will adhere at cold temperatures. If you use ordinary masking tape, mark labels on the package itself, not on the tape, which may fall off.

72

The Question: To Freeze
Before or After Baking?

There are two schools of thought on the question of whether to freeze pies before or after baking. Personally, I prefer to freeze before and bake the pie frozen. I find that the hot oven quickly sets the pastry, keeps it flaky, and prevents juices from penetrating the lower crust. Some bakers slightly increase the quantity of their pie thickener when freezing raw pies, but I only do so for especially juicy fruits (and I generally prefer tapioca to flour except for apple pie). You should note, however, that pies frozen before baking can be stored for a shorter time (4 months) than those baked first (6 months). The latter, after thawing and reheating, seem to me to have a less crisp pastry and less fresh flavor. My advice: Make two pies, perform your own test, and judge the results for yourself.

Freezing Two-Crust Fruit Pies

For especially juicy fruits or for any type of berries in 9- or 10-inch pie plates, use the full 3½ tablespoons quick-cooking tapioca or cornstarch for the thickener, rather than the minimum amount.

METHOD I:
FREEZING BEFORE BAKING

Follow any recipe for making a two-crust fruit pie. Flute the edges decoratively (page 56). Do not cut steam vents; do not glaze the pie top. Double-wrap the pie airtight in freezer-weight material, label, and freeze. If you want to glaze the pie top, apply egg glaze and a sprinkling of sugar before setting the pie in the oven. To bake a frozen unthawed pie, set it in the lower third of a preheated 450°F oven for 20 minutes. After the first 10 minutes, you can open the oven and cut steam vents in the top crust. Then lower the heat to 350°F and cover the pastry edges with a foil frame (page 22) if they seem to be browning too fast. Continue baking for an additional 40 to 45 minutes, or until the pastry is golden brown and fruit can be pierced with the tip of a knife. Cool on a wire rack.

METHOD II:
FREEZING AFTER BAKING

Follow any specific recipe for making a two-crust fruit pie. Flute the edges decoratively (page 56). Cut steam vents and glaze the pie top with egg glaze and sugar if desired. Bake according to the recipe instructions, or bake at 425°F for 15 minutes, then for an additional 40 to 45 minutes at 350°F. Cool on a wire rack. When the pie is completely cold, double-wrap it in freezer-weight material, label it, and freeze. To use, unwrap and thaw the pie; before serving, warm it for 15 to 20 minutes in a 350°F oven.

73

Freezing Do's and Don'ts

Do Not:
....

- top pies with meringue before freezing; do not freeze meringue at all *unless* baked until firm, because freezing toughens whipped egg whites.

- cut steam vents in the top crusts of fruit pies to be frozen before baking.

- glaze tops of fruit pies to be frozen before baking.

- freeze custard or cream pies unless so specified in the recipe.

- freeze cream cheese unless it is to be used in combination with other ingredients; freezing makes it grainy.

- freeze sour cream; it separates.

Do:
....

- freeze:

    mousses

    spices (fresh or dried)

    eggs (separate and freeze yolks and whites; or beat whole eggs with pinch of salt or sugar and freeze in ice cube trays; 1 cube = 1 egg)

    milk

    butter or margarine

    cream

    flour

    sugar, granulated or (to prevent lumps) brown

    nuts, whole or chopped

    crumbs (cookie, cake, cracker, bread)

    hard cheeses

piecrusts, baked, partially baked, or raw (in disks of dough or rolled into rounds or shaped into pie plates)

fruit pies and tarts, baked or unbaked

deep-dish pie or cobbler fruit mixtures.

....

Freezer Storage Timetable
....

(To be used only as a guideline)

Baked and unbaked empty pie shells	3 months
Baked fruit and berry pies	6 months
Unbaked pies	4 months
Baked chiffon pies (if recipe contains egg whites or whipped cream) and Lemon Meringue Pie *without* meringue topping	1 month
Frozen fruit pie filling	6 months

....

75

Frozen Fruit Pie Filling

. . . .

To avoid the possibility of fruit juices penetrating and softening the lower crust before a frozen two-crust pie is baked, simply freeze the filling and the crust separately and combine them immediately before baking. I prefer to roll out rounds of dough and freeze them flat between layers of foil. Pie-sized batches of seasonal fruits can be prepared quickly and easily and stored in foil packets molded to the shape of your pie plate. Fruits that freeze especially well are cooking apples, fresh apricots, peaches, nectarines, plums, rhubarb, and berries.

(*Note:* Use this recipe as well for deep-dish pie and cobbler fillings.)

SPECIAL EQUIPMENT: One 12 × 24-inch square heavy-duty aluminum foil, for each pie

FREEZING TIME: Up to 6 months without loss of flavor

YIELD: For one 9-inch pie, serves 6 to 8

> 4 to 6 cups fresh fruit—washed, peeled if necessary, hulled or cored, and sliced if necessary
> ½ to 1 cup granulated white or brown sugar (amount depends on type and sweetness of fruit)
> ½ teaspoon ground cinnamon, optional
> ½ teaspoon ground nutmeg, optional
> 1 to 3 teaspoons fresh lemon juice (amount depends on type and flavor of fruit)
> 3 to 3½ tablespoons quick-cooking tapioca, or cornstarch (amount depends on juiciness of fruit)

Toss the prepared fruit with all the remaining ingredients. Let stand for a few minutes to moisten the tapioca well and slightly soften it. Center a foil sheet over a 9-inch pie plate. Mound the fruit on the foil and pat gently to compress the fruit. Fold up the long foil flaps and make a wide double fold, pushing out the excess air. Fold over the side edges and pinch to seal. Label and date the package. Leaving the filling in the pie plate, set it on the fast-freeze shelf of your freezer (if you have one), until the fruit is hard. Remove the pie plate and return the fruit package to the freezer.

To bake, line a pie plate with a layer of thawed frozen pastry, brush with freshly made egg glaze (1 egg or egg white beaten with 1 tablespoon water) or fruit preserves. Unwrap the frozen fruit packet (do not thaw) and set it in the pastry. Cut steam vents in the rolled-out top crust (page 59). Moisten the edges of the lower crust, then cover the pie with its top crust. Fold the edges of the top crust over the lower one and pinch to seal. Mold the edge into a raised rim and flute (page 56). If you wish, glaze the pie top with brushed-on beaten egg and a light sprinkling of granulated sugar.

Bake in the lower third of a preheated 425°F oven for 25 minutes. Reduce the heat to 350°F, raise the pie to the center of the oven, and cover the pastry edges with a foil frame (page 22) if they seem to be browning too fast. Continue baking for another 30 to 35 minutes, or until the pastry is golden brown and the fruit tender. Serve warm for best texture and flavor.

(*Note:* Tapioca occasionally presents a problem when used in fruit pies topped by lattice pastry and *frozen before baking* because the tapioca sometimes does not soften sufficiently and can remain hard after baking. To avoid the problem, use cornstarch thickener for frozen lattice pies.)

Shortcut Frozen Pie and Tart Crusts

It's handy to make a double or triple batch of dough one day and have a ready supply of pie or tart crusts on hand. Prepare the pastry of your choice and roll it out (page 52) 2 or 3 inches larger than the diameter of the baking pan you will be using. Sandwich the pastry round between two layers of wax paper or regular-weight foil set on a cardboard backing. Repeat with as many layers as you like. Enclose the pastry in airtight, heavy-duty foil, then set into a large plastic bag. Label; if more than one type of pastry is included, label each round by simply writing its type (with pencil) on a slip of clean white paper set atop that piece of dough. To use, remove a dough round and set it flat to thaw for about 10 minutes, then fit it into the pie or tart pan, shape, and bake (page 55).

As an alternative, crusts can, of course, be fitted and shaped in freezer-to-oven pie plates before being frozen raw or baked.

The ultimate shortcut is, of course, to use store-bought piecrust in a pinch. The one I like best is Pillsbury's refrigerated two-crust 9-inch (15-ounce box) pastry, sold in the dairy case of the supermarket; boxes are freshness dated.

PASTRY RECIPES

· · · · · · · · · · · ·

The following collection includes a wide variety of recipes, from basic short crusts and cobbler toppings to crumb crusts and quick puff pastry. Each recipe in the main section of the book will refer you back to this collection, or to the All-Purpose Flaky Pastry recipe (and variations) that precedes it (pages 45–49). Feel free to use my suggestions or select your own choices from this collection.

Whole Wheat Pastry

. . . .

YIELD: For one two-crust 9-inch pie

    1 cup unsifted all-purpose flour
    1 cup unsifted whole wheat pastry or whole wheat all-purpose flour
    ¾ teaspoon salt
    Optional sweetener: 2 tablespoons granulated sugar
    8 tablespoons (1 stick) cold unsalted butter
    3 tablespoons cold vegetable shortening
    1 large egg yolk
    1 tablespoon fresh lemon juice or white vinegar
    4 to 5 tablespoons ice water, as needed

80

Read Basic Hand Preparation Technique (page 49).

Measure the flour, salt, and the sugar, if you are using it, into a bowl.

Cut up the butter and shortening and work them into the dry ingredients until the mixture is crumbly, with bits the size of rice.

Add the yolk and lemon juice or vinegar. Toss lightly. Add ice water, 1 tablespoon at a time, just until the dough begins to cling together in clumps.

Turn the dough out onto wax paper and form it into a ball, then flatten into a 6-inch disk, wrap, and refrigerate for at least 30 minutes before rolling out.

Whole Wheat–Wheat Germ Pastry.
Add 3 tablespoons toasted or raw wheat germ to the whole wheat flour.

Cornmeal Pastry

· · · · · · · · · · ·

Cornmeal gives this crust a special crunch but does significantly change the buttery flavor. Use with any fruit or berry pie filling. For quickest preparation, make this in the food processor.

YIELD: For one two-crust 8- or 9-inch pie

>   ⅔ cup yellow or white cornmeal
>   1⅓ cups unsifted all-purpose flour
>   Scant 1 teaspoon salt
>   2 tablespoons granulated sugar
>   12 tablespoons (1½ sticks) cold unsalted butter, cut up
>   1 large egg yolk
>   3½ to 5 tablespoons ice water, as needed

Read Basic Pastry Preparation Techniques (page 49).

Measure the cornmeal, flour, salt, and sugar into the work bowl of a processor or a mixing bowl. Pulse or whisk the dry ingredients together. Add the cut-up butter and pulse the processor, or use a pastry blender or your fingertips to work the butter into the dry ingredients, until the mixture has bits of butter the size of small peas or rice. Add the yolk and 3½ tablespoons ice water and mix just until the dough begins to look crumbly.

Turn the dough out onto a piece of wax paper and use your hands to form it into a ball; the warmth of your hands will help it come together. Sprinkle on a few more drops of water if needed. Form the dough into a 6-inch disk, wrap, and refrigerate for at least 30 minutes before rolling out.

Oil Pastry

· · · · · · · · · ·

This dough is tender, with a somewhat sandy texture. Chill it for at least 30 minutes before rolling out. For the greatest ease in handling, you can simply press it into the pie plate with your fingers. Or roll it out between two sheets of lightly floured wax paper or plastic wrap, or on a canvas pastry cloth.

YIELD: For one 8- or 9-inch pie shell; for a two-crust pie, double the recipe

> 1⅓ cups unsifted all-purpose flour
> ½ teaspoon salt
> ½ teaspoon sugar
> Optional sweetener: 2 tablespoons granulated sugar
> ⅓ cup light vegetable oil (canola or safflower, for example)
> 1 tablespoon fresh lemon juice
> 3 to 4 tablespoons ice water, as needed

Read Basic Pastry Preparation Techniques (page 49).

Whisk together the flour, salt, and ½ teaspoon sugar in a bowl. (The ½ teaspoon sugar is needed to balance the oil flavor; add optional 2 tablespoons sugar for a sweet-tasting crust.)

Add the oil and lemon juice and mix. Add 1 to 2 tablespoons ice water and stir. If the mixture is too dry, add a few more drops of water, until the dough will make a ball.

Flatten it into a 6-inch disk, wrap, and refrigerate for at least 30 minutes. Or roll out dough between two sheets of lightly floured wax paper and refrigerate in the paper for at least 30 minutes, or until you are ready to peel off the paper and line the pie plate.

Flour Paste Pastry

. . . .

Years ago, this method of making dough was the one beginning bakers were taught first. The reason: There is no guesswork or "feel" required in the recipe, and it produces a very pliable and easy-to-handle dough that bakes into a light, tender pastry layered with long flakes. The texture is slightly less fragile than All-Purpose Flaky Pastry prepared in the traditional manner. For kosher bakers, this can be made entirely with Crisco or non-dairy margarine (½ cup plus 3 tablespoons) so it will be dairy-free (pareve).

YIELD: For one two-crust 9-inch pie

> 2 cups unsifted all-purpose flour
> ¾ teaspoon salt
> ¼ cup water
> 8 tablespoons (1 stick) cold unsalted butter, cut up
> 3 tablespoons solid stick margarine or Crisco

Whisk the flour and salt together in a large bowl. Measure out ⅓ cup of this mixture and place it in a second smaller bowl.

Stir the water into the ⅓ cup flour, making a paste. In the large bowl, cut all the shortening into the remaining dry ingredients until the mixture is crumbly, with bits the size of rice. Stir in the paste, blending it well until the dough will form a ball.

Flatten it into a 6-inch disk, wrap, and refrigerate for at least 30 minutes, or until needed.

Hot Water Pastry

· · · · · · · · · · ·

Rules, like piecrusts, were made to be broken! That is the only explanation I can think of for the invention of this recipe, which breaks every rule there is for pastry crusts. But never mind. This is an old tried-and-true English recipe. It is especially easy to handle and good for pies that have moist or juicy fillings. The baked pastry has a texture halfway between a butter-crust flakiness and the sandiness of an oil crust.

Although boiling water is used to melt the fat for the dough, note that the mixture is cooled before it is added to the flour. As you would expect, the dough appears to be slightly stretchy, because the warm liquid has activated the gluten in the flour. However, chilling relaxes the gluten. Plan ahead: The dough must be refrigerated for at least 30 minutes, or for as long as overnight, before being rolled out. (*Note:* The fat for this dough can be all butter or all solid vegetable shortening solid stick margarine or Crisco. For best flavor and texture, I prefer to blend the two.

YIELD: For one two-crust 8- or 9-inch pie

> 8 tablespoons (1 stick) unsalted butter, cut into ½-inch cubes
> 4 tablespoons (½ stick) solid stick margarine or Crisco, cut into ½-inch bits
> ⅓ cup boiling water
> 2 cups unsifted all-purpose flour, or more as needed
> 1 teaspoon salt
> ½ teaspoon baking powder

Hand Mixing
or Electric Mixer Method

Put the butter and margarine in a small bowl, add the boiling water, and stir until the fat melts. Cool to lukewarm.

Sift the dry ingredients into a large mixing bowl. Gradually add the cooled liquid mixture, beating gently after each addition, until the dough forms a ball. If the dough is too sticky, sprinkle on about 1 more tablespoon flour. The dough will feel soft and slightly warm.

Form the dough into a ball, flatten it into a disk, wrap, and refrigerate for at least 30 minutes, or overnight.

Food Processor Method

Measure the butter and margarine into a small pitcher or a 2-cup measuring cup. Pour on the boiling water and stir until the fat is melted. Cool to lukewarm.

In the work bowl of the processor fitted with its steel blade, combine the dry ingredients and pulse 2 or 3 times to lighten. Pour the cooled liquid mixture slowly through the feed tube while pulsing the processor in short on/off spurts. Just as soon as the liquid has been absorbed, stop the machine and examine the dough. If it is too moist and sticky, add 1 more tablespoon flour and pulse once or twice, but not more. Do not overwork the dough. The dough will feel soft, pliable, and warm.

Form the dough into a ball, flatten it into a disk, wrap, and refrigerate for at least 30 minutes, or overnight.

Lard Pastry

. . . .

This is an old-fashioned American farm favorite. It produces a very flaky crust and can be used for any pie. Read about purchasing and storing lard, page 29.

YIELD: For one two-crust 9-inch pie

>   2 cups unsifted all-purpose flour
>   ¾ teaspoon salt
>   ⅔ cup (10⅔ tablespoons) lard, cut up
>   5 to 7 tablespoons ice water, as needed

Read Basic Pastry Preparation Techniques (page 49).

Whisk together the flour and salt in a bowl.

Work in the cut-up lard until the mixture is crumbly, with bits the size of rice. Sprinkle on 5 tablespoons of ice water and toss lightly, just until the dough begins to cling together. Add a little extra water if needed.

Turn the dough out onto wax paper. Form it into a ball, flatten it into a disk, wrap, and refrigerate for at least 30 minutes, or until needed.

Butter-Lard Pastry

. . . .

This pastry is as flaky as the all-lard recipe, but it has more flavor because of the addition of butter. The dough is very easy to handle and can be used for any sweet pie. Read about purchasing and storing lard, page 29.

YIELD: For one two-crust 9-inch pie

> **2 cups unsifted all-purpose flour**
> **¾ teaspoon salt**
> **⅓ cup (5⅓ tablespoons) lard, cut up**
> **⅓ cup (5⅓ tablespoons) cold unsalted butter, cut up**
> **5 to 6 tablespoons ice water, as needed**

Read Basic Pastry Preparation Techniques (page 49).

Whisk the flour and salt together in a bowl.

Add the lard and butter and work them into the dry ingredients until the mixture is crumbly, with bits the size of rice. Sprinkle on 5 tablespoons water and toss lightly, just until the dough holds together in clumps. Add extra water only if the dough looks too dry.

Turn the dough out onto wax paper, and form it into a ball. Flatten it into a disk, wrap, and refrigerate for at least 30 minutes, or until needed.

Rich Tart Pastry

· · · · · · · · · · ·

Because of the high quantity of sugar and egg yolk, this pastry tastes rather like a sugar cookie. It is perfect for sweet tarts or tartlets, and you can vary the flavor to complement the filling. *Note:* Instead of using all butter, you can achieve a slightly flakier version using 8 tablespoons (1 stick) cold butter plus 3 tablespoons chilled solid shortening.

YIELD: For one two-crust 9-inch pie, one 10-, 11-, or 12-inch tart shell, or seven 4½-inch tartlets

> **2 cups unsifted all-purpose flour**
> **½ teaspoon salt**
> **¼ cup sifted confectioners' sugar**
> **12 tablespoons (1½ sticks) cold or frozen unsalted butter, cut up**
> **½ teaspoon vanilla extract, optional**
> **3 large egg yolks or 2 yolks plus 1 tablespoon cream**
> **Optional flavoring: Grated zest of 1 lemon or orange (2 teaspoons) or**
> **½ teaspoon almond extract**
> **2 to 3 tablespoons orange juice, ice water, or cream, as needed**

Read Basic Pastry Preparation Techniques (page 49), selecting the hand, electric mixer, or food processor method.

Combine flour, salt, and sugar in a bowl or the work bowl, then work in the cut-up butter (or butter and shortening) until the mixture looks crumbly, with bits the size of rice.

Add the vanilla, yolks, or yolks and cream, and the optional flavoring and mix lightly. Add the cold liquid a tablespoon at a time, as needed, only until the dough begins to clump together; it should be neither powdery nor wet.

Turn the dough out onto a very lightly floured surface and use your hands to press the crumbs together into a ball. Form dough into a disk about 6 inches in diameter, wrap, and refrigerate for at least 30 minutes before rolling out. (This dough can also be pressed into a pan with your fingertips.)

Egg Yolk Pastry

This is a rich pastry, lightly lemon scented, with a texture slightly more compact and substantial than the All-Purpose Flaky Pastry. It is good for sweet tarts with moist custard or pudding fillings.

YIELD: For one two-crust 9-inch pie

> 2 cups unsifted all-purpose flour
> ½ teaspoon salt
> 3 large hard-boiled egg yolks, sieved
> 2 teaspoons grated lemon zest
> Optional sweetener: 3 tablespoons confectioners' sugar
> 12 tablespoons (1½ sticks) cold unsalted butter, cut up,
>   or 9 tablespoons butter plus 3 tablespoons solid stick margarine
> 5 to 7 tablespoons milk, as needed

Read Basic Hand Preparation Technique (page 49).

Whisk the dry ingredients together in a bowl, along with the sieved yolks, grated lemon zest, and the sugar, if using.

Work in the cut-up fat until the mixture is crumbly, with bits the size of rice. Add the milk 1 tablespoon at a time until the dough begins to clump together.

Form the dough into a ball. Flatten it into a disk, wrap, and refrigerate at least 30 minutes, or until needed.

89

Cream Cheese Pastry

· · · · · · · · · · ·

This delectable dough is sometimes called Viennese pastry. It is perfect for pies and tarts as well as for bite-sized jam-filled pastries, tartlets, and turnovers. When chilled, it is an extremely easy dough to handle. For a reduced-fat version, see variation following.

YIELD: For one two-crust 8- or 9-inch pie, or one 10-, 11- or 12-inch tart shell

> 8 ounces (1 large package) cream cheese (not low-fat), at room temperature
> 1 cup (2 sticks) unsalted butter, at room temperature (*Note:* Do not substitute margarine)
> 2 cups unsifted all-purpose flour, or more as needed
> ½ teaspoon salt

Read Basic Pastry Preparation Techniques (page 49).

Cut up the cream cheese and butter in a large bowl. With a fork or an electric mixer, blend them together until creamy.

Sift the flour and salt directly into the bowl. Blend just until the dough holds together. If it feels too sticky to handle, add a little more flour by the teaspoon.

Form the dough into a ball, flatten it into a disk, wrap, and refrigerate for at least 30 minutes, or until needed.

90

Reduced-Fat Cream Cheese Pastry
. . . .

This recipe has about half the fat and one third the cholesterol but the same ease of handling and good flavor. The secret is to melt the butter and brown it, then solidify it before blending it into the pastry. *Note:* You need to plan ahead with this recipe, allowing about 1 hour lead time, for browning and chilling the butter, and the rolled pastry.

YIELD: For one two-crust 9-inch pie or one 10-, 11- or 12-inch tart shell

> **4 tablespoons (½ stick) cold unsalted butter, cut up**
> **2 cups unsifted all-purpose flour**
> **1 teaspoon salt**
> **1 tablespoon granulated sugar**
> **⅔ cup light (not fat-free) cream cheese, chilled until very cold**
> **¼ cup canola oil, or more as needed**

Read Basic Pastry Preparation Techniques (page 49). Melt the butter in a small saucepan over low heat, then cook until the butter begins to turn golden brown and has a nutty aroma, about 4 minutes; do not allow the butter to burn, which can happen quite suddenly. Scrape the melted butter and all the browned bits into a metal bowl and freeze or refrigerate for a few minutes, until solidified.

In a large mixing bowl, toss together the flour, salt, and sugar. Add the solidified butter and cold cream cheese and use your fingertips, a fork, or a pastry blender to work the cold fat into the dry ingredients, creating small flakes. Add the oil and stir with a fork until just blended. Alternatively, you can pulse the cold fat into the dry ingredients in a food processor, then add the oil and pulse until the dough is sandy and beginning to form small beads. Turn off the machine.

Pinch the dough between your fingers to see if it holds together. Even if it looks dry and crumbly, the warmth of your hands will soften it enough to hold together. Add a few drops more oil if needed. Form the dough into a ball, flatten it into a disk, wrap, and refrigerate for at least 30 minutes, or until needed.

Sour Cream Pastry

· · · · · · · · · · ·

This traditional Hungarian recipe is especially good with fruit tarts, small jam tartlets, and fruit-filled envelopes. The sour cream contributes to the flavor as well as to the tenderness of the pastry.

YIELD: For one two-crust 9-inch pie, one 10- or 11-inch tart shell, or eight 4-inch tartlets

> **2 cups unsifted all-purpose flour**
> **¾ teaspoon salt**
> **Optional sweetener: 3 tablespoons granulated or sifted confectioners' sugar**
> **10 tablespoons (1 stick plus 2 tablespoons) cold unsalted butter, cut up**
> **4 to 5 tablespoons sour cream (or plain yogurt, top liquid drained off),**
>   **as needed**

Read Basic Pastry Preparation Technique (page 49).

Whisk the flour, salt, and the optional sugar together in a bowl.

Cut in the butter and pinch it into the dry ingredients until the mixture is crumbly, with bits the size of rice. Add the sour cream 1 tablespoon at a time, mixing lightly until the dough just begins to clump together.

Form the dough into a ball, flatten it into a disk, wrap, and refrigerate for at least 30 minutes, or until needed.

No-Rolling-Pin Pastry

· · · · · · · · · · ·

If you are reluctant to handle or roll out piecrust, this recipe will change your life. It only takes a few minutes to toss all the ingredients together and then press them in place with your fingertips. No overhandling, no rolling, no toughness—no-fail; the texture is tender, crisp and slightly flaky, with an excellent taste. Even a child can do this with ease.

This reduced-fat recipe contains zero cholesterol and, compared with an all-butter crust, about one seventh the saturated fat. Canola oil is, of course, 100 percent fat, but it is high in mono-unsaturates, which are heart-healthy.

YIELD: For one 9- or 10-inch pie shell plus pastry decorations or one 11-inch tart shell; for a two-crust 9-inch pie with extra pastry decorations, make 1½ times the recipe (3 cups flour)

> 2 cups unsifted all-purpose flour
> 1 teaspoon salt
> 1 teaspoon granulated sugar
> Scant ⅔ cup canola oil
> 3 tablespoons skim or low-fat milk, or as needed

In a mixing bowl or directly in the pie plate, toss together the flour, salt and sugar. Add the oil and milk (or stir them together first in a cup), then toss them with the flour mixture using a fork or your fingertips. As soon as the dough looks clumpy and holds together, press it out in an even layer in the baking pan. You can also cover the dough with plastic wrap and press it out in the plastic. Build up a thicker dough layer on the rim and flute or pinch into scallops (page 56).

If making a two-crust pie, roll out the top crust between two sheets of lightly floured wax paper. Peel off one sheet, position the crust over the filling, and peel off the backing paper. Cut steam vents and bake as directed in the recipe.

Brown Butter Pastry

. . . .

This reduced-fat pastry has a buttery flavor without a great deal of saturated fat. The trick is to brown a small amount of butter to increase its flavor, then chill it until solid and work it into the flour as in a traditional crust. *Note:* You need to plan ahead with this recipe, allowing about 1 hour lead time, for browning and chilling the butter, then chilling the rolled pastry.

YIELD: For one two-crust 9-inch pie, 10-inch pie shell, or 11-inch tart shell plus pastry decorations

> **2 tablespoons unsalted butter**
> **2½ cups unsifted all-purpose flour, divided (1 cup and 1½ cups)**
> **½ cup canola or other light oil**
> **¾ teaspoon salt**
> **2 tablespoons granulated sugar**
> **4 to 6 teaspoons skim or low-fat milk, as needed**

Melt the butter in a small saucepan over low heat, then cook until the butter begins to turn golden brown and has a nutty aroma, about 4 minutes; do not allow the butter to burn, which can happen quite suddenly.

In a medium bowl, combine 1 cup of the flour with the oil. Add the melted and browned butter, scraping in all the browned particles from the pan. Tossing with a fork, blend until smooth, then set in the freezer for at least 30 minutes.

Once the mixture is chilled, add the remaining 1½ cups flour, the salt, and sugar. With a pastry blender or two knives, cut the chilled mixture into the dry ingredients until the dough is in pea-sized lumps. Sprinkle on the milk 1 teaspoon at a time, adding only enough to allow the dough to hold together. Form the dough into a ball, flatten it into a disk, wrap, and refrigerate for at least 30 minutes, or until needed. Roll out the dough between sheets of lightly floured wax paper.

Linzer Pastry

· · · · · · · · · ·

This pastry comes from the town of Linz, Austria, where it was created by a pastry chef in the early 1800s. Traditionally, it is flavored with a generous amount of cinnamon and cloves and used as the shell for Linzertorte (page 230). The dough can also be formed into clove-studded ball cookies and rolled in confectioners' sugar (page 232).

YIELD: For one 11-inch tart shell plus thirty 1-inch round cookies, two 9-inch tart shells, or one 11-inch and one 8-inch tart shell

> 3 cups all-purpose flour, sifted
> ¼ teaspoon salt
> 1 cup granulated sugar
> ¾ teaspoon ground cinnamon
> ⅛ teaspoon ground cloves
> 12 tablespoons (1½ sticks) cold unsalted butter
> 1 cup (5 ounces) ground almonds (or walnuts)
> 2 teaspoons grated lemon zest
> 1 large egg plus 1 large yolk
> **Optional cookie garnish: Whole cloves**

Read Basic Pastry Preparation Techniques (page 49).

In a large mixing bowl, or a large-model food processor (with a capacity of 5 cups dry ingredients), combine the flour, salt, sugar, cinnamon, and cloves.

Cut in the butter until the mixture is crumbly, with bits the size of rice. Stir in the ground nuts and lemon zest. Finally, add the egg and yolk and mix lightly just until the dough begins to clump together.

Turn out onto wax paper and form into a ball. Flatten it into a disk, wrap, and refrigerate for at least 30 minutes, or until needed. For an 11-inch tart, use two thirds of the dough and save the rest for cookies.

Homemade Piecrust Mix

· · · · · · · · · · ·

To save time, prepare this mix ahead and store it for up to one month in the refrigerator or a cool pantry (hydrogenated vegetable shortening does not have to be refrigerated). At the last minute, you just add water, mix, and roll out the dough.

YIELD: About 9 cups mix, or six 9-inch pie shells

> **6 cups all-purpose flour, sifted**
> **1 tablespoon salt**
> **1 (1-pound) can (2⅓ cups) hydrogenated vegetable shortening, such as Crisco**

Whisk the flour and salt together in a bowl, then cut in the shortening until the mixture is crumbly, with bits the size of rice. Store in a covered container.

Crust size	Mix for 1 crust	Mix for 2 crusts	Plus ice water
8-inch	1¼ cups	2 to 2¼ cups	2 to 4 tablespoons
9-inch	1½ cups	2¼ to 2½ cups	2 to 4 tablespoons
10-inch	1¾ cups	2⅓ to 2¾ cups	3 to 5 tablespoons

To use, measure the required amount of mix into a bowl. Sprinkle on ice water and work lightly with a fork just until the mixture holds together. The quantity of water will vary with the weather and type of flour; use as little water as possible. Form a dough ball, flatten it into a disk, wrap, and refrigerate for at least 30 minutes. To roll out, form, and bake the dough, see pages 52–70.

Cobbler Topping and Dumplings

· · · · · · · · · · ·

This recipe can be spooned over hot fruit pie filling and cooked in a covered pot on the stove top or baked in the oven.

SPECIAL EQUIPMENT: 2- to 3-quart stove-top oven-proof casserole or 9-, 10-, or 11-inch deep-dish baking pan or oven-proof skillet (*Note:* For stove-top cooking, be sure the skillet has a tightly fitting lid.)

YIELD: Serves 6

> 1½ cups unsifted all-purpose flour
> ¼ teaspoon salt
> Optional sweetener: 2 tablespoons granulated sugar
> 1½ teaspoons baking powder
> 4 tablespoons (½ stick) unsalted butter or solid stick margarine,
>   at room temperature
> ⅔ cup milk
> 1 large egg, at room temperature

Sift the dry ingredients into a bowl or the work bowl of a food processor fitted with the steel blade. Cut in the fat until the mixture is crumbly (only a few pulses in the processor). Add the milk and egg, stirring only until the mixture is completely moistened. Set the batter aside until you prepare the fruit filling.

While the filling is still *hot*, spoon on the batter: *To shape dumplings*, place separate tablespoonfuls of batter slightly apart all over the filling. *To make a single-layer crust*, spoon out the batter in even-sized dabs, then gently spread it into a single layer.

Bake in a preheated 425°F oven, uncovered, for 20 to 25 minutes, or until the topping is golden. Or cover the pan tightly and place on the stove top over medium-high heat. Bring the filling mixture to a boil, then reduce the heat and simmer for 12 minutes without lifting the lid. Then peek. The topping should be puffed up and dry inside. Cook longer if necessary.

Deep-Dish Pie Topping
· · · · · · · · · · ·

Using only a top layer of crust eliminates the problem of soggy bottoms for very moist pie fillings—and also eliminates half the pastry calories and fat.

Prepare All-Purpose Flaky Pastry (page 45), using 1½ cups flour.

Roll out a single crust, about 1 inch larger than the diameter of your baking dish (page 52). Prepare the fruit filling according to the recipe instructions, fill the pie plate, and then cover with the rolled pastry.

Crimp the edges to the plate rim by pinching with your fingers and pressing with floured fork tines (page 56). For a tighter seal, you can brush the plate rim with egg glaze (page 156) before crimping the dough. Cut a hole in the center of the pastry to vent the steam. Brush with egg glaze or milk and sprinkle with granulated sugar. Decorative vine and leaf shapes, or initials, can be cut from dough scraps and applied to egg-glazed pastry. Be sure to glaze the tops of the decorative cut-outs before baking.

Bake according to the specific recipe instructions.

(*Note:* A thawed sheet of frozen store-bought puff pastry [page 112] or Quick Puff Pastry [page 110] can also be used for topping a deep-dish pie. The high rise of the dough is particularly attractive. For another alternative, use Oat–Wheat Germ or Nut-Crumb Streusel Topping [page 138 or 141]).

Crumb and Nut Crusts

Crumb crusts are most often used with unbaked fruit fillings, cold mousses, puddings, and ice cream. They are excellent for freezer pies because frozen crumbs are not quite as brittle—or as hard to cut—as frozen pastry. Crumb crusts are quick and easy to prepare using cereals, ground cookies or cracker crumbs, or nuts. When mixed with melted shortening and chilled, the crumbs hold their shape. To enhance the flavor and add a little more rigidity to the crust, you can bake it for a few minutes, though this is not always essential. Some crusts are best chilled, others best baked briefly. It takes about 30 minutes to chill a crumb crust until firm in the refrigerator. To speed this process, you can use the freezer.

Prepared cookie and cereal crumbs are available commercially. To make your own crumbs, break cookies or crackers into small pieces and place them in a heavy-duty plastic bag. Seal the bag, then tap and roll it with a rolling pin until the crumbs are finely and evenly crushed. Or process the crumbs in the blender or in the food processor fitted with the steel blade. (*Note:* To grind nuts for a nut crust, first dry out the nuts on a baking sheet in a 325°F oven for 5 to 7 minutes. In a blender, grind only ½ cup nuts at a time.)

PROCEDURE

Preheat the oven, if the crumb crust is to be baked. Combine the crumbs and the sugar, if using, in a mixing bowl (or in the pie plate itself). Pour on the melted fat and gently toss with the crumbs. Press the moistened crumbs evenly over the bottom and sides of the pie plate. Take care not to build up too thick a layer in the corners. Use the back of a large metal spoon or your fingers to press out the crumbs evenly. To make a rim, hold the thumb or forefinger of one hand horizontally on top of plate rim and, with the fingers of the other hand, press the crumbs up to it, making a firm lip. Bake as directed, in the center of the oven. Or chill as directed and do not bake.

CRUMB AND NUT CRUSTS

For one 9-inch pie shell (for other sizes, see below)	Crumbs	Granulated sugar
Graham Cracker (*Note:* Four 2 ½-inch square crackers = ¼ cup crumbs)	1¼ cups crumbs (made from 20 2½-inch squares)	2 tablespoons to ¼ cup, to taste
Reduced-Fat Graham Cracker (For 9- or 10-inch shell)	1½ cups crumbs (made from 24 2½-inch squares old-fashioned honey or cinnamon grahams or low-fat graham crackers)	2 tablespoons *plus* ¼ teaspoon cinnamon
Graham-Nut	1 cup graham cracker crumbs *plus* ½ cup ground nuts	¼ cup
Zwieback	1½ cup zwieback crumbs	2 tablespoons
Vanilla Cookie	1½ cups vanilla cookie crumbs	3 to 4 tablespoons
Almond Cookie–Nut	1¼ cups crushed Italian amaretti cookies *plus* ½ cup ground toasted almonds	¼ cup
Gingersnap	1⅓ cups gingersnap crumbs (made from 25 cookies 2 inches in diameter)	none to 2 tablespoons
Chocolate Wafer	1½ cups chocolate wafer cookie crumbs (made from 8 ounces cookies)	none to 2 tablespoons
Reduced-Fat Chocolate Crumb	1½ cups crumbs made from 25 crisp chocolate wafer cookies (8 ounces) or 24 2½-inch low-fat chocolate graham cracker squares (*Note:* For 10-inch shell, use 1¾ cups crumbs and add 1 more tablespoon melted butter and 1 tablespoon water, or as needed)	none
Oreo Crumb	1½ cups cookie crumbs (made from 18 Oreo cookies)	none
Chocolate-Almond (**or Chocolate-Pecan, Hazelnut, Peanut, or Walnut**)	¾ cups chocolate wafer crumbs (made from 4 ounces wafers) *plus* ¾ cup ground nuts of your choice	none to 2 tablespoons

Melted butter or margarine	Chill	or bake	Baking time
5⅓ tablespoons	firm	350°F	8 minutes
1 tablespoon melted butter plus 2 tablespoons canola oil or walnut oil *and* 2 tablespoons water, or fruit juice, or more if needed	firm	350°F	8 minutes
5⅓ tablespoons	firm	350°F	8 minutes
4 tablespoons	firm	——	——
5⅓ tablespoons	firm	350°F	7 minutes
5⅓ tablespoons	——	375°F (in buttered pie plate)	5 minutes
5⅓ tablespoons	firm	375°F	6 minutes
5⅓ tablespoons	firm	——	——
1 tablespoon melted unsalted butter plus 2 tablespoons canola oil *and* 1 tablespoon skim milk or water, or more if needed	firm	350°F	8 minutes
2 tablespoons	firm	——	——
5⅓ tablespoons	firm	——	——

For one 9-inch pie shell	Crumbs	Granulated sugar
Nut **(Almond, Hazelnut,** **Brazil Nut, Walnut, Pecan,** **Peanut, or a blend)** *(Note:* Instead of using added fat, you can process untoasted nuts in the food processor to form a paste. Pat the dough into the pie plate.)	1¾ to 2 cups ground nuts	¼ cup
Corn Flakes or Rice Cereal (use as wheat substitute)	1⅓ cups crumbs (made from 3 cups whole flakes) *plus* a pinch each ground cinnamon and nutmeg	none to 2 tablespoons
Granola-Nut	1 cup crushed toasted granola-style cereal *plus* ½ cup ground walnuts	3 tablespoons dark brown sugar
Coconut	2 cups finely flaked or shredded sweetened coconut	none

Quantity of crumbs required for a variety of shell sizes:
for 8-inch shell: 1 cup crumbs per recipe; reduce sugar by 1 tablespoon and butter by 2 teaspoons
for 10-inch shell: 1½ to 1¾ cups crumbs *plus* 1 tablespoon extra sugar and 7 tablespoons
    melted shortening instead of quantity indicated in recipe for 9-inch shell; for 10-inch
    Graham-Nut Crust, use 1 cup graham cracker crumbs *plus* ¾ cup ground nuts
for one 3½-inch to 4-inch tartlet: ⅓ cup crumbs
for one 4½-inch tartlet: ⅓ cup plus 1 tablespoon crumbs

Melted butter or margarine	Chill	or bake	Baking time
see Note	——	375°F	8 minutes
4 tablespoons	firm	375°F	8 minutes
5⅓ tablespoons	firm	——	——
4 tablespoons	——	325°F	15 to 20 minutes, or until light golden

Chocolate Shells

. . . .

While these chocolate candy shells are not pastry, they make a very easy and elegant substitute for piecrust when used with special fillings. Double the recipe and keep the extra batch in your freezer for instant party tartlets (page 324). Fill them with a scoop of ice cream or a dollop of vanilla pastry cream topped with fresh berries and a rosette of whipped cream or a light dusting of confectioners' sugar.

ADVANCE PREPARATION: Chocolate shells can be prepared well in advance and frozen until needed, but chocolate takes only 5 to 10 minutes to harden in the refrigerator; if you are storing them in the freezer, keep the cups in a sturdy airtight box, as they are fragile.

SPECIAL EQUIPMENT: Muffin tray and paper or foil liners of matching size (use double liners in each cup for ease of handling). (*Note:* For fanciful containers, use other cup-shaped objects like seashells, curly cabbage leaves, or small paper bags, which can be coated with chocolate as well. Try coquilles St.-Jacques–style scallop shells, covered on the *outer* surface with plastic wrap or pressed-on foil before you brush on the chocolate.)

YIELD: 6 chocolate cups, 3 inches in diameter

> **1 cup semisweet chocolate chips**
> **1 tablespoon unsalted butter or Crisco**

Melt the chocolate and butter in the top of a double boiler over hot (not boiling) water. While the chocolate is melting, set two paper or foil liners inside each muffin cup. (Or press pieces of aluminum foil or plastic wrap firmly against the outside surface of the scallop shells. Cabbage leaves or small bags must be clean and dry but do not need to be covered with foil.) When the chocolate is soft, stir well, then remove from the heat and set aside to cool for about 3 minutes; do not let it harden.

Working with one muffin cup at a time, spoon about 1½ tablespoons melted chocolate into the liner. Hold the liner at its top edge while spreading chocolate over the inside surface with the back of the spoon, drawing the chocolate up from the bottom. The coating should be fairly thick. If chocolate is too warm, it may run down to the bottom; if this happens, simply refrigerate the chocolate-lined cups for 3 to 5 minutes, then respread the chocolate. (If coating seashells, set them foil side up on a wax-paper-lined tray. Spread the melted chocolate over the shells in a generous layer.) Set the muffin tins or tray of shells in the refrigerator or freezer until the chocolate is very hard—5 minutes in the freezer, slightly longer in the refrigerator. When it is hard, set the chocolate-lined muffin cups or shells on the counter to warm up for about 2 to 3 minutes. Then peel off the paper liners; or, for shells, first remove the shell, then peel off the foil or plastic wrap. If the paper or foil sticks to the chocolate, it is still too cold. Fill the cups and serve, or refreeze in plastic bags set into a protective box until needed.

105

About Meringue

Meringue is always dramatic when used on top of a pie (page 134), but it is just as special on the bottom, baked into a light, crisp "angel" shell (page 108), filled with fruit, chilled mousse, whipped cream, ice cream, or cooked custard. However you use it, there are some important things to remember when working with meringue.

Select a cool, dry day if possible since rainy, humid weather will soften meringue. Keep all utensils scrupulously clean and dry; even a speck of fat (such as egg yolk) in the egg whites will prevent them from beating to full volume. Avoid using plastic bowls, which are impossible to keep grease-free.

Eggs separate most easily when cold, but whites beat to fullest volume when at room temperature, 70°F. Therefore, separate eggs as soon as they come from the refrigerator, then let them sit awhile; or set the bowl of whites in another bowl of warm water until they warm up. To separate eggs, see page 34. Frozen egg whites defrosted at room temperature can also be used. Acidity stabilizes egg white foam. Therefore, the trick with meringue is to add acid (cream of tartar, vinegar, or lemon juice) to the whites just before you begin beating them. To this end, you can also wipe your bowl and beater—before adding whites—with a paper towel dampened with white vinegar (this removes all traces of fat as well as adding a touch of acidity), or use a copper bowl, which imparts its own acidity.

To hold its shape, meringue must be properly beaten. For the best effect with the least personal effort, use an electric mixer with the largest balloon beater available and a bowl that fits it most closely. The object is to keep the entire mass of whites in constant movement. Length of beating time will vary, depending upon your method, from 10 to 30 minutes or more. If you have a strong arm and are a traditionalist, by all means use a large balloon whisk with a copper bowl. To avoid fatigue, try to let your arm, from the elbow down, do most of the work; otherwise, you expend most of your energy developing your pectorals. Hand beating will usually result in a greater volume of whites, and, of course, you get all the glory as well.

Beat whites until they are smooth, have a shiny satin appearance, and can hold very stiff peaks when the beater is lifted. When they are perfectly whipped, you should be able to turn the bowl of whites upside down (over a sink if you are nervous) without the whites budging. If they are overbeaten, though, the released liquid lining the bowl bottom will allow them to slide. Overbeaten whites usually become grainy or lumpy. To save them, you can try lightly beating in one fresh egg white for every 4 in the meringue.

The sugar added to meringue can be either the regular granulated type or superfine, but the latter is best because the smaller crystals dissolve faster. Sugar (and vanilla or another flavoring) should be added to the whites gradually and only *after* the whites begin to look fluffy; adding sugar too soon may prevent expansion. Beat the sugar into the whites until it is entirely dissolved, or the baked meringue may later "weep" when the sugar granules melt and ooze out. To be sure the sugar is completely melted, pinch some of the meringue between your thumb and forefinger. If it feels grainy, some sugar granules are still whole; if smooth, the sugar is dissolved. Old-timers claim weeping can be prevented by sifting a little dry cornstarch into beaten whites along with the sugar. To guarantee a perfect, nonweeping meringue, follow the recipe on page 275, adding some cooked cornstarch.

. . . .

MEASURING EGG WHITES

1 large egg white = 2 generous tablespoons
4 large egg whites = generous ½ cup
3 large egg whites, beaten stiff = 3 cups meringue = one 9-inch pie shell = eight 3-inch tartlets
4 large egg whites, beaten stiff = a generous 9-inch or regular 10-inch pie shell = ten or eleven 3-inch tartlets

. . . .

Meringue Pie Shell

· · · · · · · · · · ·

Meringue crusts or shells are used for fresh fruit tarts, chilled mousse pies, whipped cream or ice cream pies, or pies with cooked custard fillings (angel pies). Meringue shells can be baked in a buttered pie plate or in tartlet pans, or meringue can be hand-formed on a prepared baking sheet into large and small nests. Before making meringue shells, read About Meringue on page 106. To make meringue pie topping, see pages 136 and 275).

Special Equipment: 9-inch pie plate; electric mixer with balloon whisk; rubber spatula; for shells or tartlets—baking sheet lined with parchment paper or brown paper cut from paper bag, well buttered and dusted with flour; soupspoon; pastry decorating bag fitted with large star tip, optional.

Yield: One 9-inch pie shell or eight 3-inch free-form tartlets.

> 3 large egg whites, at room temperature (*Note:* For a 10-inch meringue shell, use 4 whites and the same quantities of other ingredients)
> ¼ teaspoon cream of tartar
> ⅛ teaspoon salt
> ¾ cup superfine sugar, divided (¼ cup and ½ cup)
> ½ teaspoon vanilla extract, optional

Preheat the oven to 275°F. If you are using a pie plate, butter it generously. If you are using a baking sheet, butter it well and dust with flour or line it with buttered and floured baking parchment or brown paper cut from a paper bag. Combine the egg whites, cream of tartar, and salt in a mixing bowl. Beat until fluffy. Add ¼ cup of the sugar and beat in, then gradually add the remaining ½ cup sugar, beating after each addition; add the optional vanilla with the last of the sugar. Use a rubber spatula to scrape down the whites from the side of the bowl from time to time. Beat about 7 to 10 minutes longer on medium-high speed, or longer if needed until all the sugar is dissolved (pinch the meringue to feel if it is still grainy) and the meringue is shiny satin in appearance.

If you are making a meringue piecrust, spread the meringue onto the bottom and sides of the well-buttered pie plate. Use the back of a spoon to pull up swirls around the rim, or fill a pastry bag fitted with a large star tip and pipe meringue rosettes around rim for a fancy edging. To form tartlet nests, drop large evenly spaced spoonfuls of meringue onto the prepared sheet and mold them with the back of the spoon into 3-inch-diameter cups with raised sides. Alternatively, you can pipe meringue from a pastry bag (fitted with a $\frac{1}{2}$-inch plain or star decorating tip) into 3-inch disks; then pipe a second ring around the edge of each disk to create a high rim.

Bake the pie shell or tartlet shells for 60 to 65 minutes at 275°F, or until firm and crisp. If the meringue is not hard after this time, turn off your oven, leave the door ajar slightly, and leave the meringue inside for another 30 to 45 minutes, or overnight, to dry out. Theoretically, the baked shell(s) should remain pure white, but don't worry if the color turns a very light beige. If the color darkens, the sugar is beginning to caramelize and the flavor will change.

When baked, cool the meringue pie shell in the pan on a wire rack. (*Note:* The edges of a meringue pie shell rise somewhat during baking but sink slightly when cooling. Shells may crack when cold. Never mind; the filling and topping will hide everything, and I'll never tell.) As soon as meringue tartlet shells are baked, remove them from the baking sheet with a spatula while still warm and set them on a wire rack to cool. If the meringues stick to the parchment or brown paper, simply dampen the *underside* of the paper with a wet sponge, then lift off the meringues. (They shouldn't stick, but occasionally it happens.)

Nut Meringue Shell. Just before molding the meringue into a pie shell or forming tartlets, fold in $\frac{1}{3}$ cup finely chopped toasted almonds, pecans, or other nuts. Or sprinkle finely chopped nuts over the molded meringues just before baking.

Brown Sugar–Pecan Meringue Shell. Substitute brown sugar for the white, and fold in $\frac{1}{3}$ cup finely chopped pecans just before molding the meringue.

Quick Puff Pastry

· · · · · · · · · · ·

In this speeded up, easy-to-make version of many-layered butter-filled classic puff pastry, extra butter is rolled and layered into All-Purpose Flaky Pastry (page 45). The result is startlingly successful, tastes very buttery, and rises well, though not quite as high as a classic recipe. The only trick is to keep the dough well chilled until it is baked. Try this dough with all the classic puff pastry shapes and shells (see Index).

ADVANCE PREPARATION: The dough can be frozen or shaped as directed in a specific recipe and then frozen (for up to 6 months); bake unthawed. Leftover dough can be wrapped airtight and frozen. Baked shapes can also be wrapped airtight, set in a protective box, and frozen for up to 6 months, though after 6 weeks they lose some flavor.

SPECIAL EQUIPMENT: Dough scraper; rolling pin; tape measure or ruler; pastry brush; plastic bag or foil

TEMPERATURE AND TIME: 425°F for about 20 minutes (depending on specific recipe)

YIELD: For two 8-inch piecrusts

> 2 cups unsifted all-purpose flour
> ½ teaspoon salt
> 12 tablespoons (1½ sticks) well-chilled unsalted butter, cut up,
>   plus 6 tablespoons, cut up, for rolling into dough (2 sticks plus
>   2 tablespoons total)
> 5 to 6 tablespoons ice water, as needed

Read Basic Pastry Preparation Techniques (page 49) and prepare the dough as you would for All-Purpose Flaky Pastry: Whisk the flour and salt together in a bowl, then pinch in the cold butter until mixture is coarse and crumbly, but with bits the size of big beans rather than rice. Add only enough water to enable mixture to clump together. If the dough feels too dry, add a tiny bit more water. Turn the dough out onto wax paper, form into a ball, and then flatten into a thick rectangle.

On a lightly floured surface, roll the dough out to a rectangle about 6 × 12 inches and ½ inch thick (a). Soften the remaining 6 tablespoons butter by pinching it with your fingers or tapping it with the rolling pin until it is pliable but not sticky or soft. The butter should be the same firmness as the dough; chill one or the other if either feels too soft.

Spread the softened butter in an even layer on the upper half of the rolled-out dough, coming to within ½ inch of the edges (b). Fold the bottom half of the dough up, covering the butter, and turn the dough so that the fold is on the left (c). Brush any excess flour off the dough with a pastry brush and fold the dough in thirds, as you would a letter. Turn the dough so the long open edge faces right. Roll out to about 6 × 12 inches. This is called the *first turn*. Fold the dough into thirds again, as for a letter, turn it so the open edge is to the right (d), and roll out to 6 × 12 inches to make the *second turn*. Fold the dough into thirds one more time, wrap, and refrigerate for at least 15 minutes.

After chilling, roll the dough to about 6 × 12 inches, and this time make a *book fold* by bringing the top edge of the rolled dough down to the center line and then the bottom edge up to the center (e). Brush off any excess flour, then fold the top half of the dough over the bottom, bringing the folded edges together. The dough will look like a closed book when you turn it so the open edge faces to the right (f). Wrap and chill the dough until ready to use; or, if the dough still feels cold, you can roll out and cut as needed now. (*Note:* The dough should be chilled for as long as possible if you have the time.)

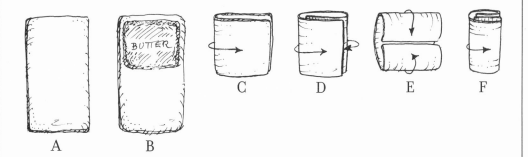

A B C D E F

To bake, follow the directions in the specific recipe. Usually this dough is set on a baking sheet lightly sprinkled with cold water to give added moisture and baked in a preheated 425°F oven for about 20 minutes.

About Puff Pastry

Eating puff pastry is a supremely sensual delight: Crisp buttery layers of ethereal flakiness that defy gravity and intrigue the tongue. Making the classical version at home is, to my mind, well worth the rather considerable effort and time when I can find it. However, it is increasingly a luxury that also defies the gravity of my schedule. As a result, I have found two substitutes: Quick Puff Pastry (page 110), which is a variation on All-Purpose Flaky Pastry, with extra butter, and store-bought frozen puff pastry sheets. In my area of New England, Pepperidge Farm frozen puff pastry sheets are available in supermarkets; a 17.3-ounce package contains two sheets, each about 9½ × 10½ inches, folded in thirds. Thaw still-wrapped frozen sheets at room temperature for 20 to 30 minutes. Unfold gently and roll out on a lightly floured surface; if the pastry cracks, press the edges together with your fingertip and continue rolling. When rolled out to about 12 inches square, a sheet is ready to use. You can use one sheet at a time and reseal and refreeze the second one in a plastic bag. If you need an amount larger than a 12-inch sheet, place one sheet on top of the other and roll both together; the double layer rolls easily to about 13 × 15 inches or slightly larger.

Frozen or Quick Puff Pastry can be used to make pie shells or two-crust pies baked in pie plates, as well as large or small freestanding pastry cases (see Index). Follow the individual recipes for specific instructions.

PUFF PASTRY SINGLE-CRUST PIE SHELL OR DOUBLE-CRUST PIE

Use either Quick Puff Pastry (page 110) or frozen puff pastry sheets. Preheat the oven to 425°F.

To make a prebaked 9-inch pie shell, roll out slightly more than half the Quick Puff Pastry Dough, or use one sheet of thawed frozen dough, on a lightly floured surface to a 12-inch square, or at least 1 inch larger all around than an overturned pie plate set on it. Lift the dough and ease it into the pie plate, fitting it comfortably onto the pan bottom and sides without stretching; drape the extra dough evenly over the edges of the plate. With a sharp knife, trim the overhanging dough flush with the edge of the plate.

Cut a 13- to 14-inch square of aluminum foil; lightly butter or spray vegetable oil on the shiny side and press that greased side down onto the pastry shell. To prevent the puff pastry from rising during baking, it must be heavily weighted. Fill the foil liner with about 3 cups (about 1½ pounds) of dry rice or dry beans reserved only for this purpose, or pie weights; the weights should fill the pie shell, coming close to the top of the plate. With the palm of your hand, compress the weights in the plate.

Bake the lined and weighted shell in the preheated oven for 15 minutes. Remove it from the oven and carefully lift out the foil and weights (taking care not to leave any stray weights behind). Return the pastry shell to the oven. *For a partially prebaked shell* (for a two-crust pie that will be baked again with filling), bake it for an additional 3 to 4 minutes, or just until the dough on the bottom looks opaque but not golden brown. Remove it from the oven and press on the puffed-up center with a pot holder to flatten it. Cool on a wire rack. *For a completely prebaked shell* that will not be baked again, the second baking time should be about 4½ to 5½ minutes, or until the bottom dough is opaque and a light golden color. Use a pot holder to press down the puffed dough after it is removed from the oven. Cool on a wire rack.

For a two-crust pie, prepare and partially prebake the bottom crust as above. Brush the bottom of the shell with a moisture-proofing egg glaze or fruit preserves, per the specific recipe. Add the filling. Roll out the remaining Quick Puff Pastry Dough or the second sheet of thawed frozen dough to a 12-inch square. Brush egg glaze or water around the rim of the bottom crust. Set the top crust in place over the fruit filling and press onto the glazed bottom crust, sealing the edges. With a sharp knife, trim the edges of the crust flush with the rim of the pie plate. Cut a ½-inch round vent hole in the center of the top crust and a few slits around it to allow steam to escape. Brush the top crust with milk or egg glaze. Bake at 425°F for the first 15 minutes, then lower the heat to 350°F and continue baking until the fruit is tender when pierced—through a vent slit—with the tip of a sharp knife, typically about 30 minutes longer. If the crust starts to overbrown, cover it with a foil frame (page 22).

About Phyllo and Strudel

P hyllo (also spelled filo or fillo), like strudel, is finely stretched paper-thin dough of indescribable delicacy. Strudel, however, is traditionally kept in one sheet and rolled over its filling, while phyllo is cut into smaller leaves—hence the name *phyllo*, which means "leaf" in Greek. The leaves are brushed with butter and stacked into layers over or around a variety of fillings before being baked into delectable golden puffs.

There is no substitute for classically homemade phyllo or strudel dough; however, since I rarely have the time, I prefer to use a perfectly satisfactory substitute for both: widely available frozen phyllo, found in most supermarkets.

To Use Frozen Phyllo Dough

Frozen phyllo dough is available in Greek, Middle Eastern, and Asian specialty shops, gourmet stores, and most supermarkets. In Greek or Armenian food shops, you may also find fresh phyllo. The frozen type is packed in 1- or 1½-pound packages containing about 25 sheets, rolled up together.

Frozen phyllo must be allowed to defrost for several hours or overnight in its own package in the refrigerator. If it is defrosted at room temperature, the outer layers may become moist from condensation inside the package and unusable. After opening, any extra dough can be rewrapped in a plastic bag and stored for several days in the refrigerator or about 3 months in the freezer.

When defrosted, phyllo appears to be very fragile, but is actually quite pliable and strong enough to withstand gentle handling—*if not allowed to dry out.* To this end, defrosted phyllo should always be set on a tray and covered immediately with a sheet of wax paper or plastic wrap topped by a dampened tea towel. Keep it this way until you brush it with butter and form it into pastries according to your recipe. When uncovered and exposed to the air too long, phyllo will crack and become impossible to handle. Small tears and cracks, however, can be ignored. These always occur; simply brush butter over the edges and press on a patching piece of dough. Since leaves of phyllo are generously brushed with butter as pastries are formed, it is best to bake pastries on a jelly-roll pan with a lip to catch the excess fat as it melts in the oven.

To use the dough, bake according to individual phyllo or strudel recipes (see Index).

PASTRY FILLINGS AND TOPPINGS

Vanilla Pastry Cream
(Crème Pâtissière)
· · · · · · · · · · ·

Traditionally, this vanilla cream is used as a filling beneath glazed fresh fruits in a completely prebaked tart or pie shell. The classic version uses as many as 6 large egg yolks for 2 cups milk; I usually use 4 yolks, but you can cut that down to only 2 or 3 yolks or 2 whole eggs and the recipe will still work. The vanilla bean imparts the best flavor to the cream, but vanilla extract, added at the end of the recipe, is a fine substitute. This cream is most often flavored with vanilla or almond, but for a change, you may wish to try some of the other flavor variations that follow.

ADVANCE PREPARATION: Pastry cream can be made ahead and refrigerated, tightly covered, for up to a week.

SPECIAL EQUIPMENT: 2½-quart heavy-bottom nonreactive saucepan; wooden spoon; whisk; strainer; mixing bowl; plastic wrap

COOKING TIME: 12 to 15 minutes

YIELD: About 2⅓ cups; enough to generously coat one 9-, 10-, or 11-inch tart or adequately coat two 9-inch tarts or pies

> **2 tablespoons all-purpose flour**
> **Scant pinch of salt**
> **⅔ cup granulated sugar**
> **2 tablespoons cornstarch**
> **4 large egg yolks (or 2 to 3 large yolks or 2 whole large eggs)**
> **2 cups milk**
> **1 vanilla bean, slit lengthwise, or 2 teaspoons vanilla extract**
> **2 tablespoons unsalted butter, cut up**

Whisk together the flour, salt, sugar, and cornstarch, in a nonreactive saucepan. In a mixing bowl, whisk the milk into the yolks (or whole eggs), then whisk them into the sugar-starch mixture. Whisk well to be sure all the cornstarch and flour is picked up off the pan bottom and dissolved. With a knife, scrape all the inner seeds out of the vanilla bean, if you are using it, and add to the pan, then add the whole vanilla bean; if you are using vanilla extract, do not add it until the end of the recipe.

Set the pan over medium heat and cook the custard mixture for about 12 minutes, until it thickens and comes to a boil: Stir with a wooden spoon on and off for the first 5 minutes, then stir constantly for about 7 minutes longer, until the mixture really thickens and reaches a boil, and you see fat heavy bubbles work up to the surface and burst between stirs. Occasionally use a whisk instead of the spoon to break up and remove any lumps. Then boil for 1 full minute (count to 60) while stirring constantly, covering the entire bottom of the pan with the spoon. Remove the pan from the heat. The cream is sufficiently cooked if it is smooth and thick and will generously coat the spoon—it should hold a clearly defined line when you draw your fingertip through the cream clinging to the back of the spoon.

Remove the vanilla bean, if used; wash and dry it for reuse. If you suspect that the cream may be lumpy, pass it through a strainer set over a bowl. Stir in the butter and the vanilla extract, if using. Spoon the cream into a bowl. To prevent a skin from forming, press a piece of buttered plastic wrap onto the surface, or dab it with butter or sift on a very light coating of confectioners' sugar. Cool, then cover and refrigerate.

Praline Pastry Cream. Fold ⅓ to ½ cup powdered peanut or almond brittle into the warm, finished pastry cream. (Grind the broken pieces of brittle to a powder in a food processor or blender or put in a plastic bag and pound with a hammer.)

Coffee Pastry Cream. Dissolve 2 tablespoons instant coffee powder in the milk before whisking it into the egg yolk mixture.

Chocolate Pastry Cream. Melt 3 to 4 ounces finest-quality semisweet, bittersweet, or unsweetened chocolate in a double boiler, then stir it into the warm, finished cream. The amount of chocolate depends on how much chocolate flavor you desire; I prefer the maximum.

Mocha Pastry Cream. Melt 3 ounces semisweet chocolate in a double boiler. Stir in 4 teaspoons instant coffee powder dissolved in 1 tablespoon hot water. Stir this into the warm, finished cream.

Almond Pastry Cream. Stir 1 teaspoon almond extract into the pastry cream along with the butter. You can also add ½ cup (2 ounces) ground blanched almonds to make this into Frangipane, an excellent filling for fruit tarts.

Orange Pastry Cream. Add 1 tablespoon grated orange zest to the custard mixture before cooking. Stir 2 to 3 tablespoons orange-flavored liqueur into the warm, finished cream.

Butterscotch Pastry Cream. Substitute ½ cup packed dark brown sugar for the granulated sugar.

Liqueur-Flavored Pastry Cream. Stir 2 tablespoons rum, kirsch, or other liqueur into the pastry cream along with the butter.

Whipped-Cream Pastry Cream. Set the pastry cream aside to cool, then chill while you whip ½ cup heavy (36% butterfat) cream until stiff. Fold the cold creams together.

Instant Pastry Cream. For desperate moments when time is precious, prepare 1 small package French vanilla pudding, *instant type,* using 1 cup milk. Whip ½ cup heavy cream (36% butterfat) until stiff and fold it into the pudding along with 1 teaspoon vanilla or almond extract. Or, for even better (although still packaged) flavor, use *cooked-style* vanilla pudding prepared as directed on the box and chilled; mix with the whipped cream, then add the vanilla or almond extract.

Light Lemon Curd
· · · · · · · · · · ·

This is a lightened version of the classic yolk-filled lemon curd on page 120; because it is thickened with starch rather than eggs and contains no butter, it has about half the calories from fat. However, the taste is fantastic and the texture rich because it is finished with a little heavy cream. Use it as a filling in any fresh fruit tart, or spoon it into a crisp Phyllo Cup (page 330) and top with fresh berries and a dusting of confectioners' sugar.

ADVANCE PREPARATION: The curd can be prepared up to 2 days in advance, covered, and refrigerated. Stir well before serving or spreading into a prebaked pie or tart shell.

SPECIAL EQUIPMENT: Medium-sized heavy-bottomed nonreactive saucepan; cup; whisk; mixing bowl; strainer

COOKING TIME: About 3 minutes, total

YIELD: 1 cup; enough to coat one 9-inch pie or tart shell or fill 4 or 5 phyllo cups.

> 1 teaspoon all-purpose flour
> Pinch of salt
> ½ cup granulated sugar
> 1½ tablespoons cornstarch
> ½ cup plus 1 tablespoon fresh orange juice
> 1 teaspoon grated lemon zest
> ¼ cup fresh lemon juice
> 2 tablespoons heavy cream

In a medium-sized nonreactive saucepan, whisk together the flour, salt, sugar, and cornstarch. In a cup, combine the orange juice, lemon zest, and lemon juice, then whisk them into the dry ingredients. Place the pan over medium heat and whisk until the mixture comes to a boil. Boil, whisking constantly, for 1 full minute (count to 60), or until thickened and clear. Remove the pan from the heat and whisk in the cream. Pass the curd through a strainer. Set the curd aside to cool, then refrigerate; it will thicken as it cools.

Classic Lemon Curd

. . . .

This traditional lemon curd filling is rich, silken, and perfectly balanced with a bright tart-sweet taste. Most classic curds are thickened exclusively with yolks, but I find the addition of a little cornstarch improves the set and the texture. Use this beneath a layer of fresh fruit in any fruit tart or pie. For delightful flavor and color variations, replace the lemon juice and zest with that of limes or blood oranges (frozen blood orange juice is available year-round from some Sources; see page 363). For an even richer pie or tart filling, you can fold ½ to 1 cup of stiffly whipped cream into the curd.

ADVANCE PREPARATION: Curd is best used the day it is made, but it should be chilled to thicken properly before being spread into a pie or tart crust. Can be made 1 day in advance. Refrigerate.

SPECIAL EQUIPMENT: Double boiler; whisk; mixing bowl; strainer

COOKING TIME: About 5 minutes.

YIELD: Scant 2 cups; enough to coat a 9- to 12-inch tart or pie shell

8 tablespoons (1 stick) unsalted butter, cut up
1 cup granulated sugar
Grated zest of 2 lemons (about 5 teaspoons)
⅓ cup fresh lemon juice
1 large egg plus 5 large egg yolks
1 tablespoon cornstarch dissolved in 2 tablespoons fresh orange juice
    or water

Melt the butter in the top of a double boiler set over simmering water. Stir in the sugar, lemon zest, and juice and whisk until the sugar is melted, about 4 to 5 minutes. In a small bowl, whisk together the whole egg and yolks, then whisk in the cornstarch mixture. Pour about ½ cup of the hot lemon mixture into the yolks while whisking hard to prevent the yolks from poaching. Pour the warmed yolks back into the rest of the hot lemon mixture, again whisking hard to blend the yolks smoothly.

Cook the curd over simmering water, whisking constantly, for about 5 minutes, until it is thick enough to coat the back of a spoon—a line drawn with your finger through the coating will not readily close. Remove the pan from the heat, turn the curd out into a bowl, and refrigerate; it will thicken as it cools. To prevent a skin from forming, dab a little cold butter on top of the hot curd or press plastic wrap against it. Once the curd is cold and thick, it can be spread into a completely baked pastry shell.

121

Almond Pastry Cream
(Frangipane)

. . . .

This almond-flavored cream is used as a filling beneath fruit in tarts and tartlets. It can be baked as a separate layer in the pastry shell, then topped with glazed fresh fruit, or it can be baked along with its fruit topping. In the latter case, the cream puffs up around the fruit, making a decorative presentation. Frangipane can also be used uncooked, spread into a prebaked pastry shell and topped with glazed fresh fruit (but be aware that it will contain an uncooked egg). For another version, see Almond Pastry Cream, page 118.

ADVANCE PREPARATION: If it is to be used right away, keep frangipane at room temperature. To store, keep it covered in the refrigerator for 2 to 3 days. If it is too stiff to stir easily after chilling, blend in a few tablespoons cream.

SPECIAL EQUIPMENT: Food processor or blender or nut mill to grind nuts; mixing bowl; baking sheet for drying out nuts

YIELD: 1 cup; enough to coat one 10- or 11-inch tart or 12 to 15 tartlets

5 tablespoons unsalted butter, at room temperature, cut up

5 tablespoons granulated sugar

1 large egg, at room temperature

½ teaspoon almond extract or 1 tablespoon dark or light rum

4 ounces blanched almonds, dried (page 41) and finely ground
   (⅔ cup ground)

1½ tablespoons all-purpose flour

HAND METHOD:

In a mixing bowl, cream the butter and sugar together until soft and smooth. Beat in the egg and extract or rum. When well blended, stir in the ground nuts and flour.

FOOD PROCESSOR METHOD:

Grind the almonds with the sugar, then add the cut-up butter and pulse 2 or 3 times. Add the egg, extract or rum, and flour and blend until smooth.

123

Hot and Sweet Cream Filling

· · · · · · · · · · ·

This is one of my favorite fillings for fresh fruit tarts—in addition to being low in fat, it's a delightful surprise to taste the mellow flavor of fresh strawberries and/or blueberries contrasted with this sweet-sour-spicy cream. Tabasco jalapeño sauce has a green color and is sold in supermarkets; you can substitute 2 to 3 tablespoons of orange liqueur and a dash of ground cayenne pepper or a drop of other hot pepper sauce.

ADVANCE PREPARATION: The filling can be prepared a day in advance, covered, and refrigerated. The flavors are best if the filling is chilled for at least 2 hours before serving.

SPECIAL EQUIPMENT: Food processor or electric mixer

YIELD: Generous 1 cup; enough to coat one 9-inch pie or tart shell.

> ⅔ cup nonfat or low-fat sour cream
> ½ cup (4 ounces) light cream cheese or Neufchâtel cheese, at room
>   temperature
> 3 tablespoons granulated sugar
> ½ teaspoon ground nutmeg
> 1 to 2 teaspoons Tabasco jalapeño sauce, or to taste

In a food processor or electric mixer, beat together all the ingredients until smooth. Begin with 1 teaspoon of the hot sauce and taste as you add more, until you reach the desired degree of heat; the flavors intensify a little on standing.

Vanilla-Yogurt Cream
. . . .

You would never guess from the taste or texture that this delicious cream is reduced in fat. You can use it as a filling in a fresh fruit tart or beneath berries in a crisp Phyllo Cup (page 330). To make Honey Vanilla-Yogurt Cream, replace 2 tablespoons of the yogurt with 2 tablespoons honey and cut the sugar in half.

ADVANCE PREPARATION: Plan ahead, because the yogurt should drain for about 15 minutes before using. The cream can be made up to 2 days in advance, covered, and refrigerated. If you prefer a thicker cream, drain the yogurt for at least 30 minutes before using and chill the cream for at least 1 hour before serving.

SPECIAL EQUIPMENT: Strainer set over a bowl; mixing bowl; electric mixer

YIELD: 2 cups or enough to coat a 9- to 12-inch pie or tart shell

> 1 cup vanilla low-fat yogurt, preferably without added gums
> 8 ounces (1 large package) low-fat cream cheese (not fat-free) or Neufchâtel cream cheese, at room temperature
> 2 tablespoons granulated sugar, or to taste
> 1 teaspoon vanilla extract

Put the yogurt in a strainer set over a bowl and drain for at least 15 minutes; discard (or drink) the liquid.

In a medium mixing bowl, combine the drained yogurt and all the remaining ingredients. Whip with an electric mixer on medium-low speed until smooth and creamy. Refrigerate until ready to use—at least 1 hour if you are using it in a pie or tart and want it to thicken enough to hold a slice.

Crème Fraîche

· · · · · · · · · · ·

This rich, slightly tangy French cream has the texture of thick sour cream, with a slightly sweeter taste. It is easy to make at home. Serve it plain or mixed with a little sugar beneath any combination of berries in a fresh fruit tart.

Special Equipment: Mixing bowl; whisk; plastic wrap; strainer lined with paper towel or coffee filter; glass jar with lid

Yield: About 1 cup

> **1 cup heavy cream**
> **½ cup (4 ounces) sour cream**

Whisk both creams together in a mixing bowl, then cover with plastic wrap and let sit at room temperature (about 68°F) for about 8 hours, until thickened.

Line a strainer with a double thickness of paper towels or a coffee filter and set it over a bowl. Turn the cream out into the strainer and drain it overnight, or up to 24 hours, in the refrigerator. Discard (or drink) the thin liquid that drains out. Store the cream in a covered glass jar, refrigerated, for up to a week.

Lemon–Double Cream Tart Filling
. . . .

This uncooked filling is quickly and easily made. The tangy lemon–cream cheese flavor is mellowed slightly by the addition of whipped cream. Spread the filling in completely prebaked tart or tartlet shells and top with any combination of glazed fresh fruits.

ADVANCE PREPARATION: The filling can be made a day or two ahead *without* the whipped cream; refrigerate. If it is too stiff to stir when chilled, add a tablespoon or two of milk or whipped cream to soften before folding in the remaining whipped cream. *With* whipped cream added, the mixture will hold refrigerated for 1 day.

SPECIAL EQUIPMENT: Food processor fitted with steel blade, electric mixer, or blender; chilled electric mixer bowl and beater for whipping cream

QUANTITY: 1½ to 1⅔ cups; enough to generously coat one 11-inch tart shell or 8 to 10 small tartlets

> 8 ounces (1 large package) cream cheese, at room temperature
> 1 cup sifted confectioners' sugar
> 2 tablespoons fresh lemon juice
> 1 tablespoon grated lemon zest
> Optional flavoring: 2 tablespoons dark rum, Grand Marnier, or other
>   fruit-flavored liqueur
> ¾ cup heavy cream (36% butterfat), chilled

Use a food processor, mixer, or blender to beat together the cream cheese, sugar, lemon juice, grated zest, and the optional flavoring until the mixture is light and smooth; turn it out into a large bowl. In a separate chilled bowl, with chilled beater, whip the cream until nearly stiff (do not overbeat). Fold it into the cream cheese mixture. Follow the specific recipe to spread into a completely prebaked pastry shell and top with glazed fresh fruit. Refrigerate.

Lemonade or Orange Juice Cream Cheese Tart Filling

. . . .

I couldn't get through a summer without this uncooked filling recipe; it is my all-occasion favorite for fresh fruit or berry tarts or pies. Quick, easy, and mixed in a minute, the filling is simply spread into a prebaked pastry shell. *Note:* Instead of using frozen lemonade or orange juice concentrate, try substituting frozen tangerine juice and grated tangerine zest, or frozen strawberry daiquiri or margarita mix.

ADVANCE PREPARATION: Filling can be made 1 to 2 days in advance and refrigerated in a covered bowl, although it is so easy it is not really necessary to make ahead. If too stiff to spread after chilling, beat well to soften slightly.

SPECIAL EQUIPMENT: Food processor, blender, or electric mixer (preferably fitted with paddle attachment)

YIELD: About 1½ cups; enough to generously coat a 9- to 11-inch tart or pie shell

> 12 ounces (1½ large packages) cream cheese (not low-fat), at room
>   temperature
> ¼ to ⅓ cup granulated sugar, to taste
> 1 tablespoon grated lemon or orange zest
> 1½ tablespoons frozen lemonade or orange juice concentrate (undiluted)
> 1 to 2 tablespoons orange-flavored liqueur or rum, optional

Cream all the ingredients in a food processor, blender, or electric mixer until light and smooth. Follow the specific recipe to spread the cream into a completely prebaked pastry shell and cover with glazed fresh fruit. Refrigerate.

About Cream
and Whipping Cream

When selecting cream for whipping, butterfat content is the single most important element to consider. The obvious choice would seem to be plain whipping cream, and it does whip up, but *not* stiff enough to hold its shape, because it contains only about 30 percent butterfat. The trick is to whip cream with 36 to 40 percent butterfat; this is generally labeled *"heavy"* or *"heavy whipping"* cream (with an average 36 percent). The butterfat content is rarely if ever marked on the carton, so you must be very careful which type you select. Light cream has a butterfat content of between 18 and 20 percent, while half-and-half has only 10½ to 12 percent; neither will whip properly.

If you purchased heavy cream but it does not hold a proper set once whipped, it is either over-ultrapasteurized or does not contain enough butterfat. To remedy this, you can add a little melted butter to the remaining (still unwhipped) heavy cream. To do this, melt 4 tablespoons of unsalted butter with ⅓ cup of the remaining cream in a small pan set over low heat. Stir well, then allow to cool to room temperature or slightly cooler (but don't allow it to solidify). In a chilled bowl, whip an additional ⅔ cup of chilled heavy cream until it just begins to form very soft peaks; continue to beat on medium speed while adding the melted butter mixture in a slow steady stream. Beat the cream until stiff peaks form. This cream will hold its shape for up to about 2 hours if refrigerated; if it must stand longer, or hold shape at room temperature for more than 30 to 45 minutes, use cream stabilized with a little gelatin (page 130).

To whip cream by hand, use a large chilled balloon whisk or a rotary beater and a large chilled bowl, preferably metal. To do the job more easily, use an electric mixer with the largest balloon-type beater available and a metal bowl. In addition to using well-chilled cream, don't forget to chill the beater and bowl, a job most quickly accomplished in the freezer. The colder the cream and utensils, the firmer the butterfat in the cream and the quicker and stiffer the whipped result. In extra-hot weather, you can beat cream in a bowl set over a pan of ice water.

Note: Cream doubles in volume when whipped; 1 cup heavy cream =
2 cups whipped cream.
When cream is whipped, it passes through several stages:

Chantilly Stage

This is the point when soft mounds appear, before the cream is really firm. Chantilly cream is best for adding to mousses and Bavarian creams and for stirring into pureed fruits for pudding-type desserts or tartlet fillings. This is the stage at which flavoring and/or sugar should be added to cream that will be whipped more stiffly. Sugar added to still-liquid cream may impede the whipping process somewhat.

Stiffly Beaten Cream

At this stage, swirl or tracking lines from the beater are clearly visible on top of the cream; they do not melt away; firm peaks hold on the beater tip when the mixer is turned off. Be careful about this stage; it occurs quickly, and beating should be halted at once. Otherwise, you may get butter, which tastes delicious but may not be what you had in mind at the time. To try to save slightly overbeaten cream, *gently* whisk in (by hand) 2 tablespoons cold milk or cream; it sometimes works.

Sugar, as noted above, is added to cream after it is partially whipped. You can use superfine, granulated, or sifted confectioners' sugar. Confectioners' sugar contains cornstarch (to prevent caking) and thus helps to stabilize the whipped cream slightly; use it if you will be holding the whipped cream for a while before serving. To hold unstabilized whipped cream for several hours before using, you can put it in a cheesecloth-lined strainer set over a bowl in the refrigerator. The strainer will keep the whipped cream separate from any liquid that drains out.

Honey can be substituted for sugar in whipped cream. Be sure the honey is liquefied and strained. Stir it gently into stiffly whipped cream.

Stabilized Whipped Cream

To make a firmer-textured cream that can be piped through a decorating bag to decorate pies and tarts and will hold shape for a long time especially in hot weather, you can add some gelatin or a commercial stabilizer made of modified food starch, gum, or gelatin. For every 1 cup heavy cream to be whipped, dissolve 1 level teaspoon unflavored gelatin in 2 tablespoons cold water. Let it sit for 2 minutes to soften, then set the gelatin over low heat and stir until completely melted; do not boil, or the setting strength will be reduced. Cool the mixture to room temperature (comfortable to the touch, not warmer). Whip the cream until soft peaks form, then slowly add the liquified gelatin while beating until stiff. Commercial products such as Whipit are sold in bakeware shops (see Sources, page 363). To use, follow package directions.

Whipped Cream Topping for Pies and Tarts

. . . .

Review About Cream and Whipping Cream, page 129. Select heavy cream, 36% butterfat, and chill it well. Unless otherwise noted in recipes below, follow this procedure: Whip the cream *just* to soft peaks, add the flavoring(s) then sift on the measured sugar, and whip to firm peaks. Chill or use immediately.

Lattice Cream. Using stabilized cream (page 130) whipped to firm peaks, and using a pastry bag fitted with a star tip, pipe a latticework pattern over the top of a one-crust open-faced pie. To finish, pipe rosettes or a ring around the rim to cover the ends of the cream "lattice" strips. Keep refrigerated until ready to serve.

Rum Cream
    1 cup heavy cream, chilled
    2 tablespoons rum or 1 teaspoon rum extract
    3 tablespoons confectioners' sugar, sifted

Amaretto Cream
    1 cup heavy cream, chilled
    2 tablespoons amaretto liqueur
    ¼ teaspoon almond extract
    2 tablespoons confectioners' sugar, sifted

Cassis Cream

1 cup heavy cream, chilled

3 tablespoons double crème de cassis liqueur (black currant flavor; tints cream pink)

2 tablespoons confectioners' sugar, sifted

Mint Cream

1 cup heavy cream, chilled

2 tablespoons white crème de menthe (green type will tint cream)

¼ teaspoon peppermint extract

¼ cup confectioners' sugar, sifted

Orange Cream

1 cup heavy cream, chilled

Grated zest of 1 orange

½ teaspoon orange extract

2 tablespoons orange-flavored liqueur (such as curaçao or Grand Marnier)

2 tablespoons confectioners' sugar, sifted

Apricot Cream

1 cup heavy cream, chilled

2 to 3 tablespoons apricot-flavored liqueur

3 tablespoons confectioners' sugar, sifted

Ginger Cream

1 cup heavy cream, chilled

½ teaspoon ground ginger, sifted

2 tablespoons confectioners' sugar, sifted

1 to 2 tablespoons finely minced candied ginger, to taste

Whip the cream to soft peaks, add the *ground* ginger and sugar and whip until stiff, then fold in the candied ginger.

Coffee Cream

1 tablespoon instant coffee powder (or instant espresso powder)
1 cup heavy cream, chilled
3 to 4 tablespoons confectioners' sugar, sifted, to taste

Dissolve the instant coffee in the chilled cream before whipping. Whip to soft peaks, add the sugar, and whip until stiff.

Chocolate Cream

1 cup heavy cream, chilled, divided (½ cup and ½ cup)
1 ounce semisweet or bittersweet chocolate, finely chopped
2 tablespoons confectioners' sugar, sifted

In a small pan, combine ½ cup of the cream and the chocolate. Stir over low heat until the chocolate melts, then stir until smooth. Transfer to a bowl, whisk in the remaining cream and then refrigerate for at least 1 hour. When very cold, whip to soft peaks, add the sugar, and whip stiff.

Mocha Cream
Prepare Chocolate Cream, but dissolve 1½ teaspoons instant coffee granules in the melting cream and chocolate.

Mocha-Praline Cream
Prepare Mocha Cream, then fold ½ cup powdered praline powder (broken almond or peanut brittle powdered in the blender or food processor) into the stiffly whipped cream.

Butterscotch Cream

1 cup heavy cream, chilled
6 tablespoons packed dark brown sugar
½ teaspoon vanilla extract

Combine all the ingredients in a chilled bowl. Stir well to soften and partly dissolve the sugar, then whip the cream until stiff.

Maple Cream

1 cup heavy cream, chilled
5 tablespoons pure maple syrup

Whip the cream to soft peaks, fold in the syrup, and whip until stiff.

About Meringue Topping

It is hard to beat the appeal of a pie topped with waves of gold-tinged meringue. To some, the magic of beaten egg whites reaches its apogee in meringue topping, but in my opinion, baked Meringue Pie Shells (page 108) turn the same ingredients into an equally delightful creation. Light clouds of creamy meringue topping are especially good, and traditionally used, on custard and cream pies. While it is not often done, meringue topping can go equally well atop baked fruit or berry pies; just replace the top crust with meringue.

Many a beginning baker has cried over trying to make a successful meringue topping. Yet frustration is unnecessary if the technique is understood and the basic rules are followed. For detailed instructions on how to beat egg whites, see About Meringue (page 106).

There are several methods of making meringue topping to prevent weeping and to insure creamy consistency. The recipe following is the classic old-fashioned technique. To make a cornstarch-stabilized meringue topping (perfect every time, but slightly more preparation time), use the recipe on page 274 (Lemon Meringue Pie).

Preheat your oven when you begin beating egg whites so the resulting meringue can be applied to the pie and baked as soon as it is completely whipped. For best results, the entire process should be done as close to serving time as possible. To apply the meringue to the pie, note first that most recipes require that the filling be hot. It should, and the reason is that the heat of the filling poaches the underside of the meringue layer, thereby preventing it from liquefying. Avoid stirring the hot pie filling once in place in its shell; stirring may release steam, which may then condense into a watery layer beneath the meringue. Mound your meringue onto the center of your pie with a rubber spatula, then spread it outward with a broad spatula or the back of a spoon, distributing it evenly to the edges all around in order to seal the beaten whites to the rim of the crust—this will prevent the meringue from shrinking during baking. Use the back of the spoon to swirl the meringue or swoop it up into peaks all over. Don't make the peaks too high, though, or the highest tips will overbrown. Alternatively, meringue topping can be piped onto a pie in a lattice, rosette, or other pattern, using a pastry bag fitted with a ½-inch star tip.

Set the pie into the preheated 325°F to 350°F oven (depending upon the recipe) and bake for 12 to 15 minutes, or just until the meringue is golden. Watch carefully and peek often, as meringue will burn easily. Cool away from drafts. To prevent the knife from sticking when you cut the meringue, dip the blade into hot water or coat it with a little vegetable oil.

Note: See About Eggs (page 31) for information on egg whites and sanitation.

. . . .

MERINGUE PIE TOPPING:
WHAT WENT WRONG AND WHY?

Meringue is too flat. Too much sugar was used (the best proportion is 2 tablespoons sugar per 1 large egg white); no acid was used (cream of tartar, lemon juice, white vinegar, or a copper bowl) to stabilize the whites; meringue was cooled in a cold draft.

Meringue is tough. Oven heat was too high (overheating causes egg protein to shrink and toughen).

Meringue "weeps" or beads on the surface after baking. Meringue was overcooked or oven heat was too high; too much sugar was used, or sugar didn't dissolve because meringue was not beaten long enough. Make stabilized meringue (page 275), using cooked cornstarch gel added to whipped meringue.

Meringue shrinks. Meringue was not spread onto edges of crust all around pie; meringue was baked in too cool an oven (under 325°F) or too hot an oven; meringue-topped pie cooled too quickly because it was set in a cold draft.

Liquefied or syrupy layer appears between meringue and pie filling. Undercooked meringue or cold pie filling failed to poach bottom surface of meringue, or hot filling stirred, releasing steam to cause condensation.

135

Classic Meringue Pie Topping

. . . .

This classic recipe is made without cornstarch. Be sure to place it on hot pie topping. Alternatively, you can make cornstarch-stabilized meringue topping, see Lemon Meringue Pie recipe, page 274.

ADVANCE PREPARATION: Meringue should be made and applied to the hot pie topping as close to serving time as possible. However, to be practical, a pie *can* be topped with meringue, baked, and successfully held at room temperature for several hours, or even frozen. For health reasons, meringue pies should be refrigerated.

SPECIAL EQUIPMENT: Copper, glass, glazed ceramic, or stainless steel round-bottomed bowl and large balloon whisk, or electric mixer with largest balloon whisk available and a deep narrow bowl; rubber scraper; spoon or spatula

TEMPERATURE AND TIME: 350°F for 12 to 15 minutes.

YIELD: Enough for one 8- to 10-inch pie

FOR ONE 8-INCH PIE:

    2 large egg whites, at room temperature
    ¼ teaspoon cream of tartar
    A pinch of salt
    ¼ cup superfine or granulated sugar

FOR ONE 9- OR 10-INCH PIE:

    4 large egg whites, at room temperature
    ¼ teaspoon cream of tartar
    A pinch of salt
    6 tablespoons to ½ cup superfine or granulated sugar

(*Note:* For a slightly less generous meringue on a 9-inch pie, you can use 3 whites with ¼ teaspoon cream of tartar, a pinch of salt, and 6 tablespoons sugar.)

Review About Meringue (page 106). Preheat the oven to 350°F.

Combine the egg whites, cream of tartar, and salt in bowl. Beat with a whisk or an electric mixer on medium speed until soft peaks form. Add the sugar 2 tablespoons at a time, beating a little after each addition. Beat 3 to 5 minutes longer (total beating time may be 4 to 6 minutes or more, depending on your mixer and the number of whites), until the whites are shiny, satiny, and hold stiff peaks on the whisk or beater when it is removed and inverted. Be sure the sugar is completely dissolved.

Apply the meringue to the pie, seal by smoothing to the edges of the crust, and make peaks with the back of a spoon. Or pipe the meringue onto the pie with a pastry bag fitted with a star tip.

Bake the meringue-topped pie in the preheated oven for 12 to 15 minutes, or until the top is golden brown. (*Note:* Meringue toppings for small tartlets can be shaped on buttered and floured foil and baked as above. Simply slide them off the foil onto the tartlets just before serving.)

Coconut Meringue Topping. Sprinkle ¼ cup sweetened shredded coconut over the meringue just before baking.

Almond Meringue Topping. Sprinkle ¼ cup slivered, sliced, or finely chopped almonds (or other nuts) over the meringue immediately before baking.

Oat–Wheat Germ Streusel Topping
· · · · · · · · · · ·

Use this crunchy topping over fruit crisps or deep-dish pies, or to replace the top pastry crust of a regular fruit pie.

ADVANCED PREPARATION: Topping can be prepared ahead and stored in a covered jar in the refrigerator or freezer for several days.

YIELD: 1⅔ cups; enough for one 9- or 10-inch pie or a 1½- to 2-quart baking dish

> 5 tablespoons all-purpose flour
> A pinch of salt
> ¼ cup granulated sugar
> ¼ cup packed dark brown sugar
> ½ cup old-fashioned rolled oats or quick-cooking type
> ¼ cup toasted wheat germ
> 5⅓ tablespoons unsalted butter or solid stick margarine,
>   at room temperature, cut up
> ¼ teaspoon ground cinnamon
> ¼ teaspoon ground nutmeg

Combine all ingredients in a large bowl and crumble them together with a fork or your fingertips.

Spread the mixture over the prepared fruit in a buttered baking dish or pie plate and bake as directed in the specific recipe.

Reduced-Fat Oat Streusel Topping

. . . .

Oats and Grape-Nuts cereal give extra crunch to this tasty topping. Use on any fruit or berry crisp or pie to replace classic buttery crumbs or a top piecrust.

ADVANCE PREPARATION: Topping can be prepared ahead and stored in a covered jar in the refrigerator or freezer for 2 or 3 days.

YIELD: About 1½ cups; enough for one 8- or 9-inch fruit crisp or pie

> ½ cup unsifted all-purpose or whole wheat flour
> ⅛ teaspoon salt
> ½ cup packed dark or light brown sugar
> ¼ cup old-fashioned rolled oats or quick-cooking type
> 2 tablespoons toasted wheat germ, optional
> 2 tablespoons Grape-Nuts cereal
> ½ teaspoon ground cinnamon
> ½ teaspoon ground nutmeg
> ½ teaspoon vanilla or almond extract
> 2 tablespoons canola or walnut oil
> 1 tablespoon plus 1 teaspoon skim milk or fruit juice, or more as needed

Combine all the ingredients in a large bowl and crumble them together with a fork or your fingertips. Add a few drops more liquid if the crumbs are too dry.

Spread the crumbs over the prepared fruit in a buttered pie plate or baking dish and bake as directed in the specific recipe.

. . . .
139

Oat Crumb Topping

· · · · · · · · · · ·

Use this simple crumb mixture on any fruit crisp or pie. The oats make the crumbs extra crisp; you can also add ½ cup chopped walnuts or pecans, if you wish.

ADVANCE PREPARATION: Topping can be prepared ahead and stored in a covered jar in the refrigerator or freezer for several days.

YIELD: 1¾ cups; enough for a 9- or 10-inch pie or a 1½- to 2-quart baking dish

> ½ cup unsifted all-purpose flour
> ½ cup granulated sugar
> ⅛ teaspoon salt
> ½ cup old-fashioned rolled oats or quick-cooking type
> ½ teaspoon ground cinnamon
> 6 tablespoons (¾ stick) cold unsalted butter, cut up

Pulse the dry ingredients in the work bowl of a food processor or toss them together in a mixing bowl. Add the butter and pulse the processor to make crumbs, or use your fingertips to pinch the mixture together in the mixing bowl until it forms crumbs.

Spread the crumbs over the prepared fruit in a buttered baking dish or pie plate and bake as directed in the specific recipe.

Nut-Crumb Streusel Topping

. . . .

This recipe makes a somewhat less crunchy topping than the Oat–Wheat Germ Streusel Topping (page 138).

ADVANCE PREPARATION: Topping can be prepared ahead and frozen or stored in a covered jar in refrigerator for several days.

YIELD: About 2½ cups; enough for one 9- or 10-inch pie or a 1½- to 2½-quart baking dish (use only 1½ to 1¾ cups topping for 9-inch pie)

> ½ cup plus 2 tablespoons unsifted all-purpose flour
> ⅔ cup granulated sugar
> 7 tablespoons unsalted butter or solid stick margarine,
>   at room temperature, cut up
> 1 cup (4 ounces) walnuts, pecans, or almonds, finely chopped
> ¼ teaspoon ground cinnamon
> ¼ teaspoon ground nutmeg

Combine all the ingredients in a bowl and crumble them together with your fingertips.

Spread mixture over the prepared fruit in a buttered baking dish or pie plate and bake as directed in the specific recipe.

Toasted Coconut Topping

· · · · · · · · · · ·

Sprinkle this topping over a vanilla or coconut cream pie, or over vanilla ice cream or yogurt.

YIELD: 1 cup; enough to top one 9-inch pie

1 cup sweetened shredded or flaked coconut (or grated fresh)

Spread the coconut on a sheet of foil with edges turned up. Bake in a preheated 375°F oven for 6 to 8 minutes, tossing the coconut occasionally so it colors evenly, until golden brown. Cool.

142

Hard Sauce

· · · · · · · · · · ·

This sauce is traditionally served with Old English plum pudding or warm Mince Pie (page 188), but it is equally good with peach, apple, or cranberry pie or tart.

ADVANCE PREPARATION: Hard Sauce can be made up to a week ahead and refrigerated in a covered container. Before serving, bring to room temperature and stir to soften slightly.

SPECIAL EQUIPMENT: Electric mixer or food processor fitted with steel blade

YIELD: 2 cups; or enough for two 9-inch pies

> 8 tablespoons (1 stick) unsalted butter
> ¼ teaspoon salt
> 4½ cups confectioners' sugar, sifted
> ¼ cup brandy *or* 2 teaspoons brandy extract plus about 3 tablespoons milk
>   or cream

With a mixer or in a food processor, beat the butter until soft.

Add the sifted confectioners' sugar a little at a time, blending until combined. Add the flavoring, and milk if needed, beating until the sauce is creamy. Serve at room temperature.

· · · · · · ·
143

Custard Sauce
(Crème Anglaise)

. . . .

This rich custard sauce is traditionally flavored with vanilla, but it may also contain orange or other liqueur or rum. Serve it warm over Apple Dumplings in Pastry (pages 340–342), or serve it with any fruit or berry pie.

ADVANCE PREPARATION: Sauce can be made early on the day it is to be served, or up to 2 days ahead, covered and refrigerated. To serve warm, reheat in a double boiler, stirring, over *warm* water.

SPECIAL EQUIPMENT: Heavy-bottomed 2-quart nonreactive saucepan; whisk or electric mixer; double boiler, optional; strainer

YIELD: 2 cups; enough to accompany a 9- or 10-inch pie

1 vanilla bean or 2 teaspoons vanilla extract
2 cups milk
4 large egg yolks
1 teaspoon cornstarch
¼ cup granulated sugar

If you are using a vanilla bean, slit it open lengthwise, scrape out the inner seeds with a knife, and put this paste and the bean in a saucepan with the milk; bring slowly to a simmer, just below a boil.

Meanwhile, beat together the yolks, cornstarch, and sugar in a bowl until very thick and light. When the milk barely begins to boil, remove it from the heat. Pour about half the hot milk onto the yolk mixture in a slow stream, whisking constantly. Then pour the warm yolk mixture back into the saucepan with the remaining milk. To be safe, you can now set the pan over a double boiler. Or watch it very closely and set directly over *low* heat. Cook, stirring constantly with a wooden spoon, until the custard is thick enough to coat the spoon and leave a clearly defined line when you draw your finger through the cream on the back of the spoon. Do not overcook, or the custard may curdle, though cornstarch helps prevent this.

Remove the custard from the heat and strain it into a bowl. Remove the vanilla bean, if used, wash, and set aside to use for another purpose. Or stir in the vanilla extract. To prevent a skin from forming, press a piece of buttered plastic wrap onto the surface of the cream or dab it with butter. To store, cool completely, then cover and chill.

Orange or Rum Custard Sauce. Stir 1 tablespoon orange-flavored liqueur or dark rum in after the custard has cooked.

145

Yogurt-Rum Sauce

. . . .

This is one of those inventions of which necessity is the mother. I ran out of cream and discovered by happy accident that the flavor of vanilla yogurt goes well with rum to make a sauce for spiced pies such as pumpkin, mince, or peach.

ADVANCE PREPARATION: Yogurt-Rum Sauce can be made a day or two in advance and refrigerated in a covered container.

YIELD: 1 cup; enough for one 9-inch pie

> 1 cup vanilla yogurt, top liquid poured off
> 1 to 2 tablespoons white or dark rum, to taste
> 2 teaspoons confectioners' sugar, sifted, or
>   granulated sugar

Beat all the ingredients together well. Store in a covered jar in the refrigerator. Serve at room temperature.

Vanilla Icing Glaze

· · · · · · · · · · ·

Use this as a drizzled glaze for fruit turnovers.

YIELD: 1/3 cup; enough for about 12 turnovers or one 9-inch pie

> 1 cup confectioners' sugar, sifted
> 3 to 4 tablespoons warm milk
> 1/4 teaspoon vanilla extract or fresh lemon juice

Blend all the ingredients until smooth. Drizzle over pastry. The glaze hardens somewhat as it dries.

147

About Chocolate

For the chocolate garnishes in this book, I have used only pure semisweet, bittersweet, or unsweetened chocolate, available in 1-ounce squares, blocks of various weights, and chips. Unless you are using premeasured 1-ounce squares of chocolate, it is handy to have a kitchen scale. However, as a guide, 2 tablespoons regular-sized chocolate chips = 1 ounce. Read about Chocolate, pages 38–40. To melt chocolate, see page 39.

Chocolate Curls and Grated Chocolate

· · · · · · · · · ·

To make easy chocolate curls, draw a swivel-type vegetable peeler across the surface of a thick candy bar or piece of block chocolate. Work over a sheet of wax paper and lift completed curls with a toothpick poked into their sides. The trick here is to have the block chocolate at the correct temperature: If it is too cold and hard, the curls will crumble or shave; if too soft, they will collapse. The easiest thing to do is to set the chocolate in a warm oven for 10 to 15 minutes; some ovens are warmed sufficiently by their pilot lights. Or in warm weather, use the sun. If the chocolate feels too soft, chill it slightly; experiment until it works. Chocolate curls can be stored in a protective airtight box in the freezer or in the refrigerator for several days, until needed.

To grate or shave chocolate as a decorative topping for pies, simply pass a piece of block chocolate, a chocolate bar, or a 1-ounce square of chocolate across the medium-sized holes of a box grater. You can do this over a piece of wax paper or directly over a pie top, but the wax paper method gives you more control in positioning the shavings. Unused grated chocolate can be stored in the freezer in an airtight container; it requires no thawing before use.

Rich Chocolate Sauce

· · · · · · · · · ·

ADVANCE PREPARATION: Can be made up to a week ahead and stored, refrigerated, in a covered container. Warm over low heat before serving.

SPECIAL EQUIPMENT: Saucepan and whisk; jar with lid

YIELD: 1 cup; 8 to 10 servings

> **1 cup (8 ounces) chopped semisweet or bittersweet chocolate (or use 4 ounces unsweetened and 4 ounces semisweet)**
> **½ cup heavy cream**
> **Optional flavoring: 1 to 2 tablespoons rum, orange-flavored liqueur, or amaretto liqueur, to taste**

Melt the chocolate in the top of a double boiler over hot (not boiling) water. Remove the chocolate from the heat just before it is completely melted.

Whisk or stir to melt completely, then very slowly whisk in the cream a little at a time, blending until smooth and thick. Stir in the flavoring, if you are using it. Serve warm.

Chocolate Leaves

· · · · · · · · · ·

Chocolate leaves are made by coating real leaves (see Note) with melted chocolate. When the chocolate is hard, the real leaf is peeled away, leaving an edible garnish for chiffon or whipped cream-topped pies and tarts or tartlets. As a bonus, you can also flavor melted chocolate with peppermint extract (or other liqueur or extract) and prepare a whole tray of chocolate leaves, to be passed as elegant after-dinner mints. Read How to Melt Chocolate, page 39.

Note: For the prettiest effect, use gracefully shaped leaves with a waxy surface and a pronounced pattern of veins on one side. Lemon, magnolia, camellia, gardenia, and even rose leaves work well. However, be aware that certain types of leaves meet all other criteria but are poisonous! If you are uncertain, check with your local agricultural extension service or a reputable botanist. Be sure leaves are pesticide- and dirt-free, rinsed, and dried thoroughly. I use lemon or camellia leaves from a local florist, who also supplies them to neighboring restaurants. Lemon leaves work well because they are strong enough to be reused without tearing. If you have a misshapen or extra-large leaf, simply cut it to the desired size with scissors before coating it with chocolate. Lemon leaves can also be cut to resemble oak, maple, or other leaf shapes.

ADVANCE PREPARATION: Chocolate leaves can be prepared well in advance and frozen for several months in a protective airtight container.

SPECIAL EQUIPMENT: Double boiler; leaves (see Note above); wax paper; tray; pastry brush or small spatula for applying chocolate, optional (I prefer to use my finger)

YIELD: As a rough guideline, 1 ounce of chocolate, melted, will coat about 6 leaves, depending upon their size; 8 ounces, then, will make roughly 50 leaves. Make as many as you wish; 6 to 8 leaves are enough to top a 9- to 11-inch pie or tart, but you should always make extras in case some break (or get eaten). Extra melted chocolate can be poured into a paper muffin cup liner and chilled, to be reused for another purpose.

8 ounces semisweet, bittersweet, or white chocolate
2 teaspoons Crisco

Melt the chocolate and shortening together in the top of a double boiler over hot (not boiling) water. Set aside to cool until the chocolate is comfortable to the touch. Set clean dry leaves, vein sides up, on a wax paper–covered tray. (*Note:* The most pronounced vein pattern is generally on the underside of the leaf.) With a pastry brush, small spatula, or your fingertip, spread a generous ⅛-inch layer of chocolate over each leaf, covering the side where the vein markings are most visible. Spread the chocolate up to, but not over, the leaf edges, and try to avoid thinning the edges too much. Set the coated leaves chocolate side up, on a wax paper-covered tray and place in the refrigerator or freezer for a few minutes, until the chocolate is hard-set.

To make curled leaves, allow the chocolate-coated leaves to cool partially, then set them into the curved surface of a French-bread pan or tube-shaped baking pan or over a rolling pin and chill to set. (If curved too soon, the melted chocolate will all run to the middle of the leaf.)

When the chocolate is completely set, remove the leaves from the refrigerator or freezer. Carefully break off any uneven chocolate edges that wrap over the front of the real leaves. Allow the chocolate to warm for about 30 seconds at room temperature, then, starting at the stem end, peel the real leaves away from the chocolate. Take care to handle the chocolate leaves as little as possible to avoid making fingerprints. Set the chocolate leaves back on the tray or in a protective container and refrigerate or freeze until needed. You can reuse real leaves, coating them with more chocolate, as long as they hold their shape.

(*Note:* If this is your first time, it is best to make a few test leaves at the start to determine the quality of the chocolate coating. Chocolate leaves should have a delicate appearance; ease up if you made the chocolate too thick. If, on the other hand, the chocolate shatters when the leaf is peeled away, apply more chocolate the next time and warm the leaf a few more seconds in your hand before peeling it off.)

Chocolate Icing
· · · · · · · · · · ·

Use this easily made icing to top Frozen Mud Pie (page 360).

QUANTITY: ½ cup

>   2 ounces chopped semisweet or bittersweet chocolate
>   or ⅓ cup semisweet chocolate chips)
>   1 tablespoon unsalted butter
>   ½ cup sifted confectioners' sugar
>   2 tablespoons hot water
>   ¼ teaspoon vanilla extract

152

In a double boiler, melt the chocolate with the butter over hot (not boiling) water. Whisk in the sifted sugar, hot water, and vanilla. Cool.

About Fruit Glazes

A fruit glaze has several purposes: It can be brushed over the top of a fresh fruit tart to impart a brilliant sheen and to prevent oxidation of the fruit, or it can be brushed inside a pastry shell to provide a light, flavorful moisture-proofing before a juicy filling is added. The finest-quality apricot preserves or red currant jelly are most commonly used for glazing because they contain a sufficient amount of pectin to stiffen somewhat when cooled after boiling.

Apricot or other fruit preserves should be warmed and strained to remove any pieces of fruit. Select preserves or jelly whose color and flavor complement the color of your pie filling or fresh fruit. Apricot gives a golden-orange hue to white, yellow, or orange fruits such as bananas, pineapples, or peaches, while red currant gives a reddish hue, best for strawberries, raspberries, cherries, and red grapes.

Both apricot preserves and red currant jelly can be flavored with kirsch or other fruit-flavored liqueur before using. Note particularly that the Plain Fruit Glaze (below) contains nothing but jelly and liqueur; it will remain intact as a coating on fresh fruit for no more than a couple of hours before it starts to soften and melt. For a glaze that holds up longer than 2 or 3 hours before serving, use Firm Fruit Glaze (page 155), which is stiffened with a little gelatin. (*Note:* Be sure fruit to be glazed is dry; do not sprinkle it with sugar, as sugar would melt and dissolve the glaze.)

Plain Fruit Glaze

· · · · · · · · · ·

YIELD: ½ cup; enough to coat one 9- to 12-inch pie or tart

½ cup apricot preserves or red currant jelly
Optional flavoring: 2 tablespoons kirsch or other fruit-flavored liqueur

If you are using apricot preserves, stir over medium heat in a small saucepan until melted, strain through a sieve (return strained fruit pieces to the preserves jar), and return the strained preserves to the saucepan. Or measure red currant jelly into a small saucepan. Add the liqueur, if you are using it, and bring the preserves or jelly to a boil over medium heat. They should cook for about 2 minutes, or until thick enough to coat a spoon. Remove from the heat and cool until the glaze begins to thicken slightly but is still luke-warm. Use a pastry brush to coat *dry* fruit on top of a pie or tart, or brush glaze over an un-filled pie shell as directed by your recipe. Chill to set the glaze. Store leftover glaze in a covered jar in the refrigerator; reheat to use.

154

Firm Fruit Glaze

. . . .

This is the recipe to use when a glazed fruit pie or tart must be held for several hours or longer before serving. The addition of a small amount of gelatin to the recipe keeps the glaze from melting, yet does not make it rubbery.

YIELD: ½ cup; enough to coat one 9- to 12-inch pie or tart

> ½ cup apricot preserves or red currant jelly
> 1½ teaspoons unflavored gelatin
> 2 tablespoons kirsch, other fruit-flavored liqueur, or fruit juice

If you are using apricot preserves, stir over medium heat in a small saucepan until melted, strain the preserves through a sieve (return strained fruit pieces to the preserves jar), and return the strained preserves to the saucepan. Or measure red currant jelly directly into a small saucepan and boil for 30 seconds; cool slightly. Add the gelatin and liqueur or fruit juice.

Stir over medium-low heat until the mixture is smooth and clear, the gelatin no longer looks granular, and is completely dissolved. Stir for a minute or two longer over medium heat; do not boil. Then cool to lukewarm. Use a pastry brush to apply glaze over *dry* fruit on top of a pie or tart. Chill to set the glaze. Store leftover glaze in a covered jar in the refrigerator; reheat to use.

Egg, Milk, and All-Purpose Pastry Glazes

Egg glazes have two purposes in pastry making: They are used to give a moisture-proof coating to pastry shells before a liquid or juicy fruit filling is added, and they are brushed over the tops of pastries to impart a rich golden luster to the finished product.

Basic Egg Glaze

. . . .

This contains egg yolk and gives a rich golden color to pastry tops.

1 large egg beaten with 1 to 2 tablespoons water

Egg Yolk Glaze

1 large egg yolk beaten with 2 tablespoons milk or water

Egg White Glaze

This is most often used for moisture-proofing crusts rather than for adding color to pastry tops. (*Note:* Water softens the protein of the egg white, so it will not produce a rubbery layer.)

1 large egg white beaten with 1 to 2 tablespoons water

Milk or Butter Glaze

. . . .

For a rustic or farm-kitchen glaze atop your fruit pie, brush milk (or melted butter) over the crust before baking. This gives a dull finish rather than the high gloss achieved with egg.

All-Purpose Glaze

. . . .

Use this glaze for topping piecrusts; it will not toughen as an egg white glaze sometimes does.

1 large egg
3 tablespoons melted unsalted butter
3 tablespoons warm milk

Beat all the ingredients together and brush over pastry. Be sure the milk is warm so that it mixes with the melted butter; cold milk will harden the butter.

FRUIT AND BERRY PIES

But I, when I undress me
Each night, upon my knees
Will ask the Lord to bless me
With apple-pie and cheese.

EUGENE FIELD
"Apple Pie and Cheese"

I t is true that almost nothing can make you feel as good as a freshly baked apple pie. And nothing so clearly symbolizes the country kitchen as an old-fashioned pie with sweet steam wafting from the vents in its sugar-glazed, golden brown crust.

As a basic rule of thumb, the procedure for making an all-American two-crust classic fruit pie is to line a 9-inch pie plate with flaky pastry and fill it with 4 to 8 cups of sliced fresh fruit mixed with spices and sugar, thickened with 2 to 3 tablespoons flour, cornstarch, or tapioca. Cover with the top crust, glaze, and bake.

There are, however, several tricks to insure perfection. First, to guarantee a crisp, rather than soggy, bottom crust, brush moisture-proofing egg glaze (page 156) on the crust before adding the filling, or sprinkle it with a handful of dry bread or cereal crumbs to absorb excess moisture. Second, to protect the oven from dripping juices, set a sheet of foil with edging turned up directly on the oven floor (under the electric heating coil if you have one). Third, to bake correctly, set it in the lower third of a preheated (425°F) oven for about 15 minutes to bake the pastry quickly. Then raise the pie to the oven center, lower the heat to moderate (350°F), and bake until the fruit filling is tender. Fourth, if the crust begins to brown too much, cover the edges with a foil frame (page 22).

My mother's technique for pies that look as good as they taste is to use an extra cup or two of fruit, piled high in the center so the top crust is dome-shaped rather than flat. For special occasions, make a classic or quick "mock" lattice top of crisscrossed pastry strips (pages 60–64). To roll out, fit, and shape pastry for two-crust pies, see pages 52–70. Bakers concerned with saving time will want to freeze pie fillings, pastry, or completely made pies (see Index).

This chapter contains a selection of classic two-crust pies as well as single-crust, deep-dish, and lattice-topped pies.

. . . .

FRUIT PIE THICKENERS

Two tablespoons flour will thicken 1 cup liquid for a medium-thick sauce or for an average 9-inch pie; 2½ to 3 tablespoons flour will thicken 1 cup liquid for a thick sauce or for a 9- or 10-inch fruit pie. Instead of flour, you can use 2 to 3 tablespoons quick-cooking tapioca to set the filling for a 9- or 10-inch pie. Use the larger amount for very juicy fruit. As other alternatives, you can use cornstarch, arrowroot, or potato starch, all of which are good thickeners with about twice the thickening power of flour. Flour produces an opaque sauce, cornstarch gives a cloudy but less opaque result, and tapioca, arrowroot, and potato starch cook to a clear sauce.

. . . .

Old-Fashioned Apple Pie

· · · · · · · · · · ·

This is IT!—what our country and flag are as American as. Since the earliest colonial days, apple pies have been enjoyed in America for breakfast, for dessert, even for an entrée. Colonists wrote home about them and foreign visitors noted apple pie as one of our first culinary specialties. According to the *American Heritage Cookbook* (Penguin Books, 1967), a Swedish parson named Dr. Acrelius wrote back to his family in 1758, "Apple-pie is used through the whole year, and when fresh apples are no longer to be had, dried ones are used. It is the evening meal of children. House-pie, in country places, is made of apples neither peeled nor freed from their cores, and its crust is not broken if a wagon wheel goes over it."

Select apples that are firm and tart such as Greenings, Jonathans, Cortlands, or Granny Smiths. In my opinion, McIntosh apples soften too much when baked in a pie. Note: To make a high-domed pie, use 8 large apples. Carefully arrange the slices, building up a compact, neat dome. Compress the dome to be sure it is stable before adding the top crust. Randomly tossed apples will sink down into air pockets during baking, causing the top crust to fall or leaving a large air pocket between fruit and the raised-up pastry. Serve apple pie warm, topped with a slice of sharp Cheddar cheese or a dollop of heavy cream.

ADVANCE PREPARATION: Apple pie is best freshly baked and warm from the oven. It will keep for a day and should be reheated to serve warm.

SPECIAL EQUIPMENT: 9-inch pie plate; rolling pin; pastry brush; aluminum foil frame (page 22)

TEMPERATURE AND TIME: 425°F for 12 to 15 minutes, 350°F for 40 to 45 minutes

YIELD: One 9-inch pie; serves 6 to 8

PASTRY:

Unbaked pastry for a two-crust 9-inch pie made with All-Purpose Flaky Pastry (page 45), Cheddar Cheese variation (page 49), Cornmeal Pastry (page 81), or Butter-Lard Pastry (page 87)

EGG GLAZE:
   1 large egg beaten with 1 tablespoon water

FILLING:
   ¼ cup plain cracker or cornflake crumbs, optional
   6 to 8 large Granny Smith or Greening apples (or a blend of these
      plus Jonathan, Golden Delicious, Rome, or other flavorful apples),
      peeled and sliced ⅛ inch thick (6 to 8 cups slices; quantity and
      compactness of slices determines pie height)
   ⅓ to ½ cup packed brown sugar (amount depends upon tartness
      of apples)
   Juice of 1 large lemon
   3 tablespoons all-purpose flour
   ½ to 1 teaspoon ground nutmeg, to taste
   ½ to 1 teaspoon ground cinnamon, to taste
   2 tablespoons unsalted butter, cut up, optional

TOPPING:
   Granulated sugar

161

Prepare the pastry, roll out half, and line the pie plate (page 52–55). Trim a ½-inch pastry overhang. To moisture-proof the lower crust, brush with egg glaze and/or sprinkle with the crumbs. Preheat the oven to 425°F.

In a large bowl, toss the sliced apples with the sugar, lemon juice, flour, and spices. Add the fruit to the pastry-lined pan and dot with the butter, if using. Brush egg glaze over the edge of lower crust.

Roll out the top crust and fit it over the fruit. Trim a ¾-inch overhang. Fold the edge under the bottom crust and pinch them together to seal, making a raised rim all around. Flute the edge as desired (page 56). Cut vent holes in the top (page 59). Brush the top of the pie with egg glaze and sprinkle with the topping sugar (or simply brush with milk or leave plain).

Set the pie in the lower third of the preheated oven and bake for 12 to 15 minutes. Reduce the heat to 350°F, raise the pie to the center of the oven, and bake for an additional 40 to 45 minutes, or until the pastry is golden brown and the fruit is tender when pierced with the tip of a knife through a vent hole. Check the pie halfway through the baking time and add a foil frame if necessary to prevent overbrowning. Cool the pie on a wire rack. Serve warm, as is or topped by slices of sharp Cheddar cheese or vanilla ice cream.

Bourbon Apple Pie. Sprinkle 2 to 3 tablespoons bourbon over the sliced apple filling before covering with the top crust.

Apple-Walnut Pie. Add ½ cup (2 ounces) coarsely chopped walnuts to the apple filling. You can also add ½ cup seedless black or golden raisins.

Apple-Cranberry-Walnut Pie. Increase the brown sugar to ¾ cup and add 1 cup whole fresh or frozen cranberries plus ½ cup (2 ounces) coarsely chopped walnuts to the apples. Top with any egg-glazed lattice topping (pages 60–64). The pie can also be baked in a 9- to 11-inch tart pan and served garnished with Orange-flavored Whipped Cream, (page 132).

Dutch Apple Pie. Cut a 1¼-inch round steam vent in the top crust of the pie. Glaze the top and bake as directed, but 5 minutes before the end of the baking time, pour ½ cup heavy cream into the vent hole. Bake 5 minutes more and serve warm.

Apple-Custard or Pear-Apple-Custard Cream Pie. This pie has a creamy custard filling blended with the apples. Use soft or medium eating apples such as McIntosh or Golden Delicious, as harder cooking apples take too long to bake for this recipe. Use ½ cup granulated sugar instead of the brown sugar, and omit the lemon juice. Just before baking, pour over the fruit in the pastry-lined pan a custard made by whisking together 1 large egg plus ¾ cup heavy cream. (*Note:* You can substitute pears, cored and sliced, for half the apples in this recipe.)

Deep-Dish Apple Pie Prepare Old-Fashioned Apple Pie or the Apple-Cranberry-Walnut variation above, but use 7 to 8 cups fruit for the filling. Prepare only half the pastry recipe. Omit the bottom crust, and place the fruit in a 7- to 8-cup (1½- to 2-quart) baking dish at least 2 inches deep. Cover the fruit with the rolled-out pastry, fitted to the edges of the pan, and cut steam vents as for a regular crust. Glaze and bake as above.

The deep-dish pie can also be topped with any lattice crust (pages 60–64) or with Oat–Wheat Germ Topping Streusel (page 138) or Nut-Crumb Streusel Topping (page 141). Follow the baking time for a regular two-crust pie.

. . . .

FRUIT MEASURING GUIDE

As a basic guide to fruit quantities, note that 3 large apples = 1 pound = 3 generous cups peeled, cored, and sliced ⅛ inch thick; 4 to 5 peaches, nectarines, or plums = 1 pound = 2½ cups pitted and sliced ¼ inch thick. For additional measurements, see Measurements and Equivalents, page 7.

. . . .

Apricot-Walnut Pie
· · · · · · · · · · ·

This open-faced pie has a tart apricot filling covered with a crunchy layer of caramelized custard and chopped nuts.

ADVANCED PREPARATION: This pie is best served the day it is baked. The apricots can be prepared ahead and refrigerated for a day or two. The pastry can be prepared ahead and frozen (page 73).

SPECIAL EQUIPMENT: 9-inch pie plate; 2-quart saucepan; strainer; 3 medium-sized bowls; aluminum foil frame (page 22)

TEMPERATURE AND TIME: 375°F for 20 minutes, 325°F for 35 to 40 minutes

YIELD: One 9-inch pie; serves 6 to 8

Unbaked pastry for a single-crust 9-inch pie made with
   All-Purpose Flaky Pastry (page 45) or Whole Wheat Pastry (page 80),

FILLING:

8 ounces packed dried apricot halves (about 2 cups)
2 cups water
2 large eggs, at room temperature
1 cup granulated sugar, divided (½ cup and ½ cup), or more as needed
1 teaspoon vanilla extract
⅛ teaspoon ground cinnamon
¼ cup heavy cream or milk
½ cup (2 ounces) walnuts, finely chopped

Prepare the pastry, roll it out, and line the pie plate (pages 52–55). Trim a ¾-inch over-hang, fold the pastry edge under, and crimp it in flutes or scallops (page 56). Be sure the edging stands up well to hold in the filling. Refrigerate the pastry-lined pan while you prepare the filling.

165

To prepare the apricots, measure them into a saucepan and cover with water. Cover the pan and bring to a boil over high heat. Lower the heat slightly and boil gently for about 15 minutes, or until the fruit is fork-tender. When soft, remove the apricots from the heat and drain well in a strainer set over a bowl. Save the juice to drink if you wish; set aside the fruit in another bowl to cool. Preheat the oven to 375°F.

To prepare the custard, beat together the eggs, ½ cup of the sugar, the vanilla, cinnamon, and cream or milk. Set aside.

Stir the remaining ½ cup sugar into the apricots. Add a little more sugar, if necessary, to your taste. Spread the apricots in an even layer over the prepared pastry shell. Sprinkle on the chopped nuts, then gently pour the custard mixture over the top.

Carefully set the pie in the lower third of the preheated oven and bake for 20 minutes. Then raise the pie to the center of the oven, reduce the heat to 325°F, and continue baking for 35 to 40 minutes longer. Check the pie after half the baking time and add a foil edging frame if necessary to prevent the crust from overbrowning. You may wish to increase the heat to 350°F for the last 10 minutes to brown the pastry if necessary. Cool on a wire rack.

Apricot-Orange Soufflé Pie

$\cdot \quad \cdot \quad \cdot \quad \cdot \quad \cdot \quad \cdot \quad \cdot \quad \cdot \quad \cdot \quad \cdot$

This baked soufflé combines meringue with orange-scented apricot puree to create a texture slightly more dense than that of a traditional soufflé, but much lighter than a fresh fruit pie. The flavor is tart and intensely apricot-y, a must for those who love this fruit. If you prefer a sweeter pie, add another ¼ cup sugar to the recipe.

ADVANCE PREPARATION: The completely prebaked pie shell can be prepared ahead and frozen (page 73). Apricot puree can be prepared as much as several days in advance and refrigerated; bring to room temperature before using. The texture of this pie is best if baked not more than several hours before serving; however, it *can* stand for several hours before serving, unlike a regular baked soufflé.

SPECIAL EQUIPMENT: 9-inch pie plate; 1½-quart nonreactive saucepan with lid; blender or food processor; grater; electric mixer; rubber spatula

TEMPERATURE AND TIME: Completely baked pie shell: 425°F for 12 minutes with pie weights, then 10 to 12 minutes empty; filled pie: 325°F for 25 minutes

YIELD: One 9-inch pie; serves 6 to 8

PASTRY:

Completely prebaked 9-inch pie shell made with All-Purpose Flaky Pastry (page 45) or Cream Cheese Pastry (page 90)

FILLING:

8 ounces packed box dried apricot halves (about 2 cups)
⅔ cup fresh orange juice or water, or more as needed
2 teaspoons grated orange zest
½ cup plus 3 tablespoons granulated sugar
3 large egg whites, at room temperature
A pinch of salt

GARNISH:

Orange Whipped Cream (page 132)

Prepare the pastry, roll it out, and line the pie plate (pages 52–55). Prick the pastry bottom with a fork, then chill for 30 minutes, until the dough is firm. Preheat the oven to 425°F. Completely prebake the shell (page 66). Cool on a wire rack. Reduce the oven heat to 325°F.

In a saucepan, combine the apricots, juice or water, orange zest, and ½ cup of the sugar. Cover and bring to a boil. Reduce the heat and simmer, covered, for 10 minutes. Remove the cover and cook 5 minutes longer, or until the fruit is fork-tender. Remove 6 nicely shaped apricot halves and set them aside on a plate for garnishing the pie. Puree the remaining apricot halves with the cooking liquid in a processor or blender until quite smooth. You should have 1 generous cup of puree.

In the bowl of an electric mixer, combine the egg whites and salt. Beat until fluffy, add the remaining 3 tablespoons sugar, and beat until stiff but not dry (page 134). Check the apricot puree; it should be a soft, spreadable consistency. If the puree feels too stiff, warm it slightly and/or stir in 2 or 3 tablespoons orange juice, water, or cream. Stir about ¼ cup of the beaten whites into the puree to lighten it, then fold in the rest. Spoon the filling into the prepared pastry shell and bake at 325°F for 25 minutes or until the filling is set and delicately browned.

To garnish, set 1 reserved apricot half (cut side down) in the pie center, then arrange the other 5 halves as petals around the center, making a flower. Serve warm or cold, with Orange Whipped Cream alongside.

167

Cherry Pie

· · · · · · · · · · ·

There are many varieties of cherries, but basically they are either sweet or sour. Some are pale, some deep ruby red, others mottled or somewhere in between. If you have fresh cherries, use them, but be sure they are unbruised and still firm enough to be holding on to their stems. Wash cherries before using to remove possible sprays. To pit, use an easy, plunger-type mechanical cherry stoner (see Sources, page 363), a sharp paring knife and fingertip, or a bent hairpin. Or, best of all, employ a willing child. If you are using canned cherries, try combining half dark sweet cherries and half tart cherries, well drained. Cherry pie is especially dramatic when baked with a lattice topping. Select any type, from classic woven strips to quick "mock" lattice, easily made on a piece of foil, baked separately, and slipped onto the pie before serving. If you are lucky enough to have fresh gooseberries, see the Gooseberry Pie variation following.

ADVANCE PREPARATION: Canned cherries can be used for quick preparation. Pastry can be prepared ahead and frozen (page 77). Pie is best served the day it is baked.

SPECIAL EQUIPMENT: Cherry stoner for fresh cherries, optional; 9-inch pie plate; pastry brush; aluminum foil frame (page 22)

TEMPERATURE AND TIME: 425°F for 15 minutes, 350°F for 25 minutes

YIELD: One 9-inch pie; serves 6 to 8

PASTRY:

Unbaked pastry for two-crust 9-inch pie made with All-Purpose Flaky Pastry (page 45) or other pastry of your choice

EGG GLAZE:

1 large egg beaten with 1 tablespoon water

TOPPING:

Granulated sugar

FILLING:

4 cups pitted fresh sweet or tart cherries, 4 cups (two 1-pound) cans sweet or tart cherries, drained, with ⅓ cup juice reserved, or 1 (20-ounce) bag frozen dry-pack sweet or tart cherries, unthawed

2¾ to 3 tablespoons quick-cooking tapioca (use 3 tablespoons if increasing sugar)

A pinch of salt

¾ cup granulated sugar, or to taste (depending on sweetness of fruit)

2 teaspoons fresh lemon juice

½ teaspoon vanilla extract

¼ teaspoon almond extract or kirsch

A drop of red vegetable food coloring, optional

2 tablespoons unsalted butter, optional

169

Prepare the pastry, roll out half, and line the pie plate (pages 52–55). To moisture-proof the lower crust, brush it with egg glaze, then place the pastry-lined pan in the refrigerator while you prepare the fruit. Preheat oven to 425°F.

In a large bowl, combine the fruit, tapioca, salt, sugar, flavorings, and the optional food coloring. If you are using drained canned fruit, add the reserved ⅓ cup fruit juice. Stir, and let the fruit mixture sit for about 5 minutes.

Spoon the fruit into the pastry-lined pan and dot with the butter, if using.

Roll out the top crust a generous ⅛ inch thick and cut into ½-inch strips, following the lattice-topping style of your choice (pages 60–64). To bake the lattice directly on the pie, moisten the rim of the lower crust with egg glaze, then arrange the pastry strips. Fold the overhanging lower crust over the ends of the lattice, pinch to make a raised rim, and flute to seal. Brush the lattice strips with egg glaze and sprinkle with a little granulated sugar.

Set the pie in the lower third of the preheated oven and bake for 15 minutes. Reduce the heat to 350°F and bake for an additional 25 minutes, or until the pastry is golden and the filling is bubbling. Check the pie after half the baking time and add a foil edging frame if needed to prevent overbrowning.

Cool on a wire rack. Serve with vanilla ice cream or plain sweetened or flavored whipped cream (page 131).

Cherry-Berry Pie. The combination of fruits in this pie produces a brilliant color without the use of food coloring. Use only 2 cups fresh cherries or 1 (1-pound) can drained tart cherries, with ⅓ cup juice reserved. Add 1 cup blueberries (fresh or whole dry-pack frozen) and 1 cup strawberries (fresh, hulled and halved, or whole dry-pack frozen). Do not thaw frozen berries, but remove any clinging frost or ice particles.

Cherry-Cranberry Pie. Use 2 cups fresh tart cherries or 1 (1-pound) can tart cherries, drained, plus 2 cups fresh or frozen whole cranberries. Replace the granulated sugar with an equal amount of packed dark brown sugar. Use 3 tablespoons tapioca. Increase the almond extract to ½ teaspoon.

Gooseberry Pie with Lattice Crust. Prepare 2-crust 9-inch All-Purpose Flaky Pastry (page 45) or Nut (almond) Pastry variation (page 48).

Roll out half the dough, line pie plate, flute edge, and chill (pages 52–55) while you prepare the filling. In a large bowl, toss together 4 cups whole fresh stemmed, rinsed, and dried gooseberries, 1½ to 1¾ cups granulated sugar (depending on sweetness of fruit), and 3½ tablespoons cornstarch.

Brush ½ cup gooseberry or apricot preserves over the bottom of the prepared pastry shell. Add gooseberry mixture.

Roll out top crust and make lattice topping of your choice (page 60). Glaze and bake as for Cherry Pie, above.

Peach or Nectarine Pie

. . . .

The bright yellow-orange color and rich sweet flavor of ripe peaches or nectarines make them prize filling for fresh fruit pies. *Note:* To peel peaches effortlessly, drop 3 or 4 at a time into a pot of boiling water. Boil for about 2 minutes, then remove with a slotted spoon to a bowl of cold water. Drain. The skins will slip off easily. Nectarines do not need peeling. Slice the fruit about ¼ inch to ⅜ inch thick and sprinkle immediately with lemon or orange juice to avoid discoloration.

ADVANCE PREPARATION: The fruit can be prepared, seasoned as described below, and frozen in individual pie-sized packets in advance (page 72). The pastry can be prepared ahead and frozen (page 71). Complete pies can also be frozen, unbaked or baked (page 73). Pie is best served the day it is baked.

SPECIAL EQUIPMENT: 9-inch pie plate; pastry brush; aluminum foil frame (page 22)

TEMPERATURE AND TIME: 425°F for 15 minutes, 350°F for 30 to 35 minutes

YIELD: One 9-inch pie; serves 6 to 8

. . . .

171

PASTRY:

**Unbaked pastry for a two-crust 9-inch pie made with All-Purpose Flaky
Pastry, Nut (almond) Pastry variation (page 48) or Cornmeal
Pastry (page 81)**

EGG GLAZE:

1 large egg beaten with 1 tablespoon water

TOPPING:

Granulated sugar

FILLING:

**2¼ pounds medium to large ripe peaches or nectarines, peeled and
sliced (see introduction above) (about 8 to 9 whole pieces of fruit,
5½ cups slices)**

Juice of 1 lemon or orange

½ to ¾ cup granulated sugar (depending on sweetness of fruit)

⅛ teaspoon ground nutmeg

¼ teaspoon ground cinnamon

3 tablespoons quick-cooking tapioca or cornstarch

2 tablespoons unsalted butter, cut up, optional

Prepare the pastry, roll out half, and line the pie plate (pages 52–55). Trim a ½-inch pastry overhang. To moisture-proof the lower crust, brush it with egg glaze. Preheat the oven to 425°F.

Toss the sliced peaches or nectarines in a large bowl with the lemon juice, sugar, spices, and tapioca or cornstarch. Add the fruit to the pastry-lined pan, mounding it in the center. Dot with the butter if using. Brush egg glaze over the edge of the lower crust. Roll out the top crust and fit it over the fruit. Trim a ¾-inch overhang. Fold the top edge under the bottom crust overhang and pinch together to seal, making a raised rim all around. Flute as desired and cut vent holes (page 59). To glaze the pie, brush with egg glaze and sprinkle with a little granulated sugar.

Set the pie in the lower third of the preheated oven and bake for 15 minutes. Reduce the heat to 350°F, raise the pie to the center of the oven, and bake for an additional 30 to 35 minutes, or until the pastry is golden brown. Check the pie halfway through baking time and add a foil edging frame to prevent overbrowning. Cool the pie on a wire rack. Serve warm or cold.

Blueberry-Peach Pie. This is an all-time favorite in my house, served by special request on my husband's birthday instead of cake. Use only 2 cups peach slices and add 2 cups fresh blueberries, washed, stemmed, and dried. Use ⅔ cup granulated sugar, the juice of 1½ lemons, and a dash each of ground cinnamon and nutmeg. Thicken with 3 tablespoons quick-cooking tapioca and top the fruit with 3 tablespoons unsalted butter, cut up. To moisture-proof the lower crust, brush with egg glaze and sprinkle with ¼ cup finely crushed cornflakes before adding the fruit. (*Note:* Since this pie is so colorful, it shows off well with a lattice crust, pages 60–64).

Peach-Plum Pie. Substitute 2 cups pitted and sliced (unpeeled) Italian prune plums or other purple plums for 2 cups of the peach or nectarine slices.

Deep-Dish Peach or Nectarine Pie. Prepare Fresh Peach or Nectarine Pie or any of the above variations but use 6 cups fruit altogether and add a little more sugar if you wish. Add only 3 tablespoons thickener, as deep-dish pies do not have to slice neatly. Prepare only half the pastry recipe; omit the bottom crust. Place the fruit in a 7- to 8-cup (1½-¼ to 2-quart) baking dish at least 2 inches deep. Cover the fruit with the rolled-out pastry, fitted to the edge of the pan, and cut steam vents as for a regular crust. Glaze and bake as for a regular two-crust pie, but for a *total* time of only 35 to 40 minutes, or until the pastry is golden brown and the fruit is fork-tender.

Peaches (or Nectarines)-and-Cream Pie. This divine pie has a creamy custard filling blended with the peaches (or nectarines). Use ½ cup sugar. Add ⅛ teaspoon ground ginger, omit the lemon juice, and use 2 tablespoons all-purpose flour as the thickener instead of tapioca or cornstarch. Pour over the fruit in the pie shell, covering the top, just before baking: custard made by whisking together 1 large egg and ¾ cup heavy cream. Cover the fruit with the top crust, cut steam vents, glaze, and bake as for a regular peach pie.

Plum Pie

· · · · · · · · · ·

Little Jack Horner
Sat in the corner,
Eating a Christmas pie;
He put in his thumb,
And pulled out a plum,
And said, "What a good boy am I!"

This familiar nursery rhyme has quite a complex history. To begin, the plum in question may not be the fruit as we know it, but rather a large currant or raisin, in which case the pie may actually have been Christmas mince, rather than "plum." No matter; whether or not it is true, it still makes a good story, involving King Henry VIII. Henry became furious, it is said, when he learned that the abbot of Glastonbury, Richard Whiting, had used church funds to enhance himself and build an elaborate new kitchen. On hearing of the King's wrath, Whiting commissioned an emissary, one Jack Horner, to take a gift of pie to the King. During the journey, Jack opened the pie and discovered it was filled not with edible plums, but with another variety: deeds to various estates or manors. He "stuck in his thumb" and pulled out the deed to the manor of Mells, which he kept for himself, and gave the rest to the king. Mells remains in the Horner family today, and the phrase *political plum*, meaning a specially favored office, has become a part of our language.

ADVANCE PREPARATION: Plums can be sliced, seasoned as described below, and frozen in individual pie-sized packets (page 72). Pastry can be prepared ahead and frozen (page 71). Complete pies can also be frozen, baked or unbaked (page 73). Pie is best served on the day it is baked.

SPECIAL EQUIPMENT: 9-inch pie plate; pastry brush; aluminum foil frame (page 22)

TEMPERATURE AND TIME: 425°F for 15 minutes, 350°F for 40 to 45 minutes

YIELD: One 9-inch pie; serves 6 to 8

PASTRY:

Unbaked pastry for a two-crust 9-inch pie made with All-Purpose
Flaky Pastry (page 45), sweetened with 2 tablespoons sugar, or other
pastry of your choice

EGG GLAZE:

1 large egg beaten with 1 tablespoon water

TOPPING:

Granulated sugar

FILLING:

About 1¾ pounds plums, unpeeled, sliced and pitted (4 to 5 cups)
(I prefer Italian prune plums for tart flavor and bright color; Damsons or
greengages can also be used with success.)
1 tablespoon fresh lemon juice
½ to ¾ cup granulated sugar (depending on tartness of fruit)
3 tablespoons quick-cooking tapioca
A pinch of salt
¼ teaspoon ground cinnamon
¼ teaspoon ground nutmeg

175

Prepare the pastry, roll out half, and line the pie plate (pages 52–55). Trim a ½-inch pastry overhang. To moisture-proof the lower crust, brush with egg glaze. Preheat the oven to 425°F.

In a large bowl, toss the sliced plums with the lemon juice, sugar, tapioca, salt, and spices. Add the fruit to the pastry-lined pan.

Roll out the top crust and fit it over the fruit. Trim a ¾-inch overhang. Fold the edge under the bottom crust and pinch together to seal, making a raised rim all around. Flute the edge as desired and cut vent holes (pages 56–60). To glaze the pie top, brush with egg glaze and sprinkle with a little granulated sugar.

Set the pie in the lower third of the preheated oven and bake for 15 minutes. Reduce the heat to 350°F, raise the pie to the center of the oven, and bake for an additional 40 to 45 minutes, or until the pastry is golden brown and the fruit is fork-tender. Check the pie halfway through baking time and add a foil edging frame if necessary to prevent overbrowning. Cool on a wire rack. Serve warm with Custard Sauce (page 144).

Plum Good Pie. This is an open-faced pie with a rich yogurt-custard filling added to the fruit. Note that honey replaces the sugar; to measure honey easily, oil the measuring cup before use so the honey runs out easily. Use Italian prune plums for the best results.

Prepare only half the pastry recipe; use only 2 cups (¾ pound) sliced plums. Omit all the other ingredients and add ⅓ cup chopped walnuts to the sliced plums; spread in the pastry-lined pan. Pour over the fruit before baking: custard made by beating together 3 large eggs, 1 cup (8 ounces) plain yogurt, 1 teaspoon vanilla extract, a pinch each ground nutmeg and cinnamon, and ¾ cup honey. Set in the center of the preheated oven and immediately turn the heat down to 375°F.

Bake for 45 minutes, or until a stainless steel knife inserted into the custard 1 inch from the edge comes out clean. The pastry edging should appear golden brown. Cool on a wire rack. Serve warm and top with a very light sifting of confectioners' sugar just before serving. (Note: This pie can also be made with a partially prebaked pie shell [page 67] moisture-proofed with egg glaze [page 156].)

Plum Crumb Pie. Omit the top crust. Before baking, top the fruit with Nut-Crumb Streusel Topping (page 141), or Oat–Wheat Germ Streusel Topping (page 138).

Grape Custard Pie. Substitute 1 pound sweet purple grapes, seeded (about 2 cups prepared grapes), for the plums.

$\mathscr{P}$ear $\mathscr{P}$ie

. . . .

$\mathbf{T}$here are more than five thousand varieties of pears and nearly as many theories on how to select and ripen them. For pies, you want ripe, flavorful pears that have not yet begun their sadly rapid decline to mush. The best moment can be about a day before you feel the fruit ready to eat fresh, because a slight firmness of flesh gives a better texture to the baked pie. Watch carefully and refrigerate ripe pears; they can go bad almost before you notice it.

ADVANCE PREPARATION: I have not had great success freezing pear pies and discourage the idea. The pastry can be prepared ahead and frozen (page 71). Pie is best served the day it is baked.

SPECIAL EQUIPMENT: 9-inch pie plate; pastry brush; aluminum foil frame (page 22)

TEMPERATURE AND TIME: 425°F for 15 minutes, 350°F for 30 to 35 minutes

YIELD: One 9-inch pie; serves 6 to 8

PASTRY:

Unbaked pastry for a two-crust 9-inch pie made with All-Purpose
Flaky Pastry, Orange or Lemon Pastry variation (page 49), Cheddar Cheese
Pastry (page 49), or pastry of your choice

EGG GLAZE:

1 large egg beaten with 1 tablespoon water

TOPPING:

Granulated sugar

FILLING:

¼ cup apricot preserves or orange or ginger marmalade
6 or 7 medium-sized Bartlett, Anjou, or red pears, peeled, cored,
and sliced ¼ inch thick, (about 5 cups slices); as soon as pears are sliced,
sprinkle them with juice of 1 lemon or orange to avoid discoloration
¼ cup granulated sugar
¼ cup packed brown sugar,
¼ teaspoon ground cinnamon
¼ teaspoon ground cardamom, optional
¼ teaspoon ground nutmeg
2½ tablespoons quick-cooking tapioca or cornstarch
2 tablespoons unsalted butter, optional

Prepare the pastry, roll out half, and line the pie plate (pages 52–55). Trim a ½-inch pastry overhang. To moisture-proof the lower crust, spread the pastry with the preserves or marmalade. Preheat the oven to 425°F.

In a large bowl, toss the pear slices with both sugars, the spices, and tapioca or cornstarch. Spread in the pastry-lined pan and dot with the butter, if using. Brush egg glaze over the edge of the lower crust.

Roll out the top crust and fit it over the fruit. Trim a ¾-inch overhang. Fold the edge under the bottom crust overhang and pinch together to seal, making a raised rim all around. Flute as desired and cut vent holes (pages 56–60). To glaze the pie top, brush with egg glaze and sprinkle with a little granulated sugar.

Set the pie in the lower third of the preheated oven and bake for 15 minutes. Reduce the heat to 350°F, raise the pie to the center of the oven, and bake for an additional 30 to 35 minutes, or until the pastry is golden brown. Check the pie halfway through the baking time and add a foil edging frame if necessary to prevent overbrowning. Cool on a wire rack. Serve warm or cold, plain or with a slice of sharp cheddar cheese or a dollop of Custard Sauce (page 144).

Pear-Raisin or Craisin Pie. Add ¾ cup seedless black raisins or Craisins (sweet dried cranberries) to the pear slices.

Pear-Apricot Pie. Add 1 cup cut-up dried apricots to the pear slices.

Ginger-Pear Pie. Add 2 to 3 tablespoons (to taste) finely minced crystallized ginger to the pear slices.

Pear Crumb Pie. Omit the top crust. Before baking, top the fruit with Nut-Crumb Streusel Topping (page 141), made with chopped pecans or walnuts.

179

Rhubarb Pie

· · · · · · · · · · ·

It is believed that the first rhubarb plants in America were imported to the territory now known as Alaska by Russian fur traders during the late 1700s. The rhubarb plant was appreciated for its ability to ward off scurvy, and it endured the cold climate in its new home just as well as it had in the tundra of Siberia. A native of Asia, rhubarb was originally used by the Chinese as a medicine. For centuries, dried and powdered medicinal forms of rhubarb roots were imported along with spices from Asia to the Mediterranean region. Because they so enjoyed eating baked rhubarb in pies and puddings at home, European settlers and travelers to the first American colonies brought rhubarb seeds with them. The plant flourished in New England as it had in Alaska, and was known as "pie plant" for obvious reasons. But beware: Only the rhubarb stalks are edible; the leaves contain oxalic acid and are poisonous.

180

ADVANCE PREPARATION: Fresh rhubarb can be sliced, seasoned as described below, and frozen in individual pie-sized packets (page 72). The pastry can be prepared ahead and frozen (page 71). Complete pies can also be frozen unbaked or baked (page 73). The pie is best served the day it is baked.

SPECIAL EQUIPMENT: 9-inch pie plate; pastry brush; aluminum foil frame (page 22)

TEMPERATURE AND TIME: 425°F for 15 minutes, 350°F for 35 to 45 minutes

YIELD: One 9-inch pie; serves 6 to 8

    Unbaked pastry for a two-crust 9-inch pie made with Whole Wheat Pastry,
       (page 80), Whole Wheat–Wheat Germ Pastry (page 80), or pastry of
       your choice

EGG GLAZE:

    1 large egg beaten with 1 tablespoon water

TOPPING:

    Granulated sugar

FILLING:

    1½ pounds fresh rhubarb stalks, trimmed and cut into 1-inch pieces
       (4 cups pieces)
    1 cup granulated white or packed light brown sugar plus ¼ cup honey or
       1¼ cups granulated white sugar
    ¼ cup all-purpose flour
    ½ teaspoon ground nutmeg or cinnamon
    A pinch of salt
    ¼ cup strawberry preserves or orange or pineapple marmalade, optional
    2 tablespoons unsalted butter, optional

181

Prepare the pastry, roll out half, and line the pie plate (pages 52–55). Trim a ½-inch pastry overhang. To moisture-proof the lower crust, brush on egg glaze. Preheat the oven to 425°F.

In a large bowl, toss the sliced rhubarb with the sugar, and the honey, if you are using it, the flour, nutmeg or cinnamon, and salt. Stir in the optional preserves or marmalade and add the fruit to the pastry-lined pan. Dot with the butter, if using. Brush the edge of the lower crust with egg glaze.

Roll out the top crust and fit it over the fruit. Trim a ¾-inch overhang. Fold the edge under the bottom crust overhang and pinch together to seal, making a raised rim all around. Flute the edge as desired and cut vent holes (pages 56–60). To glaze the pie top, brush with egg glaze and sprinkle with a little granulated sugar.

Set the pie in the lower third of the preheated oven and bake for 15 minutes. Reduce the heat to 350°F, raise the pie to the center of the oven, and bake for an additional 35 to 45 minutes, or until the pastry is golden brown. Check the pie after about half the baking time and add a foil edging frame if necessary to prevent overbrowning. Cool on a wire rack. Serve warm, topped by Custard Sauce (page 144) or vanilla ice cream or flavored whipped cream (page 131).

Strawberry-Rhubarb or Raspberry-Rhubarb Pie. Substitute 2 cups hulled fresh strawberries, whole or halved, or fresh (or whole frozen) raspberries for 2 cups of the rhubarb. Omit the preserves or marmalade. Top the pie with pastry strips woven into a lattice (pages 60–64); any style.

Quick and Creamy Rhubarb Pie. This open-faced pie or tart combines a sweet creamy filling with the tangy rhubarb. The taste is exceptional, the process quick and easy, the quantity generous; use a 10-inch pie plate or an 11-inch tart pan. Make only half the pastry recipe. Roll out the dough and prepare as for an unbaked single-crust pie or tart shell (pages 52–55). Shape a high fluted edging on the pie shell to hold in the custard. Moisture-proof the shell with egg glaze, then chill while you prepare the fruit and custard. For the filling, use the 4 cups cut-up rhubarb but omit all the other ingredients in the original recipe except 2 tablespoons of the granulated sugar. Toss the rhubarb with the sugar in a bowl and set aside for a few minutes. *Immediately before baking,* add the fruit to the prepared pastry shell and pour over it a thick custard batter made by beating together: ½ cup plus 2 tablespoons granulated sugar, ¼ cup packed dark brown sugar, ⅓ cup all-purpose flour, ¼ teaspoon ground nutmeg, a pinch of salt, ½ cup heavy cream, 1 large egg, and ¼ teaspoon almond extract. (*Note:* The custard can be made ahead and refrigerated for several hours.) Bake the center of the preheated oven for 30 minutes, then reduce the heat to 350°F and bake for 30 minutes longer, or until the top is golden brown and crackled. Check the pie after about half the baking time and add a foil edging frame if necessary to protect the crust rim from overbrowning. Cool on a wire rack. Before serving, sift on a very light sprinkling of confectioners' sugar. The flavor is best if served warm. (*Note:* This pie can also be made in a partially prebaked pastry shell, page 67).

No-Bake Pineapple Cheesecake Pie
. . . .

This rich, creamy pie with a bright pineapple flavor is a perfect choice for warm-weather entertaining and the flavor is so spectacular your guests will never guess it is low in fat (don't tell them until they taste it). It is made quickly, in advance, in a food processor or blender and then chilled to set the filling, so it is easy on the host or hostess. The recipe calls for pineapple extract, available from most supermarkets, or see Sources (page 363). As a substitute, use ¼ cup frozen pineapple juice concentrate, undiluted, and increase the gelatin to 3¾ teaspoons. *Note:* The filling can also be served without pastry, spooned into long-stemmed goblets and allowed to set in the refrigerator.

ADVANCE PREPARATION: Plan ahead: The yogurt needs to drain for at least 20 to 30 minutes before using, and the prepared pie must chill for at least 3 hours to set before serving. You can make the pie 1 day in advance. Keep refrigerated.

CHILLING TIME: 3 hours

SPECIAL EQUIPMENT: 10-inch deep-dish pie plate; strainer set over a bowl; food processor or blender; small saucepan

YIELD: One 10-inch pie, serves 8 to 10

One 10-inch Reduced-Fat Graham Cracker Crust (page 100) or any
other crumb crust made in a 10-inch deep-dish pie plate, baked at
350°F for 8 minutes, then cooled

FILLING:

1¼ cups vanilla or plain nonfat or low-fat yogurt

1 (20-ounce) can crushed pineapple, unsweetened or in light syrup

¾ cup nonfat or low-fat cottage cheese

¾ cup light (not fat-free) cream cheese

¾ cup granulated sugar

1 teaspoon vanilla extract

1½ teaspoons pineapple extract

3 tablespoons fresh lemon juice

Scant 3½ teaspoons unflavored gelatin

OPTIONAL GARNISH:

Fresh blueberries or raspberries and/or mint sprigs

184

At least 30 minutes before starting the filling (or up to a day in advance), place the yogurt
in a fine-mesh strainer set over a bowl, refrigerate, and allow to drain for 20 to 30 minutes. Discard (or drink) the drained liquid; reserve the yogurt. Rinse the strainer. Prepare
the crumb crust and set it aside.

Drain the crushed pineapple in a the rinsed strainer set over a bowl. Press firmly on the
fruit with the back of a spoon to release the juice. Transfer the pineapple to a small bowl,
and reserve ½ cup of the juice.

Place the cottage cheese in a strainer set over a bowl. Cover it with a piece of plastic wrap
and press down firmly on the cheese to force out excess liquid from the curds. Combine
the drained cottage cheese and the cream cheese in a food processor or blender and
process for at least 3 full minutes, or until absolutely smooth without a trace of graininess;
pinch between your fingers or taste to check. During the blending, stop and scrape
down the bowl sides a couple of times with a rubber spatula. Add the sugar, vanilla,
pineapple extract, and drained yogurt. Pulse well to blend. Scrape down the sides of the
bowl, then pulse several times. Add 1½ cups of the drained pineapple and pulse just to
combine.

In a small saucepan, combine the reserved ½ cup pineapple juice and the lemon juice. Sprinkle on the gelatin and allow to sit for 2 to 3 minutes to soften. Stir the mixture over low heat just until the gelatin is dissolved and no grains are visible; do not boil. With the blender or processor running, add the gelatin mixture through the feed tube.

Pour the filling into the prepared crumb crust and refrigerate for at least 3 hours, or overnight, to set. Once the top is firm to the touch, cover the pie with plastic wrap to protect the flavor. If desired, garnish the top of the pie, or each slice, with fresh blueberries or raspberries and/or mint springs just before serving.

185

No-Bake Fresh Fruit Pie

. . . .

The recipe for this delicious and speedy summer pie was given to me by a food-writing colleague, Dede Ely-Singer. The filling requires no baking, is quick to prepare, and can be varied to suit whatever combination of berries or fruits is in season. The technique is simple: Some of the fruit is first mashed and cooked into a thickened sauce. Then the remaining fresh fruit is stirred in and the entire mixture turned out into a completely prebaked pastry shell and chilled. The filling can also be served as a pudding without any pastry. For the Fourth of July, use equal quantities of strawberries or raspberries and blueberries and top the pie with whipped cream to make a patriotic red-white-and-blue pie.

ADVANCE PREPARATION: The pastry can be prebaked a day in advance. The filling should be made early in the day, and the pie filled and set to chill at least 3 hours before serving.

SPECIAL EQUIPMENT: 9-inch pie plate; food processor or bowl and fork; 2½-quart non-reactive saucepan

COOKING TIME: 7 to 10 minutes to prepare fruit filling

YIELD: One 9-inch pie; serves 6 to 8

PASTRY:

> Completely prebaked pastry for a single-crust 9-inch pie shell made with
> All-Purpose Flaky Pastry (page 45), Rich Tart Pastry (page 88), or pastry
> of your choice; if you're pressed for time, use a store-bought refrigerated
> crust, prebaked

FILLING:

> 4 cups any combination of fresh berries, picked over, washed, hulled,
> if necessary, and drained until dry, and/or cut-up peeled fresh fruit, divided
> (1½ cups and 2½ cups), (Note: Try blueberries and peaches, or
> raspberries and nectarines, or blueberries and strawberries, or plums and
> peaches with Marionberries or huckleberries; do not peel plums,
> nectarines, or pears)
>
> ⅔ to 1 cup granulated sugar (depending on sweetness of fruit)
>
> 3 tablespoons cornstarch
>
> 1 cup water
>
> 1 tablespoon fresh lemon juice, or more as needed
>
> 2 tablespoons unsalted butter

Prepare the pastry, roll it out, and line the pie plate (pages 52–55). Prick the pastry bottom with a fork and chill until firm. Preheat the oven to 425°F. Completely blind-bake the shell (page 67).

In a food processor or using a fork, mash 1½ cups of the cut-up mixed fruit or berries. Measure the sugar, cornstarch, and water into a saucepan and whisk until smooth. Stir in the mashed fruit and cook over medium-low heat for 7 to 10 minutes, or until the mixture is thick and clear. Stir in the lemon juice.

Taste the cooked sauce and correct the balance of sugar and lemon if necessary. Stir in the butter and all the remaining cut-up fresh fruit or berries. Firm fruits like apples or plums are best slightly mashed into the cooked sauce, while softer fresh fruits and berries should simply be stirred in. Chill until partially thickened, then spoon into the cooked pastry shell and chill for at least 3 hours to set. Serve with ice cream or sweetened whipped cream (page 129).

Mince Pie

· · · · · · · · · · · ·

Drink now the strong Beere,
Cut the white loafe here,
The while the meat is a shredding;
For the rare Mince-Pie
And the Plums stand by,
To fill the Paste that's a kneading.

ROBERT HERRICK,
"Christmas Mince and Plum Pie"

The future . . . seems to me no unified dream but a
mince pie, long in the baking, never quite done.

E. B. WHITE,
One Man's Meat

Minc'd" or "shrid" pie has a long and popular history that can be traced to the Crusaders, who brought back a wide variety of spices from the East. Traditionally served at Christmas, mincemeat is made in two forms: with and without shredded ("shrid") meat. All versions contain fruits, spices, sugar, brandy, and beef suet, though the quantity of the last three ingredients varies depending upon whether or not they must serve as a preservative for the long maturing period. Since you can now freeze your mincemeat if you like, you can reduce these ingredients somewhat. My recipe omits the beef and uses less suet than the eighteenth-century versions, but it is generous in all other proportions. It makes enough for three pies and thus should be packed in three separate containers if it is to be frozen. Or, instead, pack it in covered jars and refrigerate or store in a cool pantry for at least a week or two before using, to allow the flavors to mature. (*Note:* The food processor speeds the task of chopping. Flour for thickening is added to mincemeat just before the pie is baked.)

ADVANCE PREPARATION: Mincemeat filling can be made ahead and frozen, or it can be aged for a minimum of 1 to 2 weeks before baking. The pastry can be prepared ahead and frozen (page 71). Pie is best served the day it is baked, but it can successfully be served the second day.

SPECIAL EQUIPMENT: Food processor or chopping knife and board; large mixing bowl; wooden spoon; three 1-quart freezer containers or large crock for storing mincemeat; 9-inch pie plate(s); pastry brush; aluminum foil frame (page 22)

TEMPERATURE AND TIME: 425°F for 40 to 45 minutes

YIELD: 3 quarts filling, enough for three 9-inch pies; each pie serves 6 to 8

MINCEMEAT FILLING:

¼ pound blanched almonds, finely chopped (1 cup)

1 pound beef suet, ground (3½ cups packed)

3 tablespoons toasted bread or cracker crumbs

½ pound mixed candied citrus peel (orange, lemon, citron), shredded (1 cup packed)

½ pound seedless raisins, chopped (1 cup packed)

½ pound currants, chopped (1 cup packed)

1 pound (5 large) tart cooking apples, peeled, cored, and chopped (4 cups)

Grated zest and juice of 2 lemons and 1 orange

1 cup packed dark brown sugar

2 tablespoons ground cinnamon

2 teaspoons ground nutmeg

2 teaspoons ground cloves

2 teaspoons ground ginger

2 teaspoons ground mace

2 teaspoons ground allspice

1 teaspoon salt

2 cups apple cider or apple juice

½ cup dry or sweet sherry

½ cup brandy

If you are chopping the ingredients in a processor, work from dry (nuts) to moist ingredients for best results. Whatever chopping method you use, chop each ingredient in turn, then add it to the mixing bowl. Have the butcher chop or grind the suet (or grind it yourself by mixing it with 2 tablespoons of the bread or cracker crumbs to prevent sticking). After grinding, pick out any pieces of suet membrane. Chop the candied peel, then the raisins and currants, in small batches, mixed with any remaining crumbs to prevent sticking. Chop the apples.

Add the grated lemon and orange peel, then the juice, to the bowl. Or, after grating the zests, slice off white pith, remove the seeds, cut up the entire fruit, chop it in the processor, and add to the filling.

Add the sugar, spices, salt, and liquids and stir everything together well. Pack in clean, dry containers.

To Bake One Mince Pie

PASTRY:

> **Unbaked pastry for a two-crust 9-inch pie made from All-Purpose Flaky Pastry (page 45), or Butter-Lard Pastry (page 87), or pastry of your choice**

EGG GLAZE:

> **1 large egg beaten with 1 tablespoon water**

TOPPING:

> **Granulated sugar**

FILLING:

> **4 cups Mincemeat Filling (above) measured into a bowl and stirred with 1 tablespoon all-purpose flour, for thickener**

SAUCE:

> **Hard Sauce (page 143)**

Prepare the pastry, roll out half, and line the pie plate (pages 52–55). Trim a ½-inch pastry overhang. To moisture-proof the lower crust, brush with egg glaze. Preheat the oven to 425°F.

Add the mincemeat to the pastry-lined pan. Brush egg glaze over the edge of the lower crust.

Roll out the top crust and fit it over the filling. Trim a ¾-inch overhang, fold the edge under the bottom crust overhang, and pinch together to seal, making a raised rim all around. Flute the edge as desired, and cut vent holes (pages 56–60). Brush the top with egg glaze and sprinkle on some granulated sugar.

Set the pie in the lower third of the preheated oven and bake for 15 minutes. Raise the pie to the center of the oven and continue baking for another 25 to 30 minutes until pastry is golden brown. Check the pie after about half the baking time and add a foil edging frame if necessary to prevent overbrowning. Cool on a wire rack. Serve warm, with the Hard Sauce.

Quick Mincemeat Pie. To 1 jar store-bought mincemeat (1 pound 12 ounces), add: 1 whole apple peeled, cored, and chopped, the juice and grated zest of 1 lemon and 1 orange, and ½ cup (4 ounces) chopped walnuts. Use without aging. Assemble and bake the pie as directed above.

191

Concord Grape Pie

· · · · · · · · · · ·

You'll taste the full flavor of the vine in this pie, its grapey tang pointed up by a citrus accent. This is an unusual and very special autumn dessert, but surely part of my pleasure in it comes from the fact that I buy my grapes from Maple Bank Farm in Roxbury, Connecticut, a spot that is the essence of fall in New England. Smoke from the wood stove clouds the frosty air, and orange and scarlet maples crowd fruit-laden orchards surrounding a little roadside barn, which stands sentinel before the hillside farm. Sheep nibble white chrysanthemums and purple asters beyond the fence. Fresh-baked pies share counter space with the antique scale upon which copper-haired Cathleen and her husband, Howie Bronson, weigh produce when not tending the farm. Howie is the family pie baker, and he talks piecrusts as easily as he picks apples, claiming that the secret of his success is to fill the pies with original combinations of whatever fruits or berries the farm has in season including his Concord grapes.

ADVANCE PREPARATION: The pastry can be prepared ahead and frozen (page 71). The pie is best served the day it is baked.

SPECIAL EQUIPMENT: Coarse strainer; pastry brush; 2-quart nonreactive saucepan with lid; grater

TEMPERATURE AND TIME: 425°F for 15 minutes, 375°F for 35 to 40 minutes

YIELD: One 9-inch pie; serves 6 to 8

PASTRY:

Unbaked pastry for a two-crust 9-inch pie made with All-Purpose Flaky Pastry (page 45) or pastry of your choice

EGG GLAZE:

1 large egg beaten with 1 tablespoon water

TOPPING:

Granulated sugar

FILLING:

2 pounds blue or purple grapes (Concord or other slipskin variety, with seeds), stemmed, rinsed well, and drained (4 cups stemmed grapes)
1 tablespoon grated orange zest
1 tablespoon fresh orange juice
1 teaspoon fresh lemon juice
¾ cup granulated sugar (or 1 cup for a sweeter pie)
2½ tablespoons quick-cooking tapioca

Prepare the pastry, roll out half, and line the pie plate (pages 52–55). Trim a ½-inch overhang. To moisture-proof the crust, brush it with egg glaze. Refrigerate the pastry-lined pan while you prepare the filling. Preheat the oven to 425°F.

Pinch each grape between your thumb and forefinger to slip the skin from the pulp. Place the skins in a bowl and the pulp and seeds in a saucepan. Cover and cook the pulp over medium heat for 4 to 5 minutes, until soft. Strain through a coarse sieve to remove the seeds. Combine the seedless pulp with the skins in the bowl. Stir in the grated orange zest, orange and lemon juice, sugar, and tapioca. Allow to stand for 5 minutes.

Roll out the remaining dough for the top crust, or prepare any style lattice crust (pages 60–64). Moisten the rim of the lower crust with egg glaze. Fill the pie with the grape mixture. Fit the top crust or lattice over the pie. Trim ¾-inch overhang, fold the edge under the bottom crust, and pinch the edges together into a raised, fluted rim. Brush the top crust or lattice with egg glaze and sprinkle with a little granulated sugar.

Set the pie in the lower third of the preheated oven and bake for 15 minutes. Lower the heat to 375°F, raise the pie to the center shelf, and bake for 35 to 40 minutes longer, or until the crust is golden brown. Check the pie after half the baking time and add a foil edging frame if necessary to prevent overbrowning. Cool on a wire rack.

Green Tomato Pie

Although we usually think of the tomato as a vegetable, botanically speaking, it is a berry. Filled with pulp and seeds, it is the fruit of a vine and so qualifies for inclusion with other fruit pies. As a pie filling, it ranks among the least appreciated and most delicious.

With this recipe in hand, you no longer have to wrap all your green garden tomatoes in newspaper before the first frost and hope that they ripen before they rot. Save them for pie; the green tomato produces a flavor, surprisingly enough, halfway between spicy apple and peach pie. Friends Dick Parks and Jim Garland shared this recipe with us one summer Sunday at the end of a gorgeous corn chowder luncheon they had prepared. They presented it as Dick's special pie, and only after we tasted and acclaimed it, did they reveal the mystery ingredient. You can repeat this precaution if you wish, but be assured that the taste of this pie will win unanimous praise.

194

ADVANCE PREPARATION: The pastry can be prepared ahead and frozen (page 71). The pie is best served the day it is baked.

SPECIAL EQUIPMENT: 9-inch pie plate; pastry brush; large pot; colander; aluminum foil frame (page 22)

TEMPERATURE AND TIME: 425°F for 20 minutes, 375°F for 35 to 40 minutes

YIELD: One 9-inch pie; serves 6 to 8

Unbaked pastry for two-crust 9-inch pie made with All-Purpose
Flaky Pastry (page 45), or Cheddar Cheese variation (page 49), or
Whole Wheat Pastry (page 80)

EGG GLAZE:

1 large egg beaten with 1 tablespoon water

TOPPING:

Granulated sugar

FILLING:

3 tablespoons crushed cornflakes or Rice Krispies cereal
5 to 6 medium green tomatoes prepared as in step 2, (4 cups peeled
   and sliced)
1 cup packed light brown sugar
Juice and grated zest of 1 lemon
½ teaspoon ground cinnamon
½ teaspoon ground nutmeg
5 tablespoons all-purpose flour
1 tablespoon quick-cooking tapioca

195

Prepare the pastry, roll out half, and line the pie plate (pages 52–55). Trim a ½-inch overhang. To moisture-proof the lower crust, brush it with egg glaze and sprinkle with the cereal crumbs. Refrigerate the pastry-lined pan while you prepare the filling.

To peel the tomatoes, bring a large pot of water to a boil. Cut a cross-shaped slit in the skin at the bottom of each tomato. Immerse the tomatoes in the boiling water for 2 to 3 minutes. Drain in a colander, then cut around the stem ends and peel off the skin. Quarter the tomatoes, then cut them into ⅜-inch-thick slices and drain them thoroughly in a colander. Put the slices in a bowl. Preheat the oven to 425°F.

Add the sugar, lemon zest and juice, spices, flour, and tapioca to the tomatoes. Stir very gently. Note that while tomatoes vary greatly, they all contain a lot of water, so sufficient thickener must be used or the pie will be too runny.

Fill the pastry with the prepared tomato mixture. Brush egg glaze around the rim of the lower crust. Roll out the top crust and fit it over the fruit. Trim a ¾-inch overhang, fold the edge under the bottom crust overhang, and pinch together to seal, making a raised rim all around. Flute the edge as desired, and cut vent holes in the top (pages 56–60). Brush the top with egg glaze. Sprinkle lightly with a little granulated sugar.

Set the pie in the lower third of the preheated oven and bake for 20 minutes. Reduce the heat to 375°F, raise the pie to the center of the oven, and bake for an additional 35 to 40 minutes, or until the pastry is golden brown. Check the pie after half the baking time and add a foil edging frame if necessary to prevent overbrowning. Cool on a wire rack. Serve warm or at room temperature.

196

Fresh Berry Pies

· · · · · · · · · ·

Berry pies mean Vermont summer to me: prickly patches of ruby, black, or blue berries, sweet scented, plump, and dusty under the hot sun on a dirt road. Scratched ankles to be sure, but full berry baskets proudly delivered to the kitchen of our lakeside log cabin to be transformed into a pie or tart, the only thing better than eating berries directly from the bush.

Fresh berries should always be firm, plump, and clean. Discard bruised or dried-up fruit, and remove hulls, leaves, and unidentified flying objects. *Just before using*, place berries in a colander and spray with cold water to remove any dust. Spread berries on several thicknesses of paper toweling to dry. If you do this quickly and do not soak or squash the berries, their flavor and shape will remain intact. Berries can be baked between two solid pastry crusts or under a lattice topping, which I prefer, as it shows off the colorful filling. (*Note:* Adjust the amount of sugar and thickening in the basic recipe to allow for variations in the sweetness and juiciness of your own berries.).

As a general rule, the procedure for making baked berry pies is to line a 9-inch pie plate with flaky pastry and fill it with about 4 cups of sugared fresh berries thickened with about 2½ to 3½ tablespoons quick-cooking tapioca or cornstarch. Cover with a plain or lattice top crust, glaze, and bake in a hot oven (425°F) at first, to set the pastry quickly. Check after half the baking time and, if the pastry is browning too much, cover it with a foil edging frame (page 22). To complete the baking, lower the heat to moderate (350°F) and continue baking for a *total* of 50 to 55 minutes. To protect your oven from dripping juices, set a sheet of foil with the edges turned up on the oven floor (not on the oven shelf, where it will deflect heat away from the pie).

Ruth Lawrence's Blackberry Pie
· · · · · · · · · · ·

The late Ruth Lawrence of Albany, Vermont, was famous for her pies. The first one I ever tasted was a blackberry pie she served at her own fifty-fifth wedding anniversary party; although all the friends and neighbors had brought foods and baked goods, the guest of honor's pie stole the show—and the competition was stiff.

I recalled the blackberry pie vividly a few years later when I visited Ruth at berry-picking time. Not only did she share her recipe, but she gave me the berries to bake with and her secret for softening tough blackberry seeds: Cook them in a little vinegar.

ADVANCE PREPARATION: Pastry can be prepared ahead and frozen (page 71). Complete unbaked pies can also be frozen (page 73).

SPECIAL EQUIPMENT: 9-inch pie plate; pastry brush; potato ricer or large spoon for mashing fruit; 3-quart heavy-bottomed nonreactive saucepan; aluminum foil frame (page 22)

TEMPERATURE AND TIME: 425°F for 15 minutes, 350°F for 35 to 40 minutes

BERRY-COOKING TIME: 5 to 7 minutes

YIELD: One 9-inch pie; serves 6 to 8

PASTRY:

Unbaked pastry for a two-crust 9-inch pie made with Butter-Lard Pastry (page 87) or pastry of your choice

EGG GLAZE:

1 large egg beaten with 1 tablespoon water
Topping: Granulated sugar

  4 cups fresh blackberries, picked over, rinsed, and dried just before use
  1½ to 1⅔ cups granulated sugar (depending on sweetness of berries)
  ½ teaspoon cider vinegar
  3 tablespoons cornstarch
  1 tablespoon quick-cooking tapioca

Prepare the pastry, roll out half, and line the pie plate (pages 52–55). Trim a ½-inch pastry overhang. To moisture-proof the lower crust, brush with egg glaze. Refrigerate the crust while you prepare the filling. Preheat the oven to 425°F.

In a heavy-bottomed saucepan, combine the berries, sugar, vinegar, and cornstarch; add 2 tablespoons water (to prevent scorching). Mash the fruit very slightly in order to release some of the juices. Set the pan over medium-low heat and cook, stirring occasionally, just until the mixture nears the boiling point. Remove from the heat and cool completely. Stir in the tapioca.

Add the cooled fruit to pastry-lined pan. Brush egg glaze over the edge of the lower crust. Roll out the top crust and fit it over the fruit. Trim a ¾-inch overhang. Fold the top edge under the bottom crust overhang and pinch them together to seal, making a raised rim all around. Flute the edge as desired, and cut vent holes (pages 56–60). Brush the top with egg glaze. Sprinkle with sugar.

199

Set the pie in the lower third of the preheated oven and bake for 15 minutes. Reduce the heat to 350°F, raise the pie to the center of the oven, and bake for an additional 35 to 40 minutes, or until the pastry is golden brown. Check the pie after about half the total baking time and add a foil edging frame if necessary to prevent overbrowning. Cool on a wire rack. Serve warm or cold.

(*Note:* If the unbaked pie was frozen, bake it without thawing. Set the frozen pie in a preheated 375°F oven for the first 35 minutes. Cover the pastry edge with foil to prevent overbrowning if necessary. Raise the heat to 400°F for the last 15 minutes or so if needed to brown the crust; total baking time should be roughly 45 to 55 minutes.)

Currant Cream Pie

· · · · · · · · · · ·

Like Blackberry Pie (page 198), Currant Cream was a specialty of the late Ruth Lawrence, whose Albany, Vermont, farm once literally overflowed with prizewinning flowers as well as strawberries, currant and blueberry bushes, berry patches, and vegetable gardens as far as one could see. "It's hard farming, but delicious eating," Ruth once told me with a touch of pride. Ruth's daughter-in-law, Delia Lawrence, graciously picked an overflowing basket of jewel-like red currants for me to use in testing this recipe. Fresh currants are sometimes difficult to find. Check farmers' markets in midsummer if they are not in your garden. The pie is actually a custard, and the currants rise to the top during baking to give a delightfully tart flavor counterpoint and visual contrast to the sweet custardy filling.

ADVANCE PREPARATION: The partially prebaked pastry shell can be prepared in advance. Fill and bake the shell shortly before serving, or no more than 3 hours in advance; the lower crust softens on standing.

SPECIAL EQUIPMENT: Mixing bowl and whisk; 9-inch pie plate; pastry brush; stainless steel knife

TEMPERATURE AND TIME: Partially prebaked pastry shell: 425°F for 12 minutes with pie weights and foil liner, then 5 to 7 minutes empty; filled pie: 325°F for 35 to 40 minutes

YIELD: One 9-inch pie; serves 6 to 8

Partially prebaked 9-inch pie shell made with All-Purpose Flaky Pastry
(page 45) or other pastry of your choice

FILLING:

2 large eggs, at room temperature

1 cup heavy cream

⅔ cup granulated sugar

½ teaspoon all-purpose flour

A dash of ground cinnamon

1 cup fresh currants, stemmed, rinsed, and dried

Preheat the oven to 425°F.

Prepare the pastry, roll it out, and line the pie plate (pages 52–55). Do not prick the pastry with a fork. Chill the pastry until firm, then partially blind-bake (pages 66–67) for 12 minutes. Remove the liner and weights from the pastry.

In a mixing bowl, whisk together the eggs and cream. Brush the pastry with the egg-cream mixture, then return to the the oven to bake for an additional 5 minutes, or until the dough is no longer translucent. Cool on a wire rack. Reduce the heat to 325°F.

Whisk the sugar, flour, and cinnamon into the remaining egg and cream mixture. Stir in the currants. Pour the mixture into the prepared pastry shell and bake in the center of the 325°F oven for 35 to 40 minutes, or until the top is golden brown and a knife inserted into the center of the custard comes out clean. Cool on a wire rack. Serve warm or at room temperature.

Blueberry Pie

. . . .

Use this as a master recipe for whatever type of berries you have. Be sure to use firm, plump, ripe berries, picked over and hulled. Immediately before using, so as neither to soak the berries nor to lessen their flavor, gently rinse them with cold water and drain them on paper towels until dry. For the most attractive presentation, cover the pie with a lattice topping so the colorful berries show through the pastry strips. *Note:* To make Quick Fresh Blueberry *Tart*, see page 216.

ADVANCE PREPARATION: Blueberries (or other berries) can be combined with the seasonings, sugar, and thickener as described below and frozen in individual pie-sized packets (see page 72). The pastry can be prepared ahead and frozen (page 71). Complete *unbaked* pies can also be frozen (see page 73). Pie is best served the day baked.

SPECIAL EQUIPMENT: 9-inch pie plate; pastry brush; aluminum foil frame (page 22); colander; paper towels

TEMPERATURE AND TIME: 425°F for 15 minutes, 350°F for 35 to 40 minutes

YIELD: One 9-inch pie; serves 6 to 8

PASTRY:

> Unbaked pastry for a two-crust 9-inch pie made with Cream Cheese
> Pastry (page 90), All-Purpose Flaky Pastry, Orange or Lemon
> variation (page 49), or pastry of your choice

EGG GLAZE:

> 1 large egg beaten with 1 tablespoon water

TOPPING:

> Granulated sugar

FILLING:

> 4 cups fresh berries, picked over, rinsed, and dried just before using
> ½ to 1 cup granulated sugar (depending on the sweetness of the berries)
> A pinch of salt
> 3 tablespoons quick-cooking tapioca or cornstarch
> 2 tablespoons fresh lemon juice
> A pinch of ground cinnamon
> A pinch of ground nutmeg
> 2 tablespoons unsalted butter, cut up, optional

203

Prepare the pastry, roll out half, and line the pie plate (pages 52–55). Trim a ½-inch pastry overhang. To moisture-proof the lower crust, brush with egg glaze. Preheat the oven to 425°F.

In a large bowl, gently toss the berries to coat thoroughly with the sugar, salt, tapioca or cornstarch, and flavorings. Add the fruit to the pastry-lined pan and dot with the butter, if using. Brush egg glaze over the edge of the lower crust.

Roll out the top crust, and prepare a lattice of your choice (pages 60–64) or make a solid top crust and fit it over the fruit. Trim a ¾-inch overhang. Fold the edge under the bottom crust overhang and pinch together to seal, making a raised rim all around. Or cut vent holes in a solid crust and flute the edges as desired (pages 56–60). To glaze the top of the pie, brush egg glaze over the solid or lattice pastry and sprinkle on a little granulated sugar.

Set the pie in the lower third of the preheated oven and bake for 15 minutes. Reduce the heat to 350°F, raise the pie to the center of the oven, and bake for an additional 35 to 40 minutes, or until the pastry is golden brown. Check the pie after half the baking time and add a foil edging frame if necessary to prevent overbrowning. Cool on a wire rack. Serve warm or at room temperature, topped by sweetened whipped cream (page 129) or Custard Sauce (page 144).

Deep-Dish Blueberry Pie. Use 6 to 8 cups berries and increase the sugar slightly, but do not alter the other ingredients. Prepare only half the pastry recipe; omit the bottom crust. Place the prepared berries in a 1½- to 2-quart ovenproof dish at least 2 inches deep and cover with the rolled-out pastry fitted to the edge of the pan. Cut steam vents, glaze the top, and bake as for a regular two-crust pie.

Blueberry-Strawberry or Raspberry Pie. Use 2 cups blueberries and 2 cups any other berries.

Raspberry Pie. Substitute 4 to 5 cups fresh ripe raspberries for the blueberries. If the berries are very plump and juicy, use 3½ tablespoons quick-cooking tapioca or cornstarch. (*Note:* Be sure the berries are picked over, rinsed, and dried on paper towels *immediately before using*; if this is done in advance, raspberries can get soggy.)

Blackberry, Marionberry, or Huckleberry Pie. Substitute 4 to 5 cups fresh ripe blackberries, Marionberries, or huckleberries for the blueberries. If the berries are very plump and juicy, use 3½ tablespoons quick-cooking tapioca or cornstarch. (*Note:* Be sure the berries are picked over, rinsed, and dried on paper towels *immediately before using.*)

FRUIT TARTS AND GALETTES

The friendly cow all red and white,
I love with all my heart:
She gives me cream with all her might,
To eat with apple-tart.

ROBERT LOUIS STEVENSON
"The Cow"

Nothing enhances a fruit tart more than cream, whether served alongside, on top, or in a custard filling. But even unadorned, the fruit tart is a splendor. When the Knave of Hearts stole those tarts made by the Queen ("all on a summer's day") in the nursery rhyme, it was surely a crime of passion, for no one can resist the glamour of a beautifully prepared tart.

While tarts are just as easy to make as pies and use only half the pastry, they make especially elegant and dramatic presentations that can look as if you have done twice the work. Tarts come in all varieties, from classic combinations of neatly arranged fruit slices baked and glazed with preserves to quickly assembled fruit glacée tarts, in which a prebaked pastry shell is filled with a cooked vanilla or almond custard, topped with fresh fruit or berries, and glazed with fruit jelly. Classic French tart pastry is richer and less flaky than American pie pastry. It is made with an egg or yolk, plus more sugar (see Rich Tart Pastry, page 88), but any pastry recipe can be used, including commercial frozen (and thawed) puff pastry, which can be molded in pans or shaped into freestanding prebaked shells (see Puff Pastry Shells, page 112). Puff shells have a drama all their own, though they are not at all hard to create.

Tarts are either baked in pans with removable bottoms or shaped in flan rings (just a pan edging) set on a flat baking sheet. In either case, a tart bottom is perfectly flat, and must therefore be unmolded onto a flat serving platter or tray. If you lack a flat platter of sufficient diameter, simply cover a piece of stiff cardboard, or a cake disk or pizza board, with foil. Or only remove the pan sides and serve the tart right on its metal pan bottom, the most reliable alternative if the tart is at all delicate, for it prevents its being disturbed or jarred before serving.

A galette, literally any flat cake or pancake, is a tart's country cousin. My galette is simply a rustic French country tart free-formed on a flat baking sheet and served in wedges like a fruit pizza. This is the easiest tart of all to make.

French Apple Tart

· · · · · · · · · · ·

In this classic apple tart, a decorative arrangement of glazed apple slices covers thick applesauce flavored with preserves and brandy.

ADVANCE PREPARATION: The partially baked pastry shell can be prepared ahead and frozen (page 71). The tart is best when freshly made, but it can also be baked, left unglazed, and frozen (page 73). Thaw and warm in the oven, then glaze just before serving.

SPECIAL EQUIPMENT: 11-inch tart pan with removable bottom; pastry brush; food processor fitted with steel blade or a knife and cutting board; 2½-quart heavy-bottomed nonreactive saucepan; 12-inch flat serving platter

SAUCE COOKING TIME: About 25 minutes

TEMPERATURE AND TIME: Partially prebaked shell: 425°F for 12 minutes with pie weights, then 3 minutes empty; completed tart: 375°F for 35 to 45 minutes

YIELD: One 11-inch tart; serves 10 to 12

PASTRY:

>   Partially prebaked 11-inch tart shell made with All-Purpose Flaky
>   Pastry (page 45) or Rich Tart Pastry (page 88)

FILLING:

>   4 pounds (about 12 large) apples (cooking variety such as Granny Smith
>   alone or combined with Golden Delicious)
>   2 tablespoons fresh lemon juice
>   2 tablespoons granulated sugar
>   3 tablespoons unsalted butter
>   3 tablespoons water or apple or fresh orange juice
>   ⅓ cup orange marmalade or apricot preserves
>   ¼ cup Calvados, brandy, or rum, optional

FRUIT GLAZE:

>   Plain Glaze (page 153) or Firm Glaze (page 155), made with apricot
>   preserves and kirsch

Prepare the pastry, roll it out, and line the buttered tart pan (pages 52–55). Prick the bottom with a fork, chill until firm, and then partially blind-bake the shell (pages 66–67). Cool on a wire rack.

To prepare the apples and sauce, first peel and evenly thinly slice enough apples for about 3 cups of slices. Place them in a bowl and coat with the lemon juice and sugar to prevent discoloration. Peel, core, and chop (using the food processor or a knife and cutting board) the remaining apples and place them in a saucepan with the butter and water or juice. Cook over low heat, covered, for about 20 minutes, to make the applesauce. Stir in the marmalade or preserves and the brandy or rum. Raise the heat slightly and cook, uncovered, until so thick the sauce clings to the spoon and resists dripping off; do not allow the sauce to burn. Remove from the heat and stir occasionally to cool. Preheat the oven to 375°F.

Spread the applesauce in the bottom of the partially baked pastry shell. Cover the sauce with neatly overlapping rows of the apple slices arranged in concentric circles. Bake in the center of the preheated oven for 35 to 45 minutes, or until the apples are fork-tender (different types require different baking times). While the tart is baking, prepare the glaze.

Cool the baked tart for about 5 minutes, then remove the pan sides (page 55), keeping the tart on the pan bottom, and slide it onto a flat serving platter or wire rack to cool completely. Brush the lukewarm glaze over the completely cooled tart. Chill to set the glaze; serve the tart at room temperature.

Apple and Cranberry Sauce Tart. Omit the preserves and brandy. The apple-sauce is replaced by cranberry-apple sauce: Use only 1½ pounds (4 to 5 large) cooking apples.

To make the sauce, coarsely chop together 1 cup peeled, cut-up apples and 2 cups fresh or whole frozen cranberries. Put the fruit in a heavy-bottomed nonreactive saucepan with the butter, water, ½ teaspoon each ground cinnamon and nutmeg, ½ cup sugar, and 2 tablespoons quick-cooking tapioca. Cook gently, uncovered, for 10 to 15 minutes or until very thick, stirring occasionally to prevent sticking. While the sauce cooks, thinly slice the remaining apples (about 3 cups) and toss with the lemon juice and 2 tablespoons sugar.

Cool the sauce slightly and spread it in the pastry shell. Add overlapping concentric rings of the apple slices, but allow some of the underlying red sauce to show between the rows of apples. Bake and glaze as above.

209

Normandy Apple Tart

. . . .

Because Normandy produces such a bounty of excellent dairy products, the name of this classic French recipe indicates that the tart contains a rich custard.

ADVANCE PREPARATION: The unbaked pastry shell can be prepared ahead and frozen (page 71), but the tart must be assembled just before baking, or the custard will soften the lower crust. The tart is best served the day it is baked; refrigerate if baked in advance.

SPECIAL EQUIPMENT: 11-inch tart pan with removable bottom; pastry brush; mixing bowl and whisk or food processor; flat rimmed baking sheet; narrow aluminum foil frame (page 22); 12-inch flat serving platter

TEMPERATURE AND TIME: 425°F for 20 minutes, 375°F for 30 to 35 minutes

YIELD: One 11-inch tart; serves 10 to 12

PASTRY:

> Unbaked pastry for 11-inch tart shell made with All-Purpose Flaky
> Pastry, Orange or Lemon variation (page 49), or Rich Tart
> Pastry (page 88)

EGG GLAZE:

> 1 large egg white beaten with 1 tablespoon water

FILLING:

> 1 pound (3 to 4 large) apples (such as Granny Smith and/or Golden
> Delicious), peeled, cored, and sliced ⅛ inch thick (3 cups slices)
> ⅓ cup plus 1 generous tablespoon granulated sugar
> ⅛ teaspoon ground cinnamon
> ¼ teaspoon ground nutmeg, plus more for sprinkling on tart

CUSTARD AND NUTS:

> 1 large egg plus 1 large yolk
> 3 tablespoons granulated sugar
> ¼ cup all-purpose flour
> ½ cup heavy cream
> 2 teaspoons vanilla extract or 3 tablespoons Calvados, applejack,
> or dark rum
> 3 tablespoons blanched almonds, finely chopped or ground

Prepare the pastry, roll it out, and line the buttered tart pan (pages 52–55). Do *not* prick the pastry. Chill the unbaked shell until firm while you prepare the fruit. Preheat the oven to 425°F.

Toss the apples in a bowl with ⅓ cup of the sugar, the cinnamon, and nutmeg. When the pastry is firm, brush it with moisture-proofing egg white glaze and sprinkle with the remaining generous 1 tablespoon sugar. Arrange overlapping apple slices in concentric circles over the prepared pastry.

Set the tart in the lower third of the preheated oven and bake for 20 minutes. (This first baking cooks the apples to partial tenderness and prebakes the crust.) While the apples bake, prepare the custard: In a bowl or food processor, beat together the egg yolk, sugar, flour, cream, and vanilla or other flavoring.

After 20 minutes, remove the tart from the oven. Reduce the heat to 375°F. Set the tart on a flat rimmed baking sheet for ease in handling. Pour the custard over the apples and sprinkle on the nutmeg and ground almonds. Place a narrow foil edging frame over the pastry rim to prevent overbrowning if necessary. Place the tart in the center of the oven and bake for 30 to 35 minutes longer, or until the top is puffed and golden and a knife inserted into the custard 1 inch from the edge comes out clean. Cool for about 5 minutes, then remove the pan sides (page 55), keeping the tart on the pan bottom, and slide it onto a flat serving platter or wire rack to cool. Serve warm or at room temperature.

Normandy Apple-Pear Tart. Instead of all apples, use 2 large tart apples and 2 large ripe pears. Peel, core, and slice the apples ⅛ inch thick. Core and slice—do not peel—the pears, for a total of about 3 cups prepared fruit.

Almond Pear Tart

· · · · · · · · · · ·

I first tasted this tart as an art student in Paris years ago. Since then, the memory has been refined by numerous visits and at least as many different versions, the most recent sampled on a trip through Normandy during pear harvest.

ADVANCE PREPARATION: The pastry shell can be prepared ahead and frozen (page 71). The tart is best if made the day it is served.

SPECIAL EQUIPMENT: 11-inch tart shell with removable bottom; pastry brush; food processor fitted with steel blade; flat baking sheet; 12-inch flat serving platter

TEMPERATURE AND TIME: 425°F for 15 minutes, 350°F for 35 to 40 minutes

YIELD: One 11-inch tart; serves 10 to 12

> **Unbaked pastry for 11-inch tart shell made with Rich Tart Pastry, (page 88),**
> **Cream Cheese Pastry (page 90), or Cornmeal Pastry (page 81)**

ALMOND FILLING:

> ½ cup (2 ounces) whole or slivered unblanched almonds
> ⅓ cup granulated sugar
> 4 tablespoons (½ stick) unsalted butter, cut up, at room temperature
> 1 large egg
> ¼ teaspoon ground nutmeg, plus extra to sprinkle on tart
> ½ teaspoon vanilla extract
> ½ teaspoon almond extract

CREAM FILLING:

> ½ cup heavy or whipping cream
> 1 large egg plus 1 large yolk
> 1 tablespoon granulated sugar
> 1 teaspoon vanilla extract
> 2 tablespoons eau-de-vie de poire, optional

FRUIT:

> 4 large ripe pears (Bosc, Anjou, or Bartlett)

Prepare the pastry, roll it out, and line the buttered tart pan (pages 52–55). Prick the bottom with a fork and chill until firm while you prepare the filling. (*Note:* This recipe can also be made with a partially baked and completely cooled pastry shell, pages 66–67.) Preheat the oven to 425°F.

Prepare the Almond Filling: In a food processor, process the almonds with the sugar until the nuts are finely ground. Add the butter and pulse 2 or 3 times, then add the egg, nutmeg, and both extracts. Pulse 2 or 3 times to blend. Spread filling over the bottom of the chilled pastry shell. Refrigerate. Return workbowl to processor base without washing it.

Prepare the Cream Filling: In the food processor, combine the cream, egg plus yolk, sugar, vanilla, and the brandy, if you are using it. Process for a few seconds to blend. Place the flat baking sheet in the lower third of the oven to get hot.

Prepare the pears: Just before using them (to avoid discoloration), peel, cut them into quarters, and carefully core each piece. Then slice each quarter in half lengthwise, making 8 wedges. Top the almond filling on the chilled pastry with a flower-petal arrangement of pear slices, thin necks pointing inward. Pour the cream filling over the pears and sprinkle with a little nutmeg. Set the tart pan on the preheated baking sheet and bake in the lower third of the preheated oven for 15 minutes. Lower the heat to 350°F, raise the tart to the center of the oven, and continue baking for another 35 to 40 minutes, or until the filling is set and looks golden brown. Cool on a wire rack. Remove the pan sides (page 55), keeping the tart on the pan bottom, and slide it onto a flat serving platter. Serve warm or at room temperature. Store in the refrigerator.

Apricot-Almond Tart. Omit the almond extract and replace the pears with canned apricot halves, drained and positioned cut side down *after* both the almond filling *and* cream fillings are put into the shell. Brush the baked and cooled apricots with apricot Plain Fruit Glaze (page 153) shortly before serving.

215

Quick Fresh Blueberry Tart

· · · · · · · · · · · ·

Blueberry preserves make a flavorful shortcut filling beneath the fresh berries in this easy summer dessert. Make your own pastry or, in a pinch, use a store-bought refrigerated crust; the recipe makes enough for a 10- to 11-inch tart or a 10-inch pie. Serve it with vanilla ice cream or whipped cream. For a patriotic color scheme on the Fourth of July, top the tart with alternating rings of blueberries, raspberries, and piped-on whipped cream.

ADVANCE PREPARATION: Pastry can be made in advance and frozen (page 71), then baked up to 1 day ahead. Store-bought refrigerated pie pastry (sold 2 crusts to a box) keeps for at least a week, or it can be frozen, unopened, in its box. Thaw as directed before using; you will need 1½ rounds of dough to line an 11-inch tart pan. Fill the tart the day it is to be served; refrigerate.

SPECIAL EQUIPMENT: 10- to 11-inch tart pan with removable bottom or 10-inch pie plate; medium and small saucepans; pastry brush, optional; 12-inch flat serving platter

TEMPERATURE AND TIME: Completely prebaked tart shell: 425°F for 12 minutes, 350°F for 10 to 15 minutes

YIELD: One 10- to 11-inch tart or 10-inch pie; serves 8 to 10

    **Completely prebaked 10- to 11-inch tart shell or 10-inch pie shell
made with Rich Tart Pastry (page 88), All-Purpose Flaky Pastry
(page 45), or Cream Cheese Pastry (page 90)**

FILLING:

    2 tablespoons cornstarch
    3 tablespoons fresh lemon juice
    1 cup (12-ounce jar) blueberry preserves
    **2½ to 3 cups (1½ to 2 pints) fresh blueberries, picked over, stemmed,
rinsed, and well dried, divided (½ cup and 2 to 2½ cups)**

OPTIONAL: TOPPING OR GLAZE

    About 1 teaspoon confectioners' sugar *or*
    ½ cup apricot preserves

Prepare the pastry, roll it out, and line the buttered tart or pie pan (pages 52–55). Chill until firm. Preheat the oven to 425°F. Completely prebake the shell (pages 66–67). Cool on a wire rack.

In a medium nonreactive saucepan, stir the cornstarch into the lemon juice until completely dissolved, then stir in the blueberry preserves, mixing well to combine. Set over medium heat and, stirring constantly, bring the mixture to a full bubbling boil for 2 minutes, until the juice is well thickened and no longer cloudy. Stir in ½ cup of the fresh blueberries. With a table fork, mash the berries against the pan sides, then blend them into the sauce. Spread this sauce in the bottom of the cooled prebaked tart shell.

Top the blueberry sauce with the fresh berries: Either scatter them randomly or place them in a careful arrangement of concentric rings. In either case, completely cover the sauce with berries. Refrigerate.

Just before serving, sift about 1 teaspoon of confectioners' sugar over the fruit. Or, if you want the berries to have a shiny appearance, brush with apricot glaze (no more than 3 hours before serving): Melt the apricot jam in a small saucepan over low heat, strain, return to the pan, and boil for about 1 minute. Cool glaze slightly, then brush it on the berries. Refrigerate the tart to set the glaze. Remove the pan sides (page 55), keeping the tart on the pan bottom, and slide it onto a flat serving platter. Serve at room temperature.

217

Blueberry Custard Tart

. . . .

This is an irresistible summer party dessert in which fresh berries (any variety or any combination) are baked into a custard. It is a Vermont–French Canadian variation on the classic French Normandy Apple Tart (page 210).

ADVANCE PREPARATION: The partially baked pastry shell can be prepared ahead and frozen (page 71). The tart is best served the day it is made. Refrigerate if made ahead. Do not freeze.

SPECIAL EQUIPMENT: 11-inch tart shell with removable bottom; pastry brush; bowl and whisk or food processor fitted with a steel blade; flat rimmed baking sheet; narrow aluminum foil frame (page 22); stainless steel knife; 12-inch flat serving platter

TEMPERATURE AND TIME: Partially prebaked shell: 425°F for 12 minutes with pie weights, then 3 minutes empty; completed tart: 375°F for 40 to 45 minutes

YIELD: One 11-inch tart; serves 10 to 12

PASTRY:

> Partially prebaked 11-inch tart shell made with All-Purpose Flaky
> Pastry, Orange variation (page 49), Cream Cheese Pastry (page 90),
> or Rich Tart Pastry (page 88)

EGG GLAZE:

> 1 large egg beaten with 1 tablespoon water

FILLING:

> ½ cup granulated sugar
> ¼ cup unsifted all-purpose flour
> ½ teaspoon ground cinnamon
> ¼ teaspoon ground nutmeg
> A pinch of salt
> ½ cup heavy cream
> ¼ cup milk
> 1 large egg, at room temperature
> 4 cups fresh blueberries, stemmed, rinsed, and dried, or partially thawed
>   whole frozen berries (or use half blueberries and half raspberries
>   or peeled, sliced peaches or nectarines)

219

Prepare the pastry, roll it out, and line the buttered tart pan (pages 52–55). Prick the pastry with a fork, chill until firm, and then partially blind-bake the shell (pages 66–67). Brush the pastry with egg glaze after the first 10 minutes (reserve the remaining glaze) and continue baking for 3 minutes, or until the dough is no longer translucent. Cool on a wire rack. Reduce the oven heat to 375°F.

In a bowl or processor, beat together the sugar, flour, cinnamon, nutmeg, salt, cream, milk, and egg. Beat in the remaining egg glaze. Set the pastry-lined pan on a flat rimmed baking sheet for ease in handling. Spread the berries over the bottom of the shell and gently pour on the custard mix.

Set the tart on its baking sheet in the center of the preheated oven and bake for 40 to 45 minutes, or until a stainless steel knife inserted into the custard 1 inch from the edge comes out clean. Check the tart after about half the baking time and add a narrow foil edging frame if necessary to prevent overbrowning. Cool for about 5 minutes, then remove the pan sides (page 55), keeping the tart on the pan bottom, and slide it onto a flat serving platter or wire rack to cool completely. Serve at room temperature.

FRUIT TARTS AND GALETTES

Raspberry-Yogurt Tart

· · · · · · · · · · ·

The picturesque glazed berry topping conceals a flavorful layer of fruit yogurt blended with cream cheese. I devised this filling as an accompaniment for whatever fresh fruits I have available, and I like to select a yogurt flavor that complements the color and flavor of the fruit. (*Note:* A small amount of unflavored gelatin is added to set the filling so that the tart can be sliced neatly; without gelatin, you have a thick pudding good by itself without pastry or for filling individual tartlets.) Instead of raspberries, try substituting blueberries and/or strawberries, bananas, pitted grapes or cherries, sliced nectarines or peaches, and kiwis.

ADVANCE PREPARATION: The completely baked pastry shell can be made ahead and frozen (page 71). The shell should be filled with the yogurt mixture 4 or 5 hours ahead and refrigerated; it needs 4 hours chilling time to set before adding fruit topping. The tart is best prepared the morning of the day it is to be served.

SPECIAL EQUIPMENT: 11-inch tart shell; pastry brush; electric mixer or food processor fitted with a steel blade; small saucepan and spoon; paper towels; 12-inch flat serving platter

TEMPERATURE AND TIME: Completely prebaked shell: 425°F for 12 minutes, then 350°F for 15 to 20 minutes

YIELD: One 11-inch tart; serves 10 to 12

PASTRY:

Completely prebaked 11-inch tart shell made with All-Purpose Flaky Pastry, Orange or Nut (almond) variation (page 49 or 48)

FILLING:

16 ounces (2 large packages) cream cheese (not low-fat), at room temperature, cut up

2 tablespoons frozen orange juice concentrate (undiluted)

1 tablespoon grated orange zest

2 to 4 tablespoons granulated or sifted confectioners' sugar, to taste

1 cup fruit-flavored yogurt, such as raspberry, strawberry, cherry, or orange, top liquid poured off

Scant 2¼ teaspoons unflavored gelatin

¼ cup cold water or fresh orange juice

3 to 4 cups fresh raspberries, stemmed, rinsed, and dried well on paper towels just before using (or other berries or sliced fresh fruit, or canned fruit, drained well and dried)

FRUIT GLAZE:

Plain Glaze (page 153), or Firm Glaze (page 155), if the tart is to be held for longer than 2 hours before serving

Prepare the pastry, roll it out, and line the buttered tart pan (pages 52–55). Prick the pastry bottom with a fork, chill until firm, and then completely blind-bake the shell (pages 66–67). Cool on a wire rack.

In a mixer or food processor, blend together the cream cheese, orange juice concentrate, grated zest, sugar, and yogurt until thick and smooth. Set aside.

In a small saucepan, sprinkle the gelatin over the water or juice, set it aside for about 2 minutes, and then stir in 3 to 4 tablespoons of the yogurt mixture. Set the pan over medium heat and stir for about 3 minutes, until the gelatin is completely dissolved. Pinch the mixture between your fingers to be sure it is not granular. Remove from the heat and cool.

Beat the cooled gelatin mixture into the remaining yogurt mixture, then pour it into the pastry shell. Chill for at least 4 hours, or until the filling is set. Then top with an attractive arrangement of the dry berries (and/or fruit slices). Brush with the glaze and refrigerate. When ready to serve, remove the pan sides (page 55), keeping the tart on the pan bottom, and slide it onto a flat serving platter. Serve cold. Refrigerate leftovers.

Blackberry Mascarpone Tart
. . . .

Equally good as a pie or tart, this delightful, easy-to-make recipe was inspired by my friend, Linnea Milliun, a creative baker who likes to prepare it as a free-form galette, using a prebaked puff pastry shell (page 112). There are many varieties of blackberry; select those that are ripe, taste sweet and juicy, and have small and preferably tender seeds. The most fun and best flavor comes from wild berries you have picked yourself, though summer roadside fruit stands also offer tempting displays. Mascarpone cheese is a rich double cream with the texture of a thick sour cream; it is made from cows' milk and originates in the Lombardy region of Italy. While domestic mascarpone is available in some markets, I find, in my area of New England at least, that the imported brands have the best flavor. The taste of mascarpone is subtle, slightly sweet, and should be clean; if it tastes at all goat-y or bitter, it has gone off and should be discarded (or returned to the shop). As a substitute, you can blend in a food processor until smooth 6 ounces of sieved whole-milk ricotta with 16 ounces of cream cheese; or substitute all Crème Fraîche (page 126).

ADVANCE PREPARATION: The pastry shell can be prepared and baked several hours or a day in advance. The filling and fruit should be added the morning of the day the tart is to be served.

SPECIAL EQUIPMENT: 11-inch tart pan with removable bottom or 9- or 10-inch pie plate; sifter

TEMPERATURE AND TIME: Completely prebaked pastry shell: 425°F for 12 minutes, then 350°F for 15 to 20 minutes

YIELD: One 10- to 11-inch tart or 9- to 10-inch pie; serves 8 to 12

PASTRY:

**Completely prebaked 11-inch tart shell made with All-Purpose Flaky
Pastry (page 45), Rich Tart Pastry (page 88), or Cornmeal
Pastry (page 81)**

FILLING:

**2 tablespoons plus ⅓ cup blackberry preserves (plum or other seedless
berry preserves can be substituted)**

8 ounces mascarpone cheese

2 tablespoons dark rum

1 tablespoon granulated sugar, or to taste

**3 to 4 cups (about 1 quart) fresh ripe large blackberries, picked over,
rinsed, and completely dried on paper towels (if berries are small,
you may need 1 more cup)**

OPTIONAL TOPPING:

1 to 2 teaspoons confectioners' sugar

Prepare the pastry, roll it out, and line the buttered tart pan (pages 52–55). Chill, then completely prebake the shell (pages 66–67). Cool on a wire rack.

With the back of a spoon, spread 2 tablespoons of the blackberry preserves over the bottom of the cooled pastry shell. In a medium bowl, beat together the mascarpone, the remaining ⅓ cup preserves, the rum, and the sugar. Taste and add a little more sugar if desired. Spread the filling in an even layer over the pastry shell.

Top the filling with blackberries, either randomly piled on top or arranged neatly in concentric rings, completely covering the filling. Refrigerate. To serve, remove the pan sides (page 55), keeping the tart on the pan bottom, and slide it onto a flat serving platter. Immediately before serving, sift on a very faint dusting of confectioners' sugar if desired.

Fresh Fruit Tart with Lemonade or Orange Cream

· · · · · · · · · · ·

This is my summertime standby: a quick-to-prepare prebaked pastry shell filled with flavored cream cheese and topped with a colorful assortment of fresh fruits and/or berries. For visual excitement, you can arrange an assortment of berries and sliced fruits in clusters of varying heights or patterns of concentric circles of contrasting colors (raspberries and blueberries, for example). To make a Strawberry Cream Tart, arrange 1½ quarts of ripe whole strawberries (or 2 quarts *fraises des bois*, wild strawberries) stem end down, covering the whole tart, or slice the berries and arrange in overlapping concentric circles. For a reduced-fat version of this tart, see the variation following. *Note:* If you want to glaze the tart more than 3 hours before serving, use the Firm Fruit Glaze.

ADVANCE PREPARATION: The completely prebaked pastry shell can be prepared 1 day ahead, or up to 1 week ahead and frozen (page 71). The cream cheese filling can be prepared 1 or 2 days ahead, covered, and chilled in a bowl. Assemble the tart the morning of the day it is to be served, but glaze it as close as possible to serving time (or use Firm Fruit Glaze). Allow 4 hours for filling to set.

SPECIAL EQUIPMENT: 11-inch tart pan with removable bottom or 10-inch pie plate; pastry brush

TEMPERATURE AND TIME: Completely prebake shell: 425°F for 12 minutes, then 350°F for 15 to 20 minutes

YIELD: One 11-inch tart or 10-inch pie; serves 10 to 12

Completely prebaked 11-inch tart shell made with All-Purpose Flaky
Pastry (page 45) or Cream Cheese Pastry (page 90)

FRUIT GLAZE:

Plain Glaze (page 153) or Firm Glaze (page 155), either one prepared
with ¾ cup preserves

CREAM FILLING:

Lemonade or Orange Juice Cream Cheese Tart Filling (page 128), chilled

FRUIT:

4 cups fresh berries, picked over, rinsed, and completely dried on paper
towels just before using, and/or assorted fruit, such as red and green
seedless grapes, pitted sweet cherries, or peeled and sliced kiwi,
peaches, nectarines, mangoes, or pears

Prepare the pastry, roll it out, and line the buttered tart pan (pages 52–55). Chill, then
completely prebake the pastry shell (pages 66–67); cool it on a wire rack.

Prepare the fruit glaze of your choice. Brush a moisture-proofing coat of glaze over the
bottom of the prebaked pastry shell.

Prepare the Cream Filling and spread it over the pastry shell. Prepare the berries and/or
fruit and arrange them on the cream. (Slice peaches, nectarines, mangoes, or pears immediately before placing them on the cream filling so they do not discolor.) With a pastry
brush, coat the berries and fruit with the lukewarm glaze (warm it slightly if it has hardened). Refrigerate the tart to set the glaze. To serve the tart, remove the pan sides (page
55), keeping the tart on the pan bottom, and slide it onto a flat serving platter. Refrigerate
leftovers.

Fresh Fruit Tart with Reduced-Fat Cream Filling. This tart is luscious
and sparkling with flavor; you will never notice that the cream filling beneath the fruit has
between one third and one half the fat of the original recipe. Prepare the recipe above,
with the following changes:

225

**Completely prebaked 9-inch tart or pie shell made with Brown Butter
Pastry (page 94)**

FILLING:

**½ recipe (1 cup) Vanilla-Yogurt Cream (page 125), chilled, or 1 full recipe
Lemonade Cream Cheese Tart Filling (page 128), made with light cream
cheese (not fat-free), Light Lemon Curd (page 119), or Hot and Sweet
Cream Filling (page 124)**

226

Cranberry-Raisin Holiday Tart

· · · · · · · · · ·

Select only unblemished cranberries for pies. Cranberries are widely available in the autumn, but can be hard to find at other times of the year. When you see them, take advantage of the supply and buy extra bags of berries to put directly into your freezer for year-round use. Off season, if you don't find cranberries in the produce department of your market, you may locate them in the freezer section.

With its bright ruby-hued berries and rich flavor, this tart makes an especially festive holiday presentation; it can be made in advance and frozen for easy entertaining. Serve it open-faced or topped with a pastry lattice or several decorative pastry leaves baked like cookies and added at the last moment. The orange-scented, not-too-sweet filling is especially good served warm, with vanilla ice cream or Orange Whipped Cream (page 132). The recipe can also be used for tartlets or a 10-inch pie. To make a Cranberry-Apple-Raisin Tart or pie, reduce the cranberries to 2½ cups and the raisins to ½ cup; add 1½ cups peeled, cored, and chopped apples. Note: Be sure to use golden raisins, as other raisins darken the color of the tart.

ADVANCE PREPARATION: Whole fresh cranberries can be frozen until needed; use without thawing. The unbaked pastry shell can be prepared ahead and frozen (page 72). The complete but unbaked tart can be double-wrapped and frozen (page 73). Bake, without thawing, for an additional 10 minutes.

SPECIAL EQUIPMENT: 11-inch tart pan with removable bottom or eight 4½-inch tartlet pans or 10-inch pie plate; pastry brush; knife or pastry wheel for cutting lattice or leaf-shaped cookie cutter or paring knife for decorative topping cookies, optional; aluminum foil; aluminum foil frame (page 22); 12-inch flat serving platter

TEMPERATURE AND TIME: Filled tart or pie: 425°F for 15 minutes, then 350°F for 30 to 35 minutes; tartlets, 350°F for 20 to 25 minutes; decorative pastry leaves, 350°F for 10 minutes

YIELD: One 11-inch tart or 10-inch pie; serving 10 to 12, or 8 tartlets

Unbaked pastry for two-crust 10-inch pie made with All-Purpose
   Flaky Pastry (page 45); (for lattice topping, see pages 60–64)

EGG GLAZE:

1 large egg beaten with 1 tablespoon water

FILLING:

½ cup fresh orange juice

3 tablespoons quick-cooking tapioca

3 cups (12 ounces) whole fresh or frozen cranberries, picked over,
   rinsed, and dried

1 cup golden raisins

½ cup (2 ounces) chopped walnuts

1 tablespoon grated orange zest

¼ cup orange marmalade, optional

½ cup packed dark brown sugar

¾ cup granulated sugar plus 2 tablespoons extra for pastry topping

½ teaspoon ground cinnamon

½ teaspoon ground nutmeg

OPTIONAL TOPPING GLAZE:

½ cup seedless raspberry or red currant jelly, warmed

Pastry Topping: Granulated sugar

Prepare the pastry, roll out half, and line the buttered tart pan (pages 52–55). Chill until firm while you prepare the filling.

Preheat the oven to 425°F. In a small bowl, stir together the orange juice and tapioca. In a large bowl, stir together all the remaining filling ingredients. Stir in the orange juice–tapioca mixture. Brush moisture-proofing egg glaze over the bottom of the pastry shell, then add all the filling and spread it evenly.

Roll out the remaining dough and make the lattice of your choice (pages 60–64). Fold up and flute the pastry rim as desired (page 56). Or, instead of a lattice, you can cut leaf shapes with cookie cutters or make free-form leaf shapes with a paring knife (page 58). Press veins into the leaves with the back of the knife blade. Brush the lattice or leaves with egg glaze and sprinkle lightly with granulated sugar. If you've made leaves, bake them sep-

228

arately from the tart: Chill them on a piece of foil, then bake at 350°F for about 10 minutes, until golden. Set on the glazed pie top just before serving.

To bake the tart, set it in the lower third of the preheated oven and bake for 15 minutes, then reduce the heat to 350°F and bake for an additional 30 to 35 minutes (tartlets, 20 to 25 minutes), or until the pastry is golden brown and the fruit is tender. Check after about half the baking time and add a foil edging frame if needed to prevent overbrowning. Cool the tart for about 20 minutes. To add a shine and redder color, brush the filling with optional topping glaze. Remove the tart pan sides (page 55); keep the tart on the pan bottom, and slide it onto a flat serving platter or wire rack to cool. Serve warm or at room temperature.

229

$\mathcal{L}$inzertorte
· · · · · · · · · · ·

This traditional Austrian torte has a rich, sweet-and-spicy nut pastry and a cinnamon-raspberry filling that provide the perfect finish to a fireside dinner on a winter evening. To be authentic, arrange the lattice-strip pastry topping on the diagonal. The pastry was originally baked in a cake pan, hence the name *torte*. It is equally successful as a tart. The dough is also delicious by itself, baked into cookies. For this reason, the pastry recipe is large enough to make one 11-inch tart plus about 30 round cookies, which, when studded with cloves and rolled in powdered sugar, make an aromatic addition to a holiday cookie platter.

ADVANCE PREPARATION: The partially baked pastry shell can be prepared ahead and frozen, as can the plain dough (page 72) or the completely baked tart (page 71). Cookies can be frozen.

SPECIAL EQUIPMENT: 11-inch tart pan with removable bottom; wax paper; aluminum foil frame (page 22); pastry brush; 12-inch flat serving platter; flat baking sheet for cookies

TEMPERATURE AND TIME: Partially prebaked shell: 425°F for 12 minutes; completed tart: 350°F for 40 minutes; cookies: 350°F for 15 minutes

YIELD: One 11-inch tart, serving 10 to 12, plus thirty 1-inch cookies; two 9-inch tarts, each serving 6 to 8; or one 11-inch plus one 8-inch tart, serving 6 to 8

PASTRY:

Partially prebaked 11-inch tart shell made with Linzer Pastry (page 95)

FILLING:

1⅓ cups seedless raspberry jam (this will fill one 11-inch tart: If you are making the additional 8-inch tart, use 1 additional cup jam; for two 9-inch tarts, use 1 cup jam each)

¼ cup ground almonds or walnuts

EGG GLAZE:

1 large egg beaten with 1 tablespoon water

TOPPING:

2 teaspoons sifted confectioners' sugar

FOR COOKIES:

⅓ cup whole cloves
¾ cup sifted confectioners' sugar

Prepare the pastry, butter the tart pan, and divide the dough into 2 pieces, one slightly larger than the other. Wrap and refrigerate the smaller piece to use later for the lattice top and cookies. Roll out the larger piece of dough between two pieces of lightly floured wax paper to a generous ⅛-inch thickness, and fit it into the tart pan (pages 52–55). Or, simply pat the dough evenly into the buttered pan with lightly floured fingertips. Chill for 30 minutes, or until the dough is firm. Preheat the oven to 425°F while the dough chills.

Partially prebake the pastry shell (*without lining with foil and weights*) in the lower third of the preheated oven for 12 minutes, or only until the dough begins to change color. Don't let the dough brown; check it after 5 to 6 minutes, and if you see any puffed-up bubbles, prick and deflate them with a fork. Cool the shell on a wire rack. Reduce the oven heat to 350°F.

When the pastry shell is cool, spread on the preserves and sprinkle on the ground almonds.

Remove the remaining dough from the refrigerator and break off golf ball–sized lumps, one at a time. Roll each lump on a floured surface into a pencil-thick rope (roughly ⅜-inch diameter and slightly flattened) long enough to reach across the top of the tart. Brush egg glaze around the edge of the tart shell. Position 6 or 7 dough ropes at a 45° angle at equal intervals across the top of the tart. Gently press the rope ends onto the glazed pastry rim. Cut off the excess dough. Position 6 or 7 more dough ropes at a 45° angle in the opposite direction across the first ropes to make diamond-shaped spaces. (*Note:* Chilled dough is easier to handle. Dough ropes rolled too thin will break when lifted.)

To neaten the tart edge after applying the lattice, roll out additional dough ropes. Brush the tart edge again with egg glaze and press a strip of connected ropes onto the tart edge to cover the lattice ends and make a neat border, just inside, not covering, the pan edge. Brush the border, as well as the entire lattice topping, with egg glaze.

Place the tart in the center of the preheated oven and bake for 40 minutes, or until the pastry is golden brown and the preserves are bubbling. Check the tart after about half the baking time and add a narrow foil edging frame if necessary to prevent overbrowning. Cool on a wire rack. Remove pan sides (page 55), keeping the tart on the pan bottom, and slide it onto a flat serving platter. Just before serving, sift on a delicate dusting of confectioners' sugar.

To make cookies, shape the remaining dough into 1-inch balls and set them on a buttered baking sheet. Stick 1 whole clove into the top of each ball. Bake the cookies in the center of a preheated 350°F oven for about 15 minutes, or just until golden brown. Cool the cookies on a wire rack. While they are still warm, roll the cookies in sifted confectioners' sugar. When cool, sift on more sugar. Store the cookies airtight or freeze.

Fruit Tart in Puff Pastry Shell

· · · · · · · · · ·

This is a classic French tart in which a freestanding prebaked puff pastry shell is filled with pastry cream and topped with glazed fresh fruits. I have given two differently shaped shells here: the band and the square case—both are easy to form in any size following the step-by-step directions. All cases can be made successfully either with Quick Puff Pastry or store-bought frozen puff pastry, though the latter will rise somewhat higher.

ADVANCE PREPARATION: Quick Puff Pastry can be prepared ahead and frozen, or the completely prebaked pastry shell (any style) can be frozen. Thaw store-bought frozen puff pastry about 30 minutes in advance. Fill the shell with cream and fruit no more than 2 or 3 hours before serving, to prevent a soggy lower crust.

SPECIAL EQUIPMENT: Sharp knife or pizza cutting wheel; ruler; table fork; flat baking sheets; pastry brush; heavy-duty aluminum foil

TEMPERATURE AND TIME: 425°F for 20 minutes

YIELD: Two bands, each about 4½ × 14 inches (to serve 12), or nine 3-inch square cases (to serve 9) or one 10- or 11-inch square case (to serve 8)

PASTRY:

1 package (2 sheets) frozen puff pastry (page 112), thawed according to package directions, or 1 whole recipe Quick Puff Pastry (page 110)

EGG GLAZE:

1 large egg beaten with 1 tablespoon water

FRUIT GLAZE:

Plain Glaze (page 153) or Firm Glaze (page 155)

PASTRY CREAM:

Vanilla Pastry Cream (page 116) or Almond Pastry Cream variation (page 118)

FRUIT:

4 cups fresh fruit or berries (whole fruit should be peeled, pitted, neatly sliced, and patted dry; berries should be picked over, hulled if necessary, rinsed quickly and gently, and patted dry. The amount of fruit depends on the size and number of pastry shells. Poached or well drained, canned fruit can be substituted.)

234

PUFF PASTRY BANDS

On a lightly floured surface—the best is a piece of heavy-duty foil—roll the dough into a rectangle about 13 × 15 inches and ⅛ to 3/16 inch thick. If using thawed commercial frozen puff pastry, set 1 sheet on top of the other before rolling out both together. Without stretching the dough, lift it (on the piece of foil) onto a dry baking sheet and refrigerate for at least 30 minutes, or until firm. If the dough has not softened, you can skip this chilling. (*Note:* If the dough resists rolling, refrigerate it until it relaxes.)

Remove the sheet containing the foil and dough from the refrigerator, lift the foil from the sheet, and set it flat on the table. With a sharp knife held against a ruler, or using a pizza cutting wheel, cut the dough lengthwise in half. Cut cleanly without pulling the dough or cutting through the foil. Cut off about ½ inch from the narrow ends of each piece and freeze these scraps for another use (a). To make the raised borders of the band, cut a ¾- to 1-inch border strip from both long sides of each band. Carefully lift these border strips off the foil and set them aside (b).

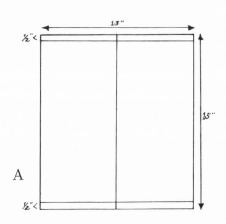

A

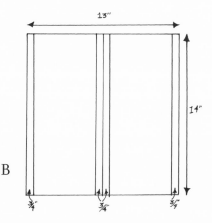

B

Lightly sprinkle the baking sheet with cold water. One at a time, transfer the bands from the foil to the dampened baking sheet as follows: Lift the foil and place it dough side down over the baking sheet, then peel the foil off the back of the dough band. The dough will thus be set *face down* on the sheet.

With a pastry brush dipped in water, moisten a ¾- to 1-inch-wide border on both long sides of each of the bands. Place the narrow dough strips on these dampened borders and press them to seal. With the back of a knife blade, scallop or indent the dough slightly at ½-inch intervals all along the outer edge of each border. These marks join the two layers and help them to rise together evenly.

235

Score the dough lightly along the *inner* edge of each border strip (c). Prick the entire central area with a fork to allow steam to escape and prevent excess rising. Brush egg glaze carefully just on the tops of the border strips. Don't let the glaze drip over the sides or they

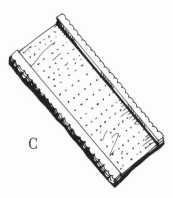

C

FRUIT TARTS AND GALETTES

will be glued together and will not rise. Chill the bands until firm. Preheat the oven to 425°F.

To bake, set the bands in the preheated oven for 20 minutes, or until the dough is risen and well browned. Press down the central (pricked) area with a pot holder if it rises too much. Cool on a wire rack.

Puff Pastry Square Case

On a lightly floured surface—the best is a piece of heavy-duty foil—roll the dough into a rectangle about 13 × 15 inches and ⅛ to 3/16 inch thick. If using thawed commercial frozen puff pastry, set 1 sheet on top of the other before rolling out both together. Without stretching the dough, lift it (on the piece of foil) onto a dry baking sheet. Refrigerate for about 30 minutes, or until firm. If dough has not softened, you can skip this chilling. *Note:* If the dough resists rolling, refrigerate it until it relaxes.)

Cut the dough to the desired size; note that each dough square is cut 1 inch larger all around than the dimensions you want after baking. For 3-inch square cases, therefore, cut 4-inch dough squares; for a 10-inch square baked case, cut an 11-inch dough square. Form as follows, whatever the size.

To make the square even, fold the dough in half diagonally, forming a right angle triangle (a). With even, clean slices (don't pull the dough), cut away a border about ¼ inch wide (dotted line, a) from both open edges. Freeze these scraps for another use.

Now, paralleling the open edges of the triangle, cut border strips ¾ inch wide as follows: Begin to cut at the fold and cut *only* to within ¾ inch of the corner (b). The edging strips *must* remain attached at the corners as shown.

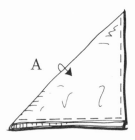

Unfold the square of dough, handling it carefully so as not to stretch it. Brush a line of water along the edge of the inner square of dough (dotted lines, b).

Lift half the cut border strip and place it face down over the moistened edge on the opposite side (c). Press the border gently to seal. Lift the remaining border strip and press it onto the opposite side (d). Press to seal. Note that one set of corners is flat and even and the other was given a decorative twist as the borders were formed. You can leave the case this way (as I prefer to do) or make all the corners flat and even by trimming off the twisted corners where the strips overlap (e). Score along the *inner* edge of the dough borders by cutting halfway through the dough with a knife tip (heavy line, f). Repeat to make additional square cases.

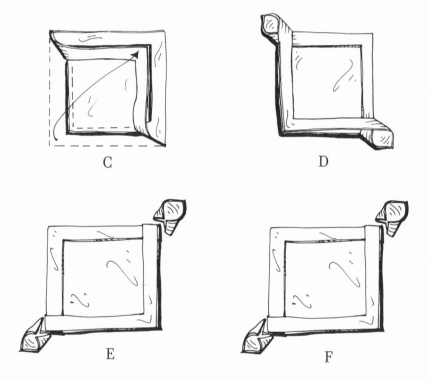

C   D

E   F

Sprinkle the baking sheet with cold water. Carefully transfer the squares to the dampened sheet and re-form the shapes if they have stretched. Prick the central area of each square all over with a fork. Brush just the tops of the borders with egg glaze; do not let the glaze drip onto the sides, or the dough won't rise. Refrigerate the dough until firm. Preheat the oven to 425°F.

To bake, set the squares in the preheated oven for 20 minutes, or until the dough is risen and golden brown. Cool on a wire rack. Use a knife tip or fork to pry out the inner pricked area if it has risen too much. Also pick out any unbaked layers of dough from this central area.

ASSEMBLY

Brush moisture-proofing fruit glaze over the bottom of the baked and cooled square pastry cases, then spread with the cold pastry cream. Top with an attractive arrangement of the prepared fruit and/or berries. Brush with fruit glaze and refrigerate to set the glaze, or until ready to serve.

238

Fresh Fig Tart with Red Wine Syrup

The fig, a native of southwestern Asia, has been cultivated since prehistoric times. The ancient Greeks considered the fruit a delicacy, as did the Romans, who spread it throughout their empire. My first experience picking figs was from a tree in the garden outside the kitchen of Sandra Calder Davidson in the Loire Valley, in France. It was a misty gray October morning, but it seemed suddenly sunny as I delighted in the purple-black pear-shaped fruits and savored their exotic sweetness and rose-hued interior—a moment for the eye of the painter and the palate of the gourmet.

I discovered this gem of a fig tart in a small pâtisserie on the Quiberon Peninsula of Brittany. It is a classic preparation in that province, wherein purple figs are poached in a red wine syrup. The red wine–fig flavor combination is sophisticated and satisfying; the presentation is elegant. (Note: If your figs have firm or very tough skins, you can peel them before poaching; if the skins are tender, leave the figs unpeeled.)

ADVANCE PREPARATION: The completely baked tart shell can be prepared ahead and frozen (page 71). The figs can be poached a day ahead and left refrigerated in their syrup. Assemble the tart the day of serving.

SPECIAL EQUIPMENT: 11-inch tart pan with removable bottom; pastry brush; 2-quart nonreactive saucepan; slotted spoon; wooden spoon; candy or jelly thermometer, optional; 12-inch flat round serving platter

TEMPERATURE AND TIME: Completely prebaked pastry shell: 425°F for 12 minutes with pie weights, then 10 to 15 minutes empty

SETTING TIME FOR GLAZED TART: 2 hours

YIELD: One 11-inch tart; serves 10 to 12

FILLING:

   1½ cups granulated sugar

   1 cup dry red wine for purple figs; if using green figs, poach them in a
      Zinfandel or dry white wine

   1 cup water

   Zest of 1 lemon, cut into wide strips with a vegetable peeler

   2 tablespoons fresh lemon juice

   1½ pounds (18 medium-sized) purple or green figs, sliced in half
      through the stem ends

   ½ cup red currant jelly

PASTRY:

   Completely prebaked 11-inch tart shell made with All-Purpose Flaky
      Pastry, Nut (almond) or Orange variation (page 48 or 49), or
      Rich Tart Pastry (page 88)

One day ahead, or at least several hours before making the tart, poach the figs in the wine syrup. To do this, combine the sugar, wine, water, strips of lemon zest and lemon juice, in a 2-quart saucepan. Heat slowly until the sugar dissolves, then bring to a boil. Add the halved figs and allow the syrup to nearly reach the boiling point. Reduce the heat slightly and slowly cook the figs for about 15 minutes, until tender when gently pierced with the tip of a knife but still holding their shape. Remove the pan from the heat and let the figs cool in the syrup. Lift out the figs with a slotted spoon and drain them on a plate, cut sides down.

You will have about 1¾ cups syrup at this point. Return the syrup to the heat and boil it down until about 1 cup remains. It will become thick and syrupy (210°F on a candy or jelly thermometer).

Remove from the heat, add the red currant jelly, and stir until completely melted. Discard the strips of lemon zest and set the glaze aside.

Prepare the pastry, roll it out, and line the buttered tart pan (pages 52–55). Prick the bottom pastry with a fork, chill until firm, and then completely blind-bake (pages 66–67), until the pastry is golden. Cool on a wire rack.

To assemble the tart, brush a generous layer of wine glaze inside the completely baked pastry shell. (*Note:* If the glaze has thickened too much upon standing, you can soften it by warming gently over low heat, stirring constantly until smooth.) Arrange the cooled halved figs cut side down in concentric circles in the tart. The fat, rounded ends of the figs should point to the outside, and each fig should touch the next. Arrange several halves in the tart center, to fill the space.

Brush wine glaze over the figs, then spoon the rest between the figs to fill up the spaces. Chill to set the glaze. Chill the tart for at least 2 hours, then remove the pan sides (page 55) keeping the tart on the pan bottom, and slide it onto a flat serving platter. Serve at room temperature.

Tart Lemon Tart

· · · · · · · · · · ·

This is what *tart* means in every sense of the word. The piquance of the velvety-smooth lemon custard comes as a surprise to your tongue—sharp and refreshing. I first tasted this some time ago at the finale of an extraordinary dinner at the now defunct Café du Bec Fin in Old Greenwich, Connecticut. A specialty of chef Harvey Edwards, it has become one of my favorites.

ADVANCE PREPARATION: The pastry shell can be prepared ahead, partially baked, and frozen. Thaw before using. Fill and bake no more than 4 hours before serving time. Glaze the lemon slices for garnish several hours ahead or the day before baking.

SPECIAL EQUIPMENT: 11-inch tart pan with removable bottom; 1½-quart nonreactive saucepan; slotted spoon; dinner plate; flat baking sheet; toothpick; sifter

TEMPERATURE AND TIME: Partially prebaked pastry shell: 425°F for 12 minutes with pie weights, then 3 to 5 minutes empty; filled tart: 375°F for 22 to 25 minutes

GLAZING LEMON SLICES: 45 minutes

YIELD: One 11-inch tart; serves 8 to 10

GLAZED LEMON SLICES:

    11 to 13 thinly sliced ($^3/_{16}$ inch) rounds cut from 1 or 2 lemons,
        seeds removed

    2 $^1/_4$ cups water

    1$^1/_4$ cups granulated sugar

PASTRY:

    Partially prebaked 11-inch pastry shell made with Rich Tart Pastry
        (page 88) or All-Purpose Flaky Pastry, Orange variation
        (page 49)

CUSTARD FILLING:

    4 large eggs, at room temperature

    1 cup granulated sugar

    $^3/_4$ cup fresh lemon juice

    $^1/_4$ cup fresh orange juice

    Grated zest of $^1/_2$ large orange

    $^1/_4$ cup heavy cream

    Topping: 2 teaspoons confectioners' sugar

To glaze the lemon slices, combine the water and sugar in a nonreactive saucepan and heat until the sugar is melted. Bring to a boil and add the lemon slices. Reduce the heat slightly and simmer, uncovered, for about 40 to 45 minutes—remove the slices *before* the pulp disintegrates. Lift them from the syrup with a slotted spoon and place them around the edges of a dinner plate to drain and cool.

Prepare the pastry, roll it out, and line the buttered tart pan (pages 52–55). Do *not* prick the pastry bottom. Chill until firm. Preheat the oven to 425°F while the dough chills. Partially blind-bake the shell (pages 66–67). Cool on a wire rack. Reduce oven heat to 375°F.

In a large bowl (or in a food processor or electric mixer), combine the eggs, sugar, lemon and orange juice, orange zest, and cream. Whisk or beat until well blended and pale in color, about 1 minute if whisking by hand.

For ease in handling, set the prepared pastry shell (in its pan) on a flat baking sheet. Pour in the lemon custard, then select 8 to 10 of the best-looking glazed lemon slices and arrange them in an evenly spaced ring about 1 inch inside the edge of the tart. Put 1 more slice in the center of the pie. (*Note:* Do not use any slices whose pulp is missing as these will sink beneath the filling). Set the tart in the center of the preheated oven and bake for

25 to 35 minutes, or until the filling no longer jiggles when the pan side is gently tapped. The custard topping will not be browned, but a toothpick inserted in the center should come out clean. Cool on a wire rack.

A few minutes before serving, sift a light dusting of confectioners' sugar over the tart. Remove the pan sides (page 55) keeping the tart on the pan bottom and slide it onto a flat platter. Serve at room temperature. *Note:* Just before cutting the tart, remove the central lemon slice so your knife can cut cleanly through mid-point of the tart. Divide so each piece contains a lemon slice.

Apple Galette
· · · · · · · · · · ·

This rustic French fruit tart is shaped by hand on a flat baking sheet instead of being molded in a tart pan. It is, in fact, a sweet fruit "pizza," ideal for picnics, tailgate parties, or casual dinners. Beginning pie makers, including children, especially enjoy making galettes since they are less intimidating and more casual than formal tarts or even pies. *Note:* The dough is rolled out on a piece of aluminum foil that is buttered so the baked galette will not stick to it when served.

Because the dough is hand-shaped, the only confining factors are the quantity of dough and fruit and the dimensions of the baking sheet. Create any shape you like: oval, rectangle, or heart, for example. Use any type of ripe seasonal fruit, fresh, poached, or canned (well drained).

ADVANCE PREPARATION: Pastry can be made up to 2 days in advance and chilled. Roll out just before using. Galette is best when baked fresh, but it can be double-wrapped and frozen before baking (page 72); bake, without thawing, for 5 to 10 minutes longer than when fresh.

SPECIAL EQUIPMENT: Heavy-duty aluminum foil or double-thickness of regular foil; rolling pin; cookie sheet with only one lip; pastry brush

TEMPERATURE AND TIME: 425°F for 15 minutes, then 350°F for 25 to 30 minutes

YIELD: One 13-inch galette; serves 10 to 12

1 recipe Cream Cheese Pastry (page 90)

TOPPING:

1 tablespoon granulated sugar

Butter, for preparing foil

FRUIT FILLING:

4 or 5 large Golden Delicious apples (or other medium-soft eating
apple), peeled, cored, and sliced about ⅛ inch thick
(generous 4 cups slices)

½ cup (2 ounces) chopped walnuts, optional

2 tablespoons fresh lemon juice

⅓ to ½ cup granulated white sugar or packed brown sugar (depends upon sweetness of fruit)

½ teaspoon ground cinnamon

½ teaspoon ground nutmeg

2½ tablespoons all-purpose flour

¾ cup apple jelly, apricot or cranberry preserves, or orange
marmalade

⅓ cup graham cracker crumbs or crushed wheat or rice flake cereal

EGG GLAZE:

1 large egg beaten with 1 tablespoon water

FRUIT GLAZE:

½ cup apricot preserves or apple jelly, warmed and strained if necessary

Prepare the pastry, form it into a disk, and chill while you prepare the fruit. In a large bowl, toss together the apples, the nuts, if used, the lemon juice, sugar, spices, and flour.

Cut an 18-inch square of heavy-duty foil or 18-inch double layer of regular foil. Turn it shiny side down. With your fingernail or a toothpick, draw a circle approximately 16 inches in diameter on the foil as a guide for rolling out the dough. In the middle, spread butter in a circle about 12-inches in diameter. Place the dough disk on the buttered area in the center of the foil and, using a lightly floured rolling pin, roll it out like a pie crust, going from the center to the outside. Roll the dough until it fills the marked circle, allowing the edges to be ragged. At least 2 inches of the dough edge should rest on plain, unbuttered foil so it won't stick. Alternatively you can cover the dough with plastic wrap and press the dough into place with your fingertips. Position a rack in the lower third of the oven and preheat it to 425°F.

Slide the foil, with the dough in place, onto a cookie sheet. With your fingertip or a toothpick, lightly mark a 2-inch border in from the edge of the dough (a); this border will later be folded up over the fruit. Brush egg glaze all over the rolled dough. Spread on some of the fruit preserves or jelly, sprinkle on the crumbs, and then top with the fruit mixture, spreading it out to fill just the marked area.

Slide your hand beneath the foil and lift it up just beneath the pastry border, using the foil as a pusher to flip the dough edge over onto the fruit (b). Allow the dough to fold over on itself naturally, like fabric making pleats as it goes around the circle. Brush the egg glaze over any pastry cracks and pinch them with your fingers to seal. Fold up the edges of the foil to make a lip to catch any drips (c).

Brush egg glaze over the top of the pastry border, then sprinkle on a topping of granulated sugar. Bake at 425°F for 15 minutes, then lower the heat to 350°F and bake for another 25 to 30 minutes, or until the pastry is golden brown and the fruit can easily be pierced with the tip of a sharp paring knife. Slide the galette, still on the foil, off the baking sheet and cool it on a wire rack. Brush the remaining fruit preserve glaze over the warm fruit filling to give it a shine. Cut the galette into wedges to serve.

247

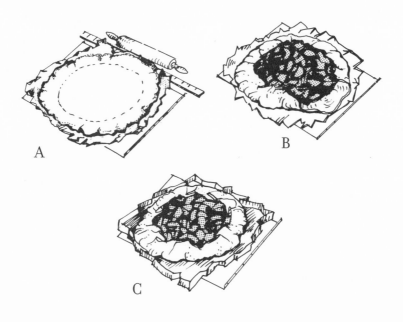

A

B

C

Plum, Pear, Nectarine, or Peach Galette: Before adding the fruit, spread the rolled and marked dough with ½ cup plum or apricot preserves, then add the crushed cereal crumbs. Replace the apples with about 4 cups pitted, sliced unpeeled plums, pears, or nectarines or peeled peaches. If desired, sprinkle the fruit with about ½ cup (2 ounces) finely chopped almonds, pecans, or walnuts and ½ cup golden raisins. Complete as directed.

248

CUSTARD AND CREAM PIES AND TARTS

· · · · · · · · · ·

Custard pies and tarts generally have delicately fla-vored fillings made with eggs, milk, and sugar. They are open-faced, and baked in a pastry or crumb shell. The filling is thickened as the egg proteins coagulate and cook gently and slowly at a very low heat; the ideal result is a well-set, creamy custard that cuts neatly and neither "weeps" nor separates. Overcooking or cooking at too high a temperature causes custard to separate and become watery.

It is easy enough to bake a custard slowly when it is prepared as a pudding in custard cups. But when it is baked in a pastry shell, the problem becomes complex: Custard requires low heat, but pastry needs high heat to set it quickly and keep it flaky. The solutions range from partially prebaking the pastry shell to baking the shell and custard separately, then slip-sliding the custard into place in the shell.

Cream pies are made with an egg-sugar-milk custard base, but they are thickened with flour or cornstarch. They can have an infinite number of flavorings.

The wide variety of pies and tarts in this section, from Southern Chess Pies to Lemon Meringue Pie, are all variations on these two basic types—custard and cream.

Because these pies have a high egg content, they should be stored in the refrigerator to avoid bacterial contamination, especially in hot weather. However, you may have noticed that some pies, custard in particular, tend to get watery when refrigerated. It occasionally happens, and the only way to avoid it seems to be to eat the whole pie so that there are no leftovers to refrigerate—not such a bad fate, really.

Custard Pie

In the Southern United States, this is known as Egg Custard Pie, but whatever you call it, it is delicious and deserves far more attention than it usually gets. True, it is an excellent and comforting family dessert, but it is equally worthy as company fare.

Anyone can bake a fine custard pudding, but it takes a little doing to bake that same custard successfully inside a crisp pastry shell—unless you know a few tricks. The problem is that a creamy egg custard that contains no starch must be baked at a low temperature to prevent scrambling the eggs, while flaky pastry requires high heat. To get around this, you have three choices: (1) Pour the custard into an unbaked pastry shell, bake both simultaneously, and risk the dreaded soggy bottom crust (not a viable option); (2) partially prebake the pastry shell, moisture-proof it with egg glaze, and then add the custard and bake again; or (3) use the slip-slide method, the only one that absolutely guarantees a crisp bottom crust and a tender, well-set custard. Partially prebaking the crust is easiest, but I urge you to try the slip-slide method at least once, even if it sounds silly. It works and is very easy to accomplish.

ADVANCE PREPARATION: The partially or completely prebaked pastry shell can be made in advance. Fill and bake the pie about 3 hours before serving; standing softens the bottom crust.

SPECIAL EQUIPMENT: 9-inch pie plate, preferably heat-proof glass (Pyrex); pastry brush; mixing bowl or electric mixer; for slip-slide method, 1 extra 8½ or 9-inch heat-proof glass pie plate (this can be slightly smaller than first plate)

TEMPERATURE AND TIME: Partially prebaked shell: 425°F for 12 minutes with pie weights, then 5 to 8 minutes empty; completely prebaked shell: 425°F for 12 minutes with pie weights, then 10 to 15 minutes empty; filled pie: 325°F for 30 to 35 minutes

YIELD: One 9-inch pie; serves 6 to 8

PASTRY:

> **Partially or completely prebaked 9-inch pie shell made with All-Purpose Flaky Pastry (page 45)**

EGG GLAZE:

> **2 egg whites (reserved from filling) beaten with 1 tablespoon water**

FILLING:

> **3 large eggs plus 2 yolks**
> **½ cup granulated sugar**
> **¼ teaspoon salt**
> **2 cups milk *or* 1 cup milk plus 1 cup heavy cream**
> **1 teaspoon vanilla extract**
> **¼ teaspoon ground nutmeg, plus a pinch more for sprinkling**
> **A pinch of ground cinnamon**
> **Butter for greasing the extra pie plate for slip-slide method**

252

In the first method described, a *partially prebaked* pastry shell is baked along with the custard. Preheat the oven to 425°F. Prepare the pastry, roll it out, and line the pan (pages 52–55). Do *not* prick the dough. Chill until firm, then partially blind-bake (pages 66–67) just until the pastry begins to look golden but is not yet browned. While warm, brush on egg glaze. Cool on a wire rack. Reduce the oven heat to 325°F. Place a flat baking sheet in the oven to get hot.

In a mixing bowl with a whisk or an electric mixer, combine all filling ingredients and beat just to blend. For ease in handling and to prevent oven spills, set the pastry shell in the center of the preheated flat baking sheet.

Pour the custard mixture into the shell and sprinkle it with a little bit more nutmeg. Set the baking sheet in the preheated oven and bake for 30 to 35 minutes, just until a knife inserted into the custard 1 inch from the edge comes out clean. The pie center may still appear soft. Do not overbake. Cool on a wire rack. Serve the pie at room temperature. Refrigerate leftovers.

For the *slip-slide method,* the pastry shell is prepared as above but completely prebaked (pages 66–67). To prepare the custard, beat together all filling ingredients with a whisk or an electric mixer. Generously butter an 8½- to 9-inch pie plate. (*Note:* This pie plate should be the same size or about ½-inch smaller than the one containing the pastry shell.) Pour the custard into the buttered plate, sprinkle with nutmeg, and bake in the center of a preheated 325°F oven for 30 to 35 minutes, until a stainless steel knife inserted into the custard 1 inch from the edge comes out clean. The center may still appear soft. Do not overbake. Remove the custard from the oven and cool on a wire rack until it is *just lukewarm*. Before it cools further, slide it into the pastry as described below.

This final step sounds much more difficult than it is. The trick is that the butter you spread in the pan under the custard remains in a separate layer so, if you work while the custard is still lukewarm, before the butter hardens, it acts as a lubricant for the custard to slide on. First run a knife blade around the edge of the custard to release it from the baking pan. Then lift the custard pan and hold it just a little bit above and directly over the baked pastry shell. Tilt the custard so it faces the far edge of the pastry shell and gently slip-slide the custard out as you pull back on the pie plate. The custard will ease itself into the pastry shell in one piece and look as if it had always been there. (It will, I promise. But if, for some reason, it falls in instead of sliding; it will still taste good.) Cool the assembled pie on wire rack. Serve at room temperature. Refrigerate leftovers.

Sugarless Custard Pie. Prepare as for the custard pie but if for dietary reasons you prefer to bake this pie without any sugar at all, increase nutmeg and cinnamon slightly. It will still have a good, eggy flavor and will slip-slide with ease.

Coconut Custard Pie. Prepare Coconut Crust (page 102), or use the Coconut variation for All-Purpose Flaky Pastry (page 49). Just before adding the custard mixture to its baking pan, blend in 1 cup flaked or shredded sweetened coconut. Top the finished pie with a sprinkling of Toasted Coconut Topping (page 142).

Lemon Custard Pie. Add 2 tablespoons fresh lemon juice and the grated zest of 1 lemon to the custard filling.

253

Old-Fashioned Pumpkin Custard Pie
. . . .

What moistens the lip, and what brightens the eye,
What calls back the past, like the rich pumpkin pie?

JOHN GREENLEAF WHITTIER,
"The Pumpkin"

Here is the answer to Whittier: Everyone's Thanksgiving memory, a rich mellow pumpkin custard pie complemented by a spoonful of Yogurt-Rum Sauce or Ginger Whipped Cream. To avoid the dreaded soggy bottom crust familiar to custard pies, partially prebake and moisture-proof the pastry shell before filling and baking with the custard.

ADVANCE PREPARATION: The partially prebaked pastry shell can be prepared in advance. Fill the shell with custard immediately before baking and no more than 3 to 4 hours before serving, or the lower crust will soften.

SPECIAL EQUIPMENT: 10-inch pie plate, preferably heat-proof glass (Pyrex); pastry brush; electric mixer or mixing bowl and spoon; flat baking sheet; stainless steel knife

TEMPERATURE AND TIME: Partially prebaked pastry shell: 425°F for 12 minutes with pie weights, then 3–5 minutes empty; filled pie: 400°F for 40 to 50 minutes

YIELD: One 10-inch pie; serves 8 to 10

PASTRY:

>**Partially prebaked 10-inch pastry shell made with All-Purpose Flaky
>Pastry (page 45) prepared with 1 whole egg instead of 1 yolk (reduce the
>water, using the minimum needed) or Whole Wheat Pastry (page 80)**

EGG GLAZE:

>**1 large egg white (reserved from filling) beaten with 1 tablespoon water**

FILLING:

>**2 large eggs plus 1 large yolk
>2 cups canned unsweetened pumpkin puree (or cooked and mashed fresh
>   sugar pumpkin)
>½ to ¾ cup granulated sugar, to taste
>1½ cups milk or cream (the heavier the cream, the richer the pie)
>2 tablespoons unsalted butter, melted
>½ teaspoon salt
>¾ teaspoon ground cinnamon
>½ teaspoon ground nutmeg
>½ teaspoon ground ginger
>⅛ teaspoon ground cloves**

TOPPING:

>**Yogurt-Rum Sauce (page 146) or Ginger Whipped Cream (page 132)**

Preheat the oven to 425°F. Prepare the pastry, roll it out, and line the pan (pages 52–55). Be sure the fluted edge is high so it will contain the custard filling. Do *not* prick the pastry bottom. Chill until firm. Partially blind-bake for 12 minutes with weighted liner (pages 66–67); then bake for about 5 minutes after removing the foil and pie weights, until the dough is no longer translucent and is beginning to look golden. Brush the warm crust with egg white glaze. Cool on a wire rack. Reduce the oven heat to 400°F. Place a flat baking sheet in the oven to get hot.

In an electric mixer or in a bowl with a whisk, beat the eggs and yolk, then add the pumpkin and beat well. Beat in the sugar, milk or cream, melted butter, salt, and spices. Set the pan containing the pastry shell on a flat baking sheet for ease in handling. Pour the filling mixture into the prepared pastry shell, and set it on the preheated flat baking sheet in the center of the preheated oven for 40 to 50 minutes, or until the top is golden brown and a knife inserted into the custard 1 inch from the edge comes out clean. Do not overbake. When the knife comes clean at the custard's edge, the pie is done even though the center

255

CUSTARD AND CREAM PIES AND TARTS

may not yet be set; the internal heat of the pie will complete the baking out of the oven. Cool the pie on a wire rack. Serve at room temperature, topped with Yogurt-Rum Sauce or Ginger-Flavored Whipped Cream. Refrigerate leftovers.

Vermont Maple Sugar Pumpkin Pie. Replace ¾ cup granulated sugar with granulated maple sugar. See Sources (page 363).

Orange Pumpkin Pie. Add ⅓ cup orange marmalade and 1 tablespoon grated orange zest to the filling.

Southern Sweet Potato Pie. This pie is a specialty of Virginia, but it is made throughout the South, where sweet potatoes are popularly used in a variety of baked goods. The preferred pie potatoes are a deep red-gold color, very rich in vitamins A and C and very sweet. You can buy sweet potatoes wherever you live when they are in season, then boil, peel, mash, and freeze them for use later in this recipe. (*Note:* 1 pound raw potatoes = 2 cups cooked and mashed.)

Prepare Old-Fashioned Pumpkin Pie, but replace the pumpkin with 2 cups cooked, mashed sweet potatoes (or a 1-pound can vacuum-packed sweet potatoes). Add ⅓ cup apricot or peach preserves and ¼ cup chopped walnuts to the filling. If you like ginger, you can add 1 to 2 tablespoons finely chopped crystallized ginger as well.

New England Squash Pie. New Englanders make this recipe to use up the over-bountiful fall squash harvest. Winter squash such as acorn, butternut, and blue Hubbard can be used; the flavor will be slightly milder than either the pumpkin or the sweet potato versions. All the above-mentioned squash can be boiled, peeled, mashed, and frozen when in season for later pie baking. (*Note:* 1 pound raw squash = 2 cups cooked and mashed.)

Prepare Old-Fashioned Pumpkin Pie, but replace the pumpkin with 2 cups cooked, mashed, and strained squash. Use 1 cup packed light brown sugar instead of granulated sugar. As optional flavoring, add the grated zest of 1 orange and/or ½ cup (2 ounces) chopped walnuts. If you are using nuts, sprinkle them over the top of the pie just before baking, to make a crunchy topping.

Vanilla Cream Pie

· · · · · · · · · · ·

This pie is outstanding unadorned or enhanced by a topping of sweetened maple-flavored whipped cream. However, the recipe is very adaptable and lends itself to any number of flavor variations. For a rich vanilla flavor, be sure to use a vanilla bean. (*Note:* For another version of vanilla cream filling, see Vanilla Pastry Cream, page 116.) The Vanilla Cream Pie filling is slightly less stiff than the Vanilla Pastry Cream and is a slightly larger recipe, but they may be used interchangeably.

ADVANCE PREPARATION: The completely prebaked pastry shell or crumb crust can be prepared ahead. Add the cream filling about 3 to 4 hours ahead and chill to set for at least 3 hours before serving. As close to serving time as possible, add the whipped cream topping. Refrigerate.

SPECIAL EQUIPMENT: 9-inch pie plate; 2½-quart heavy-bottomed nonreactive saucepan; electric mixer; rubber scraper; whisk; strainer; plastic wrap; spoon or pastry bag fitted with ½-inch star tip for whipped cream

TEMPERATURE AND TIME: Completely baked pastry shell: 425°F for 12 minutes with pie weights, 350°F for 10 to 15 minutes empty

STOVETOP CUSTARD COOKING TIME: 12 to 15 minutes

YIELD: One 9-inch pie; serves 6 to 8

PASTRY:

**Completely prebaked 9-inch pastry shell made with All-Purpose Flaky
Pastry (page 45) or 9-inch crumb crust of your choice (pages 100–103),
preferably baked for 8 minutes**

FILLING:

⅔ cup granulated sugar

¼ cup cornstarch

¼ teaspoon salt

2½ cups milk

¼ cup heavy cream

2 large egg yolks, at room temperature

1 vanilla bean, slit lengthwise, or 2 teaspoons vanilla extract

2 tablespoons unsalted butter, at room temperature

WHIPPED CREAM TOPPING:

1 cup heavy cream (36% butterfat), chilled

2 tablespoons sifted confectioners' sugar

½ teaspoon vanilla extract

Preheat the oven to 425°F. Prepare the pastry, roll it out, and line the pan (pages 52–55). Do *not* prick the pastry. Chill until firm, then completely blind-bake (pages 66–67). Cool on a wire rack. Or, prepare the crumb crust of your choice, and bake for 8 minutes, for extra solidity.

To make the filling, combine the sugar, cornstarch, and salt in a heavy-bottomed saucepan. In a bowl, whisk the milk and cream into the egg yolks.

Whisk the egg-milk mixture into the cornstarch-sugar in the pan. Whisk well to be sure all the cornstarch is picked up off the bottom of the pan and dissolved. With a knife tip, scrape the seeds and paste from inside the vanilla bean if you are using it and add the seeds and paste plus the whole bean to the pan; if using vanilla extract, do not add until the end of the recipe.

Set the pan over medium heat and cook the mixture for about 12 minutes, until thickened and brought to a boil: Stir on and off with a wooden spoon for the first 5 minutes, then stir constantly for about 7 minutes longer, until the mixture really thickens and reaches a boil and you see fat heavy bubbles work up to the surface and burst. Use the whisk instead of the spoon occasionally to remove lumps. Boil for 1 full minute while stirring constantly.

Remove from the heat. Remove the vanilla bean, if used; wash and dry it for reuse. Stir in the butter and the vanilla extract, if you are using it.

Strain the cream into a bowl, then spoon it into the prepared pastry shell. Cover the top of the hot cream filling with plastic wrap or dab with butter to prevent a skin from forming. Set it aside to cool, then chill until shortly before serving.

In a chilled bowl, with chilled beaters, whip the cream to soft peaks, add the sugar and vanilla, and whip to stiff peaks. Decorate the top of the pie with rosettes of cream piped through a pastry bag fitted with star tip, or spoon mounds of cream around the edge of the pie and stripe them with a fork. Chill until serving time. Refrigerate leftovers.

Banana Cream Pie. Thinly slice 1 or 2 ripe bananas over the pastry shell just before adding the finished cream. Top with whipped cream.

Fruit Cream Pie. Prepare 1 to 1½ cups fresh fruit slices (well drained and blotted dry) or berries, and arrange them in the pie shell before spooning on the cream filling. Successful fruits include sliced strawberries, ripe peeled peaches or nectarines, or berries. Top with whipped cream.

Chocolate Cream Pie. Increase the sugar in the filling to 1 cup. In a double boiler, melt 4 ounces semisweet or bittersweet chocolate. Stir the chocolate into the warm finished cream filling along with the butter. For a more intense chocolate flavor, add 3 tablespoons sifted Dutch-processed cocoa to the cornstarch at the beginning of the recipe, in addition to the melted chocolate. Top with whipped cream and chocolate curls or grated chocolate (page 148).

Butterscotch Cream Pie. Substitute ¾ cup packed dark brown sugar for the granulated sugar.

Quick Coconut Cream Pie. Add 1½ cups flaked sweetened coconut to the finished cream along with the butter. Spoon the filling into the pastry shell and top with Toasted Coconut Topping (page 142). You can also use All-Purpose Flaky Pastry, Coconut variation (page 49), for the pastry shell.

$\mathcal{A}$pricot-$\mathcal{R}$aisin-$\mathcal{S}$our $\mathcal{C}$ream $\mathcal{P}$ie

. . . .

$\mathbf{A}$t pie-tasting parties in preparation for this book, this recipe was consistently selected as one of the favorites. The rich custard-cream filling is easy to prepare and has a cheesecake-like texture. The raisins and apricots lend a sparkle of color as well as delicious flavor.

ADVANCE PREPARATION: The unbaked pastry shell can be prepared in advance and frozen (page 71); thaw before filling. You can fill and bake the pie 1 day in advance, but it is best baked on the day it is served. Refrigerate until 1 to 2 hours before serving, then bring to room temperature.

SPECIAL EQUIPMENT: 10-inch pie plate; strainer or colander; electric mixer or whisk; stainless steel knife

TEMPERATURE AND TIME: 425°F for 15 minutes, 375 for 25 to 30 minutes

YIELD: One 10-inch pie; serves 8 to 10

PASTRY:

    Unbaked pastry for a 10-inch pie shell made with All-Purpose Flaky
       Pastry (page 45) or pastry of your choice.

FILLING:

    ⅓ cup packed golden raisins

    ⅔ cup (about 4½ ounces) packed dried apricot halves

    2 cups sour cream

    2 large eggs, at room temperature

    1 cup granulated sugar

    ¼ cup unsifted all-purpose flour

    ¼ teaspoon salt

    Grated zest of 1 orange

    1 teaspoon vanilla extract

TOPPING:

    Confectioners' sugar

Measure the raisins into a small bowl, cover them with boiling water, let stand 20 minutes. Prepare the pastry, roll it out, and line the pie plate (pages 52–55). Chill while you prepare the filling.

Cut the apricots into quarters, put into a saucepan and cover with water. Cover the pan and bring to a boil, then lower the heat slightly and simmer for 10 minutes or until fork-tender. Drain the apricots in a strainer, discard the liquid. Preheat the oven to 400°F.

With an electric mixer or whisk, beat together the sour cream, eggs, sugar, flour, salt, orange zest, and vanilla. Strain the raisins, discarding the liquid, and add them to the sour cream mixture along with the prepared apricots. Stir well, then pour it into the prepared pastry shell.

Bake in the lower third of the preheated oven for 15 minutes, then reduce the heat to 375°F and continue baking 25 to 30 minutes, or until light golden on top and a stainless steel knife inserted into the custard 1 inch from the edge comes out clean. Cool on a wire rack. The pie filling will puff somewhat as it bakes, then sink as it cools. Serve at room temperature. Just before serving, sift a light dusting of confectioners' sugar over the top of the pie. Refrigerate leftovers.

Vermont Maple-Walnut Pie

· · · · · · · · · · · · ·

This recipe comes from Vermont's Northeast Kingdom, a region known both for its extraordinarily picturesque alpine scenery and its delicious maple syrup. As the February thaw begins, there is scarcely a wooded area that doesn't have a sugar shack tucked within, its jauntily angled chimney billowing steam into the frosty air as the sap (thirty gallons for one of syrup) is boiled down over a wood fire. Because maple syrup and maple sugar are readily available, Vermonters use both in their daily cooking. *Note:* For this recipe, be sure to use *pure* maple syrup rather than flavored corn syrup blends sold in imitation of the real thing.

ADVANCE PREPARATION: The partially prebaked pastry shell can be prepared ahead and frozen (page 71). If possible, the filling should be added and the pie baked no more than 4 hours in advance of serving so the bottom crust does not soften.

SPECIAL EQUIPMENT: 9-inch pie plate; pastry brush; electric mixer; flat baking sheet

TEMPERATURE AND TIME: Partially prebaked pastry shell: 425°F for 12 minutes with pie weights, about 3 to 5 minutes empty; filled pie: 375°F for 30 to 40 minutes

YIELD: One 9-inch pie; serves 6 to 8

PASTRY:

**Partially prebaked 9-inch pie shell made with Butter-Lard Pastry (page 87)
or Whole Wheat–Wheat Germ Pastry (page 80)**

FILLING:

3 large eggs, at room temperature
¼ teaspoon salt
⅓ cup granulated sugar
4 tablespoons (½ stick) unsalted butter, melted
1 cup pure maple syrup
1 cup (4 ounces) walnut pieces

Preheat the oven to 425°F. With a whisk or an electric mixer, beat together the eggs and salt at this point so they can be used for a glaze before adding to the pie filling. Set the bowl aside. Prepare the pastry, roll it out, and line the pie plate (pages 52–55). Do *not* prick the pastry bottom with a fork. Chill, then partially blind-bake (pages 66–67). Moisture-proof the crust bottom by brushing with some of the previously beaten eggs before baking the empty shell for the final 3 to 5 minutes. Cool on a wire rack. Reduce the oven heat to 375°F. Place a flat baking sheet in the oven to get hot.

Add the sugar, melted butter, and maple syrup to the beaten eggs and salt. Mix well, but do not make the mixture too frothy. For ease in handling, set the pan containing the pastry shell on the preheated flat baking sheet. Pour the filling into the prepared pie shell and top with the nuts.

Bake in the center of the preheated oven for 30 to 40 minutes, or until a stainless steel knife inserted into the filling 1 inch from the edge comes out clean. Cool on a wire rack. Serve at room temperature, topped by plain or Maple Whipped Cream (page 133).

Maple-Pecan Pie. Replace the walnuts with pecan halves.

263

Kentucky Bourbon Chess Pie

· · · · · · · · · · ·

Kentucky-born writer Joan Moore shared this old family recipe with me. It is an authentic Southern specialty, right down to the white cornmeal in the filling and the bourbon in both the filling and topping. We affectionately call this "killer pie"—it's rich, marvelous, and a unique dinner party finale.

ADVANCE PREPARATION: The partially prebaked pastry shell can be prepared ahead and frozen (page 71). Fill and bake the pie no more than 4 hours before serving so bottom crust will not soften.

SPECIAL EQUIPMENT: 9-inch pie plate; pastry brush; electric mixer; stainless steel knife; aluminum foil frame (page 22); chilled bowl and beater for whipping cream; pastry bag fitted with star tip, optional

TEMPERATURE AND TIME: Partially prebaked pastry shell: 425°F for 12 minutes with pie weights, then 3 to 5 minutes empty; filled pie: 350°F for 30 minutes

YIELD: One 9-inch pie; serves 6 to 8

PASTRY:

Partially prebaked 9-inch pie shell made with Cornmeal Pastry (page 81)

EGG GLAZE:

1 large egg white (reserved from filling) beaten with 1 tablespoon water

FILLING:

4 large egg yolks, at room temperature

1 cup granulated sugar

¼ teaspoon salt

1½ tablespoons white cornmeal

1½ tablespoons all-purpose flour

8 tablespoons (1 stick) unsalted butter, melted and cooled

¼ cup Kentucky straight bourbon whiskey, or less, to taste

¼ cup heavy cream or milk

1 teaspoon vanilla extract

OPTIONAL TOPPING:

½ cup heavy cream (36% butterfat), chilled

1 tablespoon sifted confectioners' sugar

1 tablespoon Kentucky straight bourbon whiskey

Preheat the oven to 425°F. Prepare the pastry, roll it out, and line the pie plate (pages 52–55). Do *not* prick the pastry bottom. Chill, then partially blind-bake (pages 66–67). Brush moisture-proofing egg glaze on the pastry shell as soon as it is removed from the oven. Cool on a wire rack. Reduce the oven heat to 350°F.

With an electric mixer, beat the yolks and sugar together until thick and light colored. Beat in the salt, cornmeal, flour, melted butter, bourbon, cream or milk, and vanilla.

Pour the mixture into the prepared pastry shell and bake in the center of the preheated 350°F oven for 30 minutes, or until the filling is puffed and golden brown and a stainless steel knife inserted in the center comes out clean. (*Note:* Monitor your oven temperature. If baked at too high a heat, the custard may separate.) Check the pie after half the baking time and add a foil edging frame to prevent overbrowning. Cool on a wire rack.

Shortly before serving, whip the cream. When soft peaks form, add the sugar and bourbon, then beat to stiff peaks. Spoon around the top edge of the pie, or pipe a decorative pattern using a pastry bag fitted with a star tip. Serve at room temperature. Refrigerate leftovers.

265

Pineapple Chess Tart

. . . .

The tangy flavor of pineapple is a refreshing addition to this sweet chess pie. It makes an appealing dinner party dessert when served topped by rosettes of whipped cream garnished with mint sprigs or toasted almond slices. The same recipe will also make eight 4 ½-inch-diameter tartlets.

ADVANCE PREPARATION: The partially prebaked tart shell can be prepared ahead and frozen (page 71). Fill and bake the pie no more than 4 hours before serving so the bottom crust will not soften.

SPECIAL EQUIPMENT: 11-inch tart pan with removable bottom (or 10-inch pie plate); pastry brush; strainer; electric mixer or bowl and whisk; flat baking sheet; stainless steel knife; spoon or pastry bag fitted with star tip for applying whipped cream garnish

TEMPERATURE AND TIME: Partially prebaked tart shell: 425°F for 12 minutes with pie weights, 3 to 5 minutes empty; filled tart: 325°F for 50 to 60 minutes

YIELD: One 11-inch tart or 10-inch pie; serves 8 to 12

PASTRY:

>   Partially prebaked 11-inch tart shell made with All-Purpose Flaky
>   Pastry (page 45) or Butter-Lard Pastry (page 87), which is the
>   more traditional Southern choice.

EGG GLAZE:

>   1 large egg beaten with 1 tablespoon water

FILLING:

>   1 (20-ounce) can pineapple chunks, drained (for 12 ounces of prepared fruit)
>   1½ tablespoons all-purpose flour
>   8 tablespoons (1 stick) unsalted butter, at room temperature, or
>   half butter/half solid stick margarine
>   ⅓ cup granulated sugar
>   ⅓ cup packed dark brown sugar
>   1 teaspoon vanilla extract
>   ¼ teaspoon salt
>   3 large eggs, at room temperature
>   ½ cup sour cream or plain yogurt (top liquid poured off)
>   Ground nutmeg

TOPPING:

>   1 cup heavy cream (36% butterfat), chilled
>   2 tablespoons sifted confectioners' sugar

OPTIONAL GARNISH:

>   Mint sprigs or lightly toasted almond slices

Preheat the oven to 425°F. Prepare the pastry, roll it out, and line the buttered pan (pages 52–55). Do *not* prick the pastry bottom. Chill, then partially blind-bake (pages 66–67). Brush moisture-proofing egg glaze on the pastry shell as soon as it is removed from the oven. Cool on a wire rack. Reduce the oven heat to 325°F.

Drain the pineapple in a strainer set over bowl. Cut the pineapple chunks in thirds, then put the fruit into a bowl and toss with the flour.

With an electric mixer or whisk, cream together the butter, both sugars, the vanilla, and salt, beating until smooth and light textured. Add the eggs one at a time, beating after each addition. Beat in the sour cream or yogurt. Stir in the pineapple. Don't worry if the mixture looks curdled; baking will make the filling smooth and creamy.

For ease in handling, set the pastry shell in the center of a flat baking sheet. Spoon the filling into the prepared pastry shell and top with a light sprinkling of nutmeg. Bake in the center of the preheated oven for 50 to 60 minutes, or until the top looks golden brown. (*Note:* Monitor your oven temperature. If baked at too high a heat, custard may separate.) Cool on a wire rack.

A short time before serving, whip the cream until it forms soft peaks, add the sugar, and then whip until stiff. Spoon onto the pie in an edging ring or pipe through a pastry bag fitted with a star tip, making rosettes over the pie top. Garnish with mint sprigs or sliced almonds if you wish. Refrigerate leftovers.

268

Pecan Pie

. . . .

Pecan pie is the prototype of the Southern classic "transparent pie": a variation on Chess Pie that is rich in eggs, butter, sugar, and another regional specialty—pecans. This recipe contains brown sugar and molasses, traditional Southern sweeteners, as well as corn syrup, a latecomer to chess pie filling. I have added a touch of lemon to cut the sugar and eliminate the cloying taste often associated with pecan pie.

If the sweetness of this pie has always put you off, try the Pecan-Cranberry variation that follows; the tartness of the berries gives a delightful sweet-sour balance to the pie. Or try blending pecans with a variety of nuts such as dry-roasted peanuts, black walnuts, pine nuts, toasted hazelnuts, or macadamia nuts, for example. Northern Vermont cooks replace the corn syrup with maple syrup, for their own flavor variation. This pie can also be baked in a tart pan.

ADVANCE PREPARATION: The partially prebaked pastry shell can be prepared ahead and frozen (page 71). Because of the high sugar content, pecan pie will keep well, but should be refrigerated if left overnight. It can be prepared ahead of serving, but be aware that the crust will soften on standing longer than a day.

SPECIAL EQUIPMENT: 9-inch pie plate (or 9- or 10-inch tart pan with removable bottom); mixing bowl and whisk or electric mixer; stainless steel knife

TEMPERATURE AND TIME: Partially prebaked pastry shell: 425°F for 12 minutes with pie weights; filled pie: 400°F for 20 to 25 minutes

YIELD: One 9-inch pie; serves 6 to 8

PASTRY:

> **Partially prebaked 9-inch pie shell made with Whole Wheat Pastry (page 80) or pastry of your choice**

FILLING:

> ¾ cup packed dark brown sugar
> 3 large eggs, at room temperature
> 6 tablespoons (¾ stick) unsalted butter, melted
> ⅔ cup dark corn syrup
> 1 tablespoon unsulfured molasses
> 1 teaspoon fresh lemon juice
> 1 teaspoon vanilla extract
> ¼ teaspoon salt
> 1 cup (4 ounces) pecan halves

Preheat the oven to 425°F. Prepare the pastry, roll it out, and line the pan (pages 52–55). Do *not* prick the pastry bottom. Chill, then partially blind-bake for only 12 minutes (pages 66–67). Cool on a wire rack. Lower the oven heat to 400°F.

To prepare the filling, combine the brown sugar and eggs in a mixing bowl and whisk or beat with an electric mixer until well blended and free of lumps. Mix in the melted butter, corn syrup, molasses, lemon juice, vanilla, and salt.

Pour the filling into the prepared pastry shell and arrange the nuts over the top—either carefully positioned in concentric circles or simply scattered at random. Bake the pie in the center of the preheated oven for 20 to 30 minutes, or until a stainless steel knife stuck into the center comes out clean. Cool on a wire rack. Serve at room temperature, topped by vanilla ice cream or slightly sweetened whipped cream (page 131).

Cranberry-Pecan Pie. Add ¾ cup coarsely chopped fresh or frozen cranberries and use only ¾ cup (3 ounces) pecan halves.

Black Walnut Pie. Replace the pecans with 1 cup (4 ounces) chopped black walnuts and use light corn syrup instead of dark.

Hawaiian Macadamia Nut Pie. Replace the pecans with 1 cup (4 ounces) unsalted macadamia nuts, coarsely chopped.

Peanut Pie Add ½ cup (2 ounces) finely chopped or ground peanuts to the pastry (page 48, All-Purpose Flaky Pastry, Nut Pastry variation), and replace the pecans with peanuts as follows:

Coarsely chop ½ cup (2 ounces) lightly salted dry-roasted peanuts and add to the filling mixture. Sprinkle an additional 1 cup (4 ounces) of whole dry-roasted, lightly salted peanuts over the top of the filled pie before baking. Peanut Pie can be made with either dark or light corn syrup.

Pennsylvania Dutch Shoofly Pie

· · · · · · · · · · · ·

Shoofly Pie is a well-known Pennsylvania Dutch specialty with a spicy molasses and gingerbread flavor. It is thought that the name comes from the fact that flies love molasses and have to be shooed away when you make this pie. The pie filling can be assembled and baked in different ways: When the pastry lining is topped by alternating layers of crumbs and molasses custard, with the crumbs ending up on top, the texture is cake-like and the name is "Gravel Pie," for obvious reasons. When the molasses custard remains in a separate layer beneath the crumb topping as described in the following directions, the result is "Wet-Bottom Shoofly Pie," also for obvious reasons. Either way, serve it plain for breakfast, or for afternoon tea topped with Yogurt-Rum Sauce (page 146) or sweetened whipped cream (page 131).

ADVANCE PREPARATION: The unbaked pie shell can be prepared ahead and frozen (page 71). The pie is best when served warm from the oven.

SPECIAL EQUIPMENT: 9-inch pie plate; electric mixer; 2 mixing bowls; toothpick or cake tester

TEMPERATURE AND TIME: 375°F for 35 to 40 minutes

YIELD: One 9-inch pie; serves 6 to 8

PASTRY:

Unbaked pastry for a 9-inch pie shell made with All-Purpose Flaky Pastry (page 45) or Butter-Lard Pastry (page 87)

CRUMB TOPPING:

1 cup unsifted all-purpose flour

½ cup packed dark brown sugar

¼ teaspoon salt

¼ teaspoon ground cinnamon

¼ teaspoon ground nutmeg

¼ teaspoon ground ginger

¼ teaspoon ground cloves

¼ teaspoon ground mace, optional

5 tablespoons unsalted butter or solid stick margarine

MOLASSES CUSTARD:

½ cup unsulfured molasses

2 large eggs, at room temperature

½ cup boiling water

½ teaspoon baking soda

Prepare the pastry, roll it out, and line the pie plate (pages 52–55). Set the pastry-lined pan in the refrigerator to chill while you prepare the filling. Preheat the oven to 375°F.

In a large bowl, combine the flour, brown sugar, salt, and spices for the topping. Cut in the butter or margarine until the mixture looks like coarse meal. Spoon about ⅓ cup of this mixture into an even layer in the pastry-lined pan.

In a second bowl with a whisk or with an electric mixer, beat together the molasses and eggs. Measure the boiling water into a small bowl, and stir in the baking soda until it is dissolved. The mixture will bubble up. Immediately stir the soda-water into the molasses-egg mixture and beat well, then pour over the crumbs in the pastry-lined pie plate. Sprinkle on all the remaining crumb topping, making an even coating with a nearly bare spot in the pie's center to allow the filling to rise and expand. Don't delay in getting this into the oven, or the rising power of the baking soda will be dissipated.

Bake the pie in the center of the preheated oven for 35 to 40 minutes, or until well browned and a cake tester inserted into the center comes out clean. Serve warm or at room temperature, plain, with Yogurt-Rum Sauce, or with sweetened whipped cream.

Lemon Meringue Pie

· · · · · · · · · · ·

This is everybody's favorite, and it is equally good, if not better, flavored with orange or blood orange for Orange Meringue Pie. The filling is an easy stove-top custard pudding set into a crumb or pastry crust (your choice), topped with a tall fluffy cloud of never-fail meringue. I like an extra-tall meringue and use 5 egg whites in the topping; the recipe works well, with just a slight decrease in volume, if you use 4 whites. Read About Meringue (page 106).

Remove the eggs from the refrigerator before starting the recipe; room-temperature whites will whip to greater volume than cold whites. Be sure the bowl and beater used for whipping the whites are absolutely grease-free. You will need 3 to 4 large lemons for the full recipe.

ADVANCE PREPARATION: The completed pie should be served the same day it is baked.

SPECIAL EQUIPMENT: 9-inch pie plate; 1½- to 2-quart heavy-bottomed saucepan; small saucepan; large metal spoon; electric mixer

TEMPERATURE AND TIME: Crumb crust 350°F for 7 to 8 minutes; meringue: 350°F for 12 to 15 minutes; Stove top custard: cooking time about 13 minutes

YIELD: 9-inch pie, serves 6 to 8

PASTRY:

> Cookie-Coconut Crumb Crust, below; or completely prebaked pastry for 9-inch pie shell made with All-Purpose Flaky Pastry, Orange or Lemon variation (page 49); or 9-inch store-bought refrigerated pie crust completely prebaked

COOKIE-COCONUT CRUMB CRUST (OPTIONAL):

> 1¼ cups Nabisco 'Nilla Wafer or graham cracker crumbs
>
> 2 tablespoons granulated sugar
>
> ½ cup shredded sweetened coconut (or ½ cup additional cookie crumbs)
>
> 6 tablespoons (¾ stick) unsalted butter, melted (7 tablespoons if using 1¾ cups crumbs and no coconut)

FILLING:

> 1 cup granulated sugar
>
> ⅓ cup cornstarch
>
> ¼ teaspoon salt
>
> 1½ cups water
>
> Grated zest from 1 lemon (about 1½ tablespoons)
>
> ½ cup fresh lemon juice
>
> 4 large egg yolks, at room temperature
>
> 2 tablespoons unsalted butter, at room temperature, cut up, optional

MERINGUE TOPPING:

> ½ cup granulated or superfine sugar, divided (2 tablespoons and 6 tablespoons)
>
> 1 tablespoon cornstarch
>
> ½ cup water
>
> 4 or 5 large egg whites, at room temperature
>
> ⅛ teaspoon salt
>
> ¼ teaspoon cream of tartar
>
> ½ teaspoon vanilla extract

275

Preheat the oven to 350°F. If making the crumb crust, toss together the crumbs, sugar, coconut, and melted butter in a bowl. Turn out the crumbs into the pie plate and use the back of a large metal spoon to press them in an even layer against the pan sides, then flat on the bottom. Bake the crust for 7 to 8 minutes, until golden. Remove the pan from the oven and set it aside. You can turn off the oven now and re-heat it shortly before baking the meringue topping.

Prepare the filling: In a medium heavy-bottomed saucepan, whisk together the sugar, cornstarch, and salt. Whisk in the water, lemon zest, and juice; scrape into the pan corners to incorporate all the dry ingredients. Place over medium heat and cook, stirring, for 7 to 8 minutes, until the mixture comes to a boil. Whisk constantly while boiling for 1 full minute (count to 60), until it thickens, looks clear, and generously coats a spoon. Remove from the heat.

In a medium bowl, whisk the yolks well, then whisk in about ½ cup of the hot lemon pudding to warm the yolks (work quickly so the yolks do not poach). Scrape the warm yolks into the hot lemon pudding in the pan, simultaneously whisking hard to blend in the yolk mixture before the eggs overcook. Return the lemon pudding to the stove over the very lowest heat and stir continuously for about 4 minutes, to cook the yolks and ensure a stable pudding. Remove from the heat and stir in the butter, if using, mixing until it melts. Leave the pudding in the pan and set it aside.

Prepare the meringue topping: In a small saucepan, stir together 2 tablespoons of the sugar, the cornstarch, and water until the cornstarch dissolves. Stir constantly over medium-high heat for 2 to 3 minutes until the mixture bubbles up into a boil; it will immediately start to thicken and look almost clear. Quickly remove the pan from the heat and set it aside. Preheat the oven to 350°F.

Whip the egg whites: Place the egg whites in the large absolutely grease-free bowl of an electric mixer. Add the salt and cream of tartar. With the electric mixer on medium speed, whip the whites until foamy. Gradually add the remaining 6 tablespoons sugar while beating continuously. When the whites look thick and foamy, increase the speed to high and whip until they look smooth and satiny and you begin to see beater tracks on the surface. When the mixer is turned off and the beater is lifted, the foam should make a soft, slightly droopy peak. Add the vanilla, turn the mixer on to medium speed, and begin beating in spoonfuls of the cooked cornstarch mixture from the small pan. Then beat on high a little longer, until the whites are smooth, satiny, and hold very stiff peaks.

276

Rewarm the lemon pudding by stirring it over very low heat just until it is *almost* hot to the touch; it must be hot enough to poach the surface of the meringue that will rest on it. Spoon the hot pudding into the pie plate. Add about half the meringue, spreading it out onto the edges of the crust to seal it and prevent shrinking. Pile on the remaining meringue and shape medium-high swirls with the back of a big spoon.

Bake the pie at 350°F for 12 to 15 minutes, or just until the meringue swirls begin to look golden brown. Cool the pie on a wire rack, and serve at room temperature. Refrigerate leftovers.

Orange or Blood Orange Meringue Pie. Replace the lemon juice with regular or blood orange juice, adjust the sugar to taste, and use 2 tablespoons grated regular or blood orange zest instead of the lemon zest. *Note:* See Sources, (page 363).

    Frozen blood orange juice is available from Frieda's, Inc.

Lime Meringue Pie. Replace the lemon juice with lime juice and the lemon zest with lime zest.

Key Lime Pie

. . . .

In this quick pie, the filling is made with condensed milk instead of a cooked custard. The flavor and texture of this pie is excellent, and it only takes a moment to prepare. To make a cooked lime custard pie with meringue topping, see Lime Meringue Pie, page 277.

ADVANCE PREPARATION: The crumb crust can be prepared ahead. The custard should be added to the crust at least 3 hours in advance and chilled.

SPECIAL EQUIPMENT: 9-inch pie plate; electric mixer or food processor fitted with a steel blade; rubber spatula

TEMPERATURE AND TIME: Crumb crust: 350°F for 8 minutes

CHILLING TIME: Completed pie: 2 to 3 hours

YIELD: One 9-inch pie; serves 6 to 8

9-inch Graham Cracker Crumb Crust (page 100), baked for 8 minutes

FILLING:

4 large egg yolks, at room temperature

1 (14-ounce) can sweetened condensed milk

½ cup fresh Key lime juice (or juice of regular limes)

2 teaspoons grated lime zest (Note: *Key limes are yellow-green rather than dark green in color; if you feel your pie is not really "lime" unless it looks green, you can add a drop of green vegetable food coloring to the cream filling*)

Preheat the oven to 350°F. Prepare the crumb crust and bake it as directed. Set on a wire rack to cool.

In an electric mixer or food processor, combine the egg yolks, condensed milk, lime juice, and grated zest. Blend until thick and smooth. Scrape the filling into the prepared crust and refrigerate for about 3 hours, until set. Store in the refrigerator. If you wish, serve with sweetened whipped cream (page 131).

279

Key Lime Cheese Pie. Omit the egg yolks. Use only ⅓ cup lime juice, and add 8 ounces (1 large package) cream cheese, at room temperature, beaten into the mixture along with the condensed milk and grated lime zest until perfectly smooth. Top with sweetened whipped cream (page 131).

Ricotta Cheese Pie

· · · · · · · · · · ·

*T*orta di ricotta is an Italian cheesecake pie made with ricotta cheese and flavored with either chopped candied fruits or small chunks of bittersweet chocolate (my favorite). In many regions of Italy, it is served as a Christmas specialty. *Note:* Fresh dairy ricotta often has much more liquid in it than commercially processed ricotta; either one works well in this pie, as long as the liquid is completely drained.

ADVANCE PREPARATION: The partially prebaked pie shell can be prepared ahead. Bake the pie shortly before serving, as it is best warm, though it can also be chilled and served cold.

SPECIAL EQUIPMENT: 9-inch pie plate or quiche pan; strainer set over bowl; whisk and mixing bowl or electric mixer; pastry brush; food processor fitted with a steel blade or a wooden board and chopping knife

TEMPERATURE AND TIME: Partially prebaked shell: 425°F for 12 minutes with pie weights, then 3 to 5 minutes empty; completed pie: 350°F for 40 to 45 minutes

YIELD: One 9-inch pie; serves 6 to 8

Partially prebaked 9-inch pie shell made with All-Purpose Flaky
   Pastry, either Sherry variation or Nut variation (pages 49 or 48), or
   Cream Cheese Pastry (page 90)

FILLING:
   1 pound (2 cups) whole-milk ricotta cheese
   3 large eggs, at room temperature
   1 cup granulated sugar
   3 ounces (1 small package) cream cheese (not low-fat), at room
      temperature
   1 teaspoon almond extract
   1 cup mixed candied fruits, chopped, or ½ cup chopped semisweet or
      bittersweet chocolate, or a combination of half fruit and half chocolate

Prepare the pastry, roll it out, and line the pie plate (pages 52–55). Trim a ¾-inch pastry overhang, fold over the edge, and flute as desired (page 56). Be sure the fluted rim is high, as it must contain a generous amount of filling. Preheat the oven to 425°F. Prick the pastry bottom with a fork, chill until firm, then partially blind-bake (pages 66–67). Cool on a wire rack. Reduce the oven heat to 350°F.

Measure the ricotta into a strainer set over a bowl and press out any excess fluid.

In an electric mixer or mixing bowl, beat the eggs well. Then brush some of the beaten eggs over the bottom of the pie shell to moisture-proof it. Add the sugar to the remaining eggs and beat for 2 to 3 minutes, until thick and a light yellow color. Add the drained ricotta, cream cheese, and almond extract and beat until smooth.

Sprinkle about half the fruit and/or chocolate mixture over the glazed pie shell. Stir the remaining fruit and/or chocolate into the egg-cheese mixture, then spoon this into the pie shell. Bake in the center of the preheated oven for 40 to 45 minutes, until the top is puffy and golden brown. Cool on a wire rack. Serve warm or chilled. Refrigerate leftovers.

Mississippi Mud Pie

· · · · · · · · · · ·

This pie is fun to make both because it is easy to prepare and because its name always stimulates dinner table conversation. The flavor is a chocoholic's dream, although it looks rather like what you might expect: a mudpie that has dried in the sun, crusty and cracked on top, soft inside. The touch of coffee in the filling is just enough to take the edge off the sweetness. Serve at room temperature with a dollop of vanilla yogurt or vanilla ice cream, or sweetened whipped cream (page 131).

This recipe for Mississippi Mud Pie was shared with me by Connecticut friend, good cook, and artist-in-clay Elizabeth MacDonald. For a Reduced-Fat Mud Pie, see variation following. For a Frozen Mud Pie made with ice cream, see page 360.

ADVANCE PREPARATION: The unbaked pastry shell can be prepared ahead and frozen (page 71); thaw before filling. The baked pie can also be frozen, although it tastes best when freshly baked.

SPECIAL EQUIPMENT: 10-inch pie plate; double boiler; electric mixer, mixing bowl, or food processor fitted with a steel blade; rubber scraper

TEMPERATURE AND TIME: 350°F for 35 to 45 minutes

YIELD: One 10-inch pie; serves 8 to 10

Unbaked 10-inch pie shell made with All-Purpose Flaky Pastry,
Nut Pastry (hazelnut, walnut or almond) variation (page 48)

FILLING:

8 tablespoons (1 stick) unsalted butter

2 ounces unsweetened chocolate

1 ounce semisweet chocolate

3 large eggs, at room temperature

1 tablespoon instant coffee powder, dissolved in 2 tablespoons
   sour cream

1⅓ cups granulated sugar

3 tablespoons light corn syrup

1 teaspoon vanilla extract

Prepare the pastry, roll it out, and line the pie plate (pages 52–55). Chill the pastry-lined pan while you prepare the filling. Preheat the oven to 350°F.

Melt the butter and chocolate in the top of a double boiler over hot (not boiling) water. Remove from the heat and stir to cool.

With an electric mixer or a processor, or with a bowl and whisk, beat together all the remaining ingredients until well blended. Stir in the melted and partly cooled chocolate-butter mixture. Pour into the prepared pie shell.

Bake in the lower third of the preheated oven for 35 to 45 minutes, or until the filling puffs up and forms a crisp, deeply crackled crust and the pastry edges look golden brown. Cool on a wire rack. The filling will sink down as it cools and the inner layer will set but remain softly chewy. (*Note:* The shorter baking time of 35 minutes leaves the inner layer more creamy than chewy, an effect I personally prefer.) Serve at room temperature, topped by vanilla yogurt, vanilla ice cream, or whipped cream.

Mississippi Mud Pie, Reduced-Fat Variation

· · · · · · · · · · ·

Warm from the oven, this pie is soft and silken; when cold, it is a solid, creamy fudge. You would never guess this version has nearly half the fat of the original recipe.

ADVANCE PREPARATION: This pie is good warm or chilled but should not be frozen.

SPECIAL EQUIPMENT: 9-inch pie plate; double boiler; electric mixer or food processor; rubber scraper

TEMPERATURE AND TIME: 350°F for 40 to 45 minutes

YIELD: One 9-inch pie; serves 6 to 8

9-inch Reduced-Fat Graham Cracker or Reduced-Fat Chocolate
  Crumb Crust (page 100)

FILLING:

2 tablespoons unsalted butter, at room temperature
1 ounce unsweetened chocolate
½ ounce semisweet chocolate
½ cup unsifted unsweetened cocoa, preferably Dutch-processed
Pinch of salt
Pinch of ground nutmeg
1 tablespoon plus 1 teaspoon cornstarch
½ cup granulated sugar
½ cup packed dark brown sugar
1 tablespoon instant espresso powder or regular instant coffee powder
⅓ cup light cream cheese (not fat-free), at room temperature
1 large egg plus 2 large whites, at room temperature
¼ cup nonfat or low-fat sour cream
¼ cup dark corn syrup
1 tablespoon vanilla extract

285

Prepare the crumb crust and press it into an even layer over bottom/up the sides of the pie plate. In the top of a small double boiler, combine the butter and both chocolates and place over simmering (not boiling) water until melted. Stir the chocolate mixture, then set it aside to cool slightly.

With an electric mixer or in a food processor, blend all the dry ingredients. Add the cream cheese and beat or pulse until smoothly blended. Add all the wet ingredients and beat. Scrape in the melted butter-chocolate mixture and blend until smooth; don't over-beat.

Spoon the filling into the crumb crust and bake for 40 to 45 minutes, until the top puffs up slightly, looks shiny, and feels dry to the touch. The top may be crackled. It will sink down and flatten as it cools. Serve warm, at room temperature, or cool completely, refrigerate, and serve cold. Refrigerate leftovers.

Mocha Hazelnut Tart

. . . .

The sophisticated taste of this tart blends chocolate, espresso, and toasted hazelnuts in a rich, creamy filling. Its preparation is quick and easy using a food processor; you can substitute an electric mixer, but in that case, the nuts must be chopped separately. You will need a total of approximately 11¾ ounces (2⅓ cups) whole hazelnuts; be sure to toast them first for maximum flavor, as directed in the first step.

ADVANCE PREPARATION: The pastry can be made a day in advance and refrigerated. Prepare the filling and bake the tart the day it will be served, or no more than 1 day in advance. Refrigerate.

SPECIAL EQUIPMENT: 10½- or 11-inch tart pan with removable bottom; jelly-roll or roasting pan for toasting nuts; food processor fitted with steel blade; nut chopper, optional; pastry brush; sifter; pint-size self-sealing plastic bag; small saucepan

TEMPERATURE AND TIME: 425°F for 12 minutes, then 375°F for 15 to 18 minutes

YIELD: One 11-inch tart; serves 12 to 14

HAZELNUT PASTRY:

   ½ cup (2½ ounces) whole hazelnuts (see first step)

   1½ cups unsifted all-purpose flour

   ½ teaspoon salt

   9 tablespoons (1 stick plus 1 tablespoon) cold unsalted butter

   1 large egg yolk

   1 tablespoon fresh lemon juice or white vinegar

   3 to 5 tablespoons ice water, as needed

FILLING:

   1 cup (5 ounces) whole hazelnuts

   ¾ cup granulated sugar

   8 tablespoons (1 stick) unsalted butter, cut up, at room
      temperature

   2 tablespoons instant espresso powder or regular instant
      coffee powder

   2 tablespoons unsweetened cocoa powder

   ¼ cup boiling water

   2 large eggs, at room temperature

   1 teaspoon vanilla extract

   ¼ teaspoon salt

COCOA ICING GLAZE:

   1¼ cups confectioners' sugar

   1 tablespoon unsweetened cocoa powder

   1 teaspoon vanilla extract

   2 tablespoons mocha essence, reserved from filling

GARNISH:

   ¼ cup (1½ ounces) semisweet or bittersweet chips or solid chocolate, finely
      chopped, optional

   About 30 whole toasted hazelnuts

287

Toast the hazelnuts: You will need a total of about 2⅓ cups (about 11¾ ounces) hazelnuts for the pastry, filling, and garnish. Spread all the hazelnuts in a jelly-roll or roasting pan and bake them at 350°F 10 to 12 minutes, tossing them a few times, until aromatic. Rub the nuts in a towel to remove most of the skins. You can chop the nuts in a nut chopper or with the food processor as described below.

Prepare the pastry: In the work bowl of a food processor, blend the flour, salt, and the ½ cup nuts until the nuts are very finely chopped. Add the butter and pulse only until the texture resembles coarse meal. Add the yolk, lemon juice or vinegar, and 2 to 3 table-spoons ice water through the feed tube, and pulse a few times. Add 1 or 2 tablespoons more water if needed, stopping the machine as soon as the dough begins to look clumpy. Turn the dough out onto a lightly floured board and gather it into a ball. The warmth of your hands will help it come together; add a drop more water if dough feels too dry. Flatten the dough into a 6-inch disk, wrap, and refrigerate for at least 30 minutes, or until no longer soft. Return the work bowl to the processor base without washing it.

Roll out the dough and line the buttered tart pan (pages 52–55). Refrigerate the pastry-lined pan while you make the filling.

Preheat the oven to 425°F. Prepare the filling: In the food processor, pulse 1 cup of toasted hazelnuts with the sugar until the nuts are chopped medium-fine. Add the butter and blend until a paste forms. Turn off the machine and scrape down the bowl. In a cup, mix together the coffee powder and cocoa, then stir in the boiling water until the coffee dissolves. Reserve 2 tablespoons of this mocha essence for the icing glaze, and pour the remainder into the processor, pulsing to blend it with the nut paste. Add the eggs, vanilla, and salt and pulse to blend.

Spoon the filling into the prepared pastry shell, smooth the top, and bake it at 425°F for 12 minutes. Then reduce the heat to 375°F and bake for an additional 15 to 18 minutes, or until the filling begins to puff slightly; the pastry edges will look golden and a knife in-serted in the center of the filling should come out clean. Set the baked tart on a wire rack to cool for about 5 minutes, until the filling settles and flattens out.

While the tart bakes, prepare the icing glaze: In a medium bowl, sift together the confec-tioners' sugar and cocoa, then whisk in the vanilla and the reserved 2 tablespoons mocha essence. The glaze should have the consistency of softly whipped cream; add a drop or two of water if it feels too thick.

While the tart is still very warm, spoon the icing glaze on top and use a pastry brush to spread it into an even coating; the warmth of the tart will melt the glaze so it flows on evenly. Refrigerate the tart for at least 30 minutes, or until the glaze is set.

For an added (but optional) touch of chocolate, you can put the chocolate chips into a small plastic bag, seal the top, and drop it into a saucepan of very hot (140°F) water. After about 3 or 4 minutes, the chocolate should liquefy. Dry the outside of the bag thoroughly. With scissors or a sharp knife, cut a tiny hole in one corner of the bag. Remove the tart from the refrigerator and drizzle fine chocolate lines over the glazed top (or, if you wish, write a special greeting). Be careful not to touch the glaze; fingerprints show. Arrange the remaining toasted hazelnuts in a ring around edge of tart. Let the tart sit at room temperature until ready to serve, or in warm weather, refrigerate. Bring to room temperature before serving. Remove the pan sides (page 55), keeping the tart on the pan bottom, and slide it onto a flat serving plate. Refrigerate leftovers.

289

A chiffon pie is a light fluffy confection in which flavoring, usually in an egg-yolk base, is supported by stiffly beaten egg whites and/or whipped heavy cream. Often gelatin is added as well, as a stabilizer. Without gelatin, the chiffon is essentially a *mousse,* a French term meaning, literally, "froth" or "foam." Dessert mousses and mousse pies are served chilled from the refrigerator, or frozen, in which case they are called frozen soufflés and have a texture similar to creamy ice cream. When gelatin is added to the egg yolk base along with whipped cream, but without egg whites, it becomes, strictly speaking, a Bavarian cream. Bavarian creams can be frozen, but they should be thawed overnight in the refrigerator before serving cold.

Rum-Pumpkin Chiffon Pie

. . . .

This light but richly flavored pie is a family favorite, made by my mother, Frances Joslin Gold. It has been part of our Thanksgiving since I can remember. Equally good without the rum, it is an elegant variation on traditional pumpkin custard pie.

ADVANCE PREPARATION: The crumb crust can be prepared in advance, or the complete pie can be made a minimum of 3 hours or up to a day ahead and refrigerated. Add the whipped cream garnish shortly before serving. The complete but un-garnished pie can also be chilled overnight, then double-wrapped and frozen; thaw overnight in the refrigerator.

SPECIAL EQUIPMENT: 9-inch pie plate; double boiler; small saucepan; large mixing bowl containing ice cubes and cold water; chilled bowl and beater for whipping cream; rubber scraper; plastic wrap; pastry bag fitted with ½-inch star tip, optional

CHILLING TIME: Crumb crust: 30 minutes minimum; filled pie: 3 hours minimum, or overnight

YIELD: One 9-inch pie; serves 6 to 8

CRUMB CRUST:

> 9-inch Gingersnap Crumb Crust (page 100) prepared without
> additional sugar, chilled until firm

FILLING:

> 2¾ teaspoons unflavored gelatin
>
> ¼ cup cool water
>
> 3 large eggs, at room temperature
>
> ⅔ cup granulated sugar, divided (⅓ cup and ⅓ cup)
>
> ½ teaspoon salt
>
> ¾ teaspoon ground cinnamon
>
> ¾ teaspoon ground nutmeg
>
> ¾ teaspoon ground ginger
>
> 3 to 4 tablespoons dark rum (or Triple Sec), to taste, optional
>
> 1¼ cups canned unsweetened pumpkin puree
>
> ½ cup heavy cream (36% butterfat), chilled

GARNISH:

> Whipped Cream (page 131), flavored with rum or Triple Sec
>   if desired
>
> Almond slices or slivers of candied ginger
>
> Ground nutmeg

Prepare the crumb crust and set it in the refrigerator to chill while you prepare the filling. Sprinkle the gelatin over the cool water in a small saucepan, let sit for 2 minutes to soften, and then stir over low heat until thoroughly dissolved. Set aside to cool. Separate the eggs (page 34), placing the yolks in the top of a double boiler and the whites in the large bowl of an electric mixer.

Whisk ⅓ cup of the granulated sugar into the yolks until the mixture is thick and light lemon colored. Whisk in the salt, spices, the rum, if using, and the dissolved gelatin. Set the double boiler over (not touching) boiling water and stir constantly over medium heat until the mixture becomes very thick and generously coats the back of a spoon.

Remove from the heat and stir in the pumpkin; whisk to combine thoroughly. Turn the mixture into a medium-sized metal bowl, then set it into a large bowl containing ice water. Whisk for about 15 minutes to cool the pumpkin mixture until it feels thick, mounds on the spoon, and looks as if it is beginning to set—about the consistency of raw egg whites. Do not chill until it sets hard; remove it from the ice water. (*Note:* The ice water speeds this process, but if you are not in a hurry, you can simply leave the mixture in the refrigerator for about 45 minutes, until it cools and thickens; however, do not let it set completely.)

Beat the egg whites until fluffy, then add the remaining ⅓ cup sugar a little at a time, beating until stiff peaks form and the whites are very satiny. With a chilled bowl and beater, whip the heavy cream until medium-stiff peaks form.

Fold the cooled, thickened (but not hard-set) pumpkin mixture into the whipped cream, then fold this into the stiffly beaten whites. Spoon the mixture into the prepared shell, then chill for at least 3 hours, or overnight, to set.

Garnish the pie shortly before serving with plain or rum-flavored whipped cream spooned into a ring around the edge of the pie or piped into rosettes through a pastry bag fitted with star tip. Decorate with almond slices or slivers of candied ginger and sprinkles of ground nutmeg.

Piña Colada Pie

· · · · · · · · · · ·

Like the cocktail for which it is named, this light refreshing chiffon pie is redolent of tropical island flavors: rum, coconut, lime, and pineapple.

ADVANCE PREPARATION: The crumb crust can be prepared ahead and frozen. The complete pie can be prepared a day ahead and refrigerated; or it can be double-wrapped and frozen; thaw overnight in the refrigerator before serving.

SPECIAL EQUIPMENT: 10-inch pie plate; 2½-quart heavy-bottomed nonreactive saucepan; small saucepan; large bowl containing ice cubes and cold water; electric mixer; chilled bowl and beater for whipping cream; plastic wrap; paper towels; strainer; pastry bag fitted with ½-inch star tip, or spoon and fork, for applying whipped cream

TEMPERATURE AND TIME: Coconut crust: 325°F for 20 minutes

CHILLING TIME: Filled pie: 3 hours minimum

YIELD: One 10-inch pie; serves 8 to 10

One 10-inch Coconut Crumb Crust (page 102) prepared with 2½
cups flaked or shredded coconut and ⅓ cup melted unsalted butter
(5⅓ tablespoons)

FILLING:

1 (20-ounce) can crushed pineapple

½ cup canned sweetened coconut cream (Coco Lopez, for
example)

3 large eggs, at room temperature

1 tablespoon unflavored gelatin

⅓ cup granulated sugar

1 tablespoon cornstarch

¼ cup dark rum, divided (3 tablespoons and 1 tablespoon)

2 tablespoons fresh lime juice

½ teaspoon coconut extract, optional

⅓ cup sifted confectioners' sugar

1 cup heavy cream (36% butterfat), chilled

TOPPING:

½ cup heavy cream (36% butterfat), chilled

1 tablespoon sifted confectioners' sugar

1 tablespoon dark rum or ½ teaspoon coconut extract

OPTIONAL GARNISH:

Fresh mint sprigs

Toasted Coconut Topping (page 142)

Thin-sliced lime cartwheels

Prepare the coconut crust and set aside to cool on a wire rack while you make the filling. Put the pineapple in a strainer set over a bowl. You should have about 1⅔ cups fruit and ¾ cup juice. Set the fruit aside and measure ¼ cup juice into a small saucepan. Stir the canned coconut cream into the remaining ½ cup of juice.

Separate the eggs (page 34), putting the whites in the large bowl of an electric mixer and whisking the yolks into the coconut-cream–pineapple juice mixture. Sprinkle the gelatin on the juice in the small pan, let sit for 2 minutes to soften, and then stir over low heat until the gelatin is thoroughly dissolved; do not boil.

In a saucepan, combine the granulated sugar and cornstarch. Stir, then whisk in the pineapple juice–yolk mixture. Set over medium heat and stir constantly with a wooden spoon for 4 to 5 minutes, until the mixture comes to a boil and thickens. Stir constantly while boiling for 1 full minute (count to 60). Remove from the heat. Stir in 3 tablespoons of the rum, the lime juice, the coconut extract, if using, and the dissolved gelatin. Measure and stir in 1½ cups pineapple pieces. Reserve the remaining pineapple for garnish.

Turn the pineapple mixture into a medium-sized metal bowl, then set it in a large bowl containing ice water. Whisk for about 15 minutes, until the mixture feels thick and looks as if it is beginning to set—about the consistency of raw egg whites. Then remove from the ice water. Do not allow it to set hard. (*Note:* The ice water speeds this process, but if you are not in a hurry, you can simply leave the mixture in the refrigerator for about 45 minutes, until it cools and thickens; however, do not let it set completely.)

Beat the egg whites until they are foamy, then add the confectioners' sugar and beat until stiff peaks form. In a chilled bowl, with chilled beater, whip the heavy cream until it forms soft peaks, then stir in the remaining 1 tablespoon rum and whip until medium-stiff. Fold the cream into the pineapple mixture, then fold in the beaten whites.

Turn the filling into the prepared shell. Cover with plastic wrap and refrigerate for at least 3 hours, until set.

The pie can be served plain or shortly before serving, *either* garnish with the reserved pineapple pieces (blotted well on paper towels) arranged around the edge of the pie and alternating with sprigs of mint *or* whip the ½ cup cream, stir in the sugar and rum or coconut extract and beat stiff. Decorate the pie with rosettes of whipped cream piped through a pastry bag fitted with a star tip. Alternatively, you can spoon mounds of the cream around the edges of the pie and stripe them with a fork. Garnish the cream with sprinkled on Toasted Coconut Topping, a few mint sprigs, and thin lime slices alternating with bits of pineapple, for color. Refrigerate and serve chilled.

Mango Mousse Pie

. . . .

Mangoes are a tropical fruit widely available in local supermarkets as well as Asian, Indian, and specialty fruit markets. They are seasonally available from May through September, but they are imported year-round. Generally an elongated round or oval shape, the mango has a smooth peel that is firm to the touch and green or yellow-green when unripe; it turns a mottled gold-orange-red as the fruit ripens. A fully ripe mango should yield gently to the pressure of your finger. The ripe flesh is aromatic, sweet, and juicy, with an exotic multilayered flavor reminiscent of a blend of apricots, peaches, cantaloupe, honey, and sweet pineapple. To achieve the best flavor and texture for this mousse, it is essential that the mangoes be fully ripe, so it is necessary to plan ahead. I generally buy my mangoes at least a week before I want to make the pie to be sure the fruit will be ready. Typically sold while partly green and hard, mangoes can be ripened at home on a window sill or in a paper bag at room temperature for several days or up to a week.

The Graham Cracker–Coconut Crumb Crust should be baked for a short time to enhance its flavor and give a crisp texture; toasted coconut blends well with the mango, but if you prefer, you can use all graham crackers (1¾ cups).

For the most elegant and tasty presentation, be sure to have on hand an extra ripe mango to slice on top of the pie as a garnish. Note: The mango mousse is equally successful served alone as a dessert without any crust, in long-stemmed goblets, topped by fresh ripe mango slices and sprigs of mint or a few blueberries or raspberries.

ADVANCE PREPARATION: The piecrust can be prepared several hours in advance. The filled pie needs to be refrigerated for about 3 hours to set. Pie is best served the day it is made, but will keep for at least 1 day, refrigerated.

SPECIAL EQUIPMENT: 9-inch pie plate; food processor or blender; small saucepan; chilled bowl and beater for whipping cream

TEMPERATURE AND TIME: Crust: 350°F for 8 minutes

CHILLING TIME: Mousse: 3 hours minimum, or overnight

YIELD: One 9-inch pie; serves 6 to 8

     1¼ cups graham cracker crumbs

     2 tablespoons granulated sugar

     ½ cup shredded sweetened coconut

     6 tablespoons (¾ stick) unsalted butter, melted

FILLING:
     3 extra-large or 4 to 5 medium-size completely ripe mangoes (about
        3 pounds total weight, to make 3½ cups puree. Canned mango puree
        can be substituted for fresh puree; ripe peaches or nectarines, peeled,
        pitted, and pureed can replace up to 1 cup of the mango puree.)

     ¼ cup fresh lemon or lime juice

     Pinch of salt

     ¼ cup granulated sugar

     ¼ cup plus 2 tablespoons frozen lemonade concentrate, undiluted,
        or frozen orange juice concentrate, undiluted

     2¾ teaspoons unflavored gelatin

     ½ cup heavy cream (36% butterfat), chilled

     2 tablespoons Grand Marnier or other orange-flavored liqueur,
        optional

OPTIONAL GARNISH:
     2 medium or 1 large very ripe mango, peeled and thinly sliced,
        or substitute ripe peaches or nectarines, peeled, pitted, and sliced

     ½ cup apricot preserves, strained and warmed, optional

     Mint sprigs

     ¼ cup fresh blueberries or raspberries

Prepare the crumb crust. Position a rack in the center of the oven and preheat it to 350°F. In a bowl, toss together the crumbs, sugar, coconut, and melted butter. Turn the crumbs out into the pie plate and press them over the bottom and up the sides into an even layer using the back of a large metal spoon. Bake the crust 8 minutes; cool on a wire rack.

Wash the mangoes. There is a large oval seed in the center of the mango. With a sharp knife, cut completely through the fruit on each side of this seed, then cut off the flesh remaining on the edges of the seed. With a teaspoon, scoop the flesh from the skin and place it in the workbowl of a food processor or blender. Discard the skin. Repeat with remaining mangoes. Puree the mango flesh; reserve 3½ cups of puree for the mousse and save any extra for another purpose (or eat as a cook's bonus). Blend in the fresh lemon or lime juice, salt, and the granulated sugar. Turn the mixture out into a bowl.

Measure the lemonade concentrate into a small saucepan, sprinkle on the gelatin, stir, and let sit 2 minutes to soften. Stir over low heat several minutes until gelatin is thoroughly dissolved and no longer looks granular; do not boil. Cool it slightly. Whisk about ½ cup of the mango mixture into the gelatin to blend it well, then scrape all the gelatin mixture into the mango puree and whisk to blend thoroughly.

With a chilled bowl and beater, whip the heavy cream to medium peaks, add the optional liqueur if used, and whip another second or two to make the cream slightly more firm. Fold the whipped cream into the mango mixture and spoon it into the cooled crumb crust. Refrigerate for at least 3 hours to set the mousse.

To garnish the pie shortly before serving, peel and thinly slice the ripe flesh of 1 or 2 mangoes. Arrange the slices in slightly overlapping concentric rings either over the whole pie top or around the outer edge only. If you wish, glaze the fruit slices by brushing on the warm, strained, apricot preserves. To add color, dot the slices with some fresh blueberries or raspberries, or a sprig of mint leaves. Refrigerate the pie and serve chilled.

299

Lemon Mousse Pie

· · · · · · · · · · ·

This light, tart, refreshing dessert is especially appreciated after a heavy meal, though it is also an appropriate finale for a spring luncheon, served with fresh sweet strawberries. For easy entertaining, prepare the pie a day ahead and refrigerate it until serving time. For variety, you can replace the lemon with orange or blood orange, lime, or tangerine.

ADVANCE PREPARATION: The crumb crust can be prepared ahead and frozen, the complete pie can be prepared in advance and refrigerated overnight, or for at least 3 hours before serving. Or the complete pie can be chilled overnight, then double-wrapped and frozen; thaw overnight in the refrigerator before serving.

SPECIAL EQUIPMENT: 9-inch pie plate; grater; strainer; cup; double boiler; electric mixer; whisk; large mixing bowl containing ice cubes and cold water, optional; rubber scraper; medium-sized bowl; plastic wrap; chilled bowl and beater for whipping cream

CHILLING TIME: Crumb crust: 20 minutes minimum; filled pie: 3 hours minimum

YIELD: One 9-inch pie; serves 6 to 8

9-inch Graham Cracker or Graham-Nut Crust (page 100)

FILLING:

3½ lemons, for a total of about 4½ tablespoons grated zest and
   ½ cup juice

2¼ teaspoons unflavored gelatin

¼ cup cold water or fresh orange juice

2 large eggs, at room temperature, separated, plus 1 large yolk

1 cup superfine sugar

1 teaspoon cornstarch

3 tablespoons orange-flavored liqueur (such as Grand Marnier
   or Cointreau)

A pinch of salt

½ cup heavy cream (36% butterfat), chilled

2 tablespoons sifted confectioners' sugar

Prepare the crumb crust and set it in the refrigerator to chill while you prepare the filling. Grate the lemons, reserving about 1½ teaspoons of the zest to garnish the pie and
putting the rest in a cup or small bowl. Squeeze the lemons, strain the juice, and add to the
zest in the cup. Set aside for the filling.

In the top of a double boiler, sprinkle the gelatin over the cold water or orange juice, stir,
and let sit for about 2 minutes to soften. Then set the pan over hot water on medium heat
and stir until the gelatin dissolves; do not boil. Remove from the heat.

Put all the egg yolks in one bowl of an electric mixer and the two whites in another bowl.
Add the sugar to the yolks and immediately begin to beat, continuing for about 5 minutes,
until the mixture is thick and light colored and forms a flat ribbon, falling back upon itself, when the beater is lifted. (*Note:* If the yolk mixture seems too dry and granular to become creamy after beating for 3 minutes, add 2 to 3 teaspoons water and continue beating.)

Add the cornstarch to the lemon juice and zest. Stir until the cornstarch is dissolved,
then whisk it into the melted gelatin in the top of the double boiler. Little by little, whisk
in the beaten yolk-sugar mixture, then set the pan back over medium heat and cook *over*
(not touching) hot water, whisking constantly, for about 9 to 12 minutes, or until the mixture thickens enough to generously coat the back of a spoon. Stir in the liqueur, if using,
and cook for about 1 minute longer; do not boil. Remove from the heat and spoon into a
medium-sized metal bowl.

To chill the lemon mixture, set it in a larger bowl containing ice water. Whisk for about 10 to 15 minutes, until it feels thick, will mound on a spoon, and looks as if it is beginning to set—about the consistency of raw egg whites. Immediately remove it from the ice water and set it aside. Do not chill the mixture until it sets hard. (*Note:* The ice water speeds the chilling process, but if you are not in a hurry, you can simply refrigerate the mixture for about 45 minutes, stirring occasionally until it cools and thickens; do not let it set completely.)

Whip the egg whites with the pinch of salt until stiff peaks form. Use a chilled bowl and beater to whip the cream to soft peaks, then add the confectioners' sugar and whip the cream until medium-stiff. Fold the lemon mixture a little at a time into the cream, then fold the mixture into the whites. Spoon the filling into the prepared shell. Garnish with the reserved lemon zest. Refrigerate to set for at least 3 hours. When the top of the pie is set, cover it with plastic wrap to protect the flavor, especially if the pie will be refrigerated overnight or longer. Refrigerate and serve chilled.

Raspberry Bavarian Cream Pie

. . . .

This delightful summertime pie is rich and creamy with a full fruit flavor. Serve it garnished with rosettes of raspberry-flavored whipped cream topped with whole fresh berries. You can be creative with this recipe and substitute different berries or a whole fruit puree. Or prepare the recipe in the form of eight 4½-inch tartlets.

ADVANCE PREPARATION: The nut or crumb crust can be prepared ahead and frozen. The complete pie can be prepared in advance and refrigerated overnight. Garnish with whipped cream shortly before serving.

SPECIAL EQUIPMENT: 9-inch pie plate (or eight 4½-inch-diameter tartlet pans); non-reactive heavy-bottomed saucepan; strainer; large mixing bowl filled with ice cubes and cold water; chilled mixing bowl and beater for whipping cream; rubber scraper; plastic wrap; spoon or pastry bag fitted with ½-inch star tip for applying whipped cream

CHILLING TIME: For the nut or crumb crust: 30 minutes minimum; for filled pie: 3 hours minimum, or overnight

YIELD: One 9-inch pie; serving 6 to 8; or eight 4½-inch tartlets

NUT OR CRUMB CRUST:

**9-inch Hazelnut or Almond Crust (page 102) or tartlet pans
lined with crumb crust**

FILLING:

1 tablespoon unflavored gelatin

¼ cup cold water

½ cup boiling water

1½ tablespoons fresh lemon juice

**2 to 4 tablespoons granulated sugar (depending upon sweetness
of fruit)**

¼ teaspoon salt

**1 cup fresh raspberry puree, strained, or 1 (12-ounce) bag whole
frozen raspberries, thawed and strained (add a little water if needed
to make 1 cup)**

**3 tablespoons fruit-flavored liqueur (such as Chambord raspberry
liqueur or double crème de cassis)**

¾ cup heavy cream (36% butterfat), chilled

TOPPING:

½ cup heavy cream (36% butterfat), chilled

1 tablespoon sifted confectioners' sugar

2 tablespoons fruit-flavored liqueur (same as in pie)

½ cup fresh whole raspberries, rinsed and dried, for garnish

Prepare the nut or crumb crust and set it in the refrigerator to chill while you prepare the filling.

Sprinkle the gelatin over the cold water in a small saucepan. Let it sit for 2 minutes to soften, then stir in the boiling water and stir until dissolved. Stir in the lemon juice, 2 tablespoons of the sugar, salt, and berry puree. Taste and add more sugar if necessary. Set the pan over low heat and stir well until the sugar is dissolved completely; do not boil.

Transfer the fruit mixture to a medium-sized metal bowl and stir in the liqueur. Set the bowl over ice water and stir or whisk for 10 to 15 minutes, until the mixture feels thick, mounds on the spoon, and looks as if it is beginning to set—about the consistency of raw egg whites. Remove it from the ice water. Do not allow it to set hard. (*Note:* The ice water speeds this process, but if you are not in a hurry, you can simply leave the mixture in the refrigerator for about 45 minutes, until it cools and thickens; however, do not let it set completely.)

With a chilled bowl and beater, whip the ¾ cup heavy cream until *nearly* stiff. Fold the whipped cream into the cooled, thickened raspberry mixture. Spoon the filling into the prepared shell. Cover with plastic wrap to protect the flavor and chill for at least 3 hours, or overnight.

Shortly before serving, whip the ½ cup heavy cream until soft peaks form. Add the confectioners' sugar and liqueur. Beat to stiff peaks and spoon into a decorative ring around the edge of the pie. Or pipe rosettes of cream through a pastry bag fitted with a star tip. Garnish with whole berries set into the whipped cream.

305

Chocolate Honey Chiffon Pie

. . . .

There are two surprises in this light, creamy pie: the honey, which adds richness to the chocolate flavor, and the lack of sugar and cream, which means fewer calories than in other chiffon pies (not exactly dietetic, but the thought is there).

ADVANCE PREPARATION: The crumb crust can be prepared ahead and frozen (as can the completely prebaked pastry shell). The complete pie can be prepared in advance and refrigerated overnight.

SPECIAL EQUIPMENT: 9-inch pie plate; rubber scraper; electric mixer with largest balloon beater; double boiler; plastic wrap

CHILLING TIME: Crumb crust: 30 minutes minimum; filled pie: 3 hours minimum, or overnight

YIELD: One 9-inch pie; serves 6 to 8

CRUMB CRUST:

> 9-inch Chocolate-Almond Crumb Crust (page 100) or completely
> prebaked 9-inch pastry shell made with All-Purpose Flaky Pastry,
> almond variation (page 48)

FILLING:

> 2 large eggs, at room temperature
> ½ cup sour cream
> 6 ounces semisweet chocolate, chopped
> ¼ teaspoon salt
> ⅓ cup honey

TOPPING:

> Chocolate Curls or Grated Chocolate (page 148)

Prepare the crumb crust and set it in the refrigerator to chill while you prepare the filling. Separate the eggs (page 34), placing the yolks in a small bowl and the whites in the bowl of an electric mixer fitted with the largest balloon beater available. Spoon the sour cream into a measuring cup and place near the stove, along with the egg yolks; you'll need them handy when working with the chocolate.

307

Melt the chocolate in the top of a double boiler over hot (not boiling) water. While the chocolate is melting, begin preparing the egg whites. Add the salt to the whites; measure the honey and set it nearby. Beat the whites until stiff but not dry, then very gradually add the honey while continuing to beat until stiff peaks form. Do not despair if the whites look soft after you add the honey. Beat for 4 or 5 minutes, and they will stiffen beautifully. The bigger the beater and the more powerful the mixer, the easier and quicker this job is; but no matter what type beater you use, it will work if you just keep at it.

As soon as the chocolate is melted, remove it from heat, add the yolks, and whisk vigorously. Then replace over the heat and whisk for about 30 seconds, or slightly more, until the mixture forms a ball and pulls away from the sides of the pan. Immediately remove the top of the double boiler from the heat. Stir in the sour cream and beat until smooth.

When the egg whites are stiff, gently and gradually fold them into the chocolate mixture. Spoon the mixture into the prepared shell and cover with plastic wrap to protect the flavor. Chill in the refrigerator for at least 3 hours, or overnight, to set. Garnish with Chocolate Curls or Grated Chocolate. Refrigerate and serve chilled.

Quick Mocha Cream Pie

· · · · · · · · · · ·

This is one of the easiest, quickest, and best-tasting chocolate pies ever, made basically of melted chocolate folded into coffee-flavored whipped cream. The only way it could be simpler is to have a crumb crust or prebaked pastry shell already in your freezer. The one trick to this pie is to be sure the melted chocolate is cool enough before mixing it with the whipped cream. For entertaining, make the pie days or weeks ahead and freeze it, but thaw it overnight in the refrigerator before serving. If you prefer a texture closer to ice cream, remove the pie from the freezer only about 15 minutes before serving. Add the whipped cream topping just before serving.

ADVANCE PREPARATION: The prepared crumb shell can be made ahead and frozen (page 71). The filled pie can be prepared and frozen until needed, then thawed overnight in the refrigerator before serving, or frozen until 15 minutes before serving.

SPECIAL EQUIPMENT: 9-inch pie plate; double boiler; electric mixer; chilled bowl and beater for whipping cream; rubber scraper; pastry bag fitted with ½-inch star tip for decorating, optional

CHILLING TIME: Crumb crust: 30 minutes; filled pie: about 3 to 4 hours in the refrigerator, or 2 hours minimum in the freezer (to serve as a frozen pie)

YIELD: One 9-inch pie; serves 6 to 8

CRUMB CRUST:

CRUMB CRUST:

    9-inch Chocolate Wafer Crumb Crust (page 100) or completely prebaked
       9-inch pie shell made with pastry of your choice

FILLING:

    8 ounces semisweet or bittersweet chocolate or one 8-ounce
       semisweet or milk chocolate candy bar, cut up
    1 cup heavy cream (36% butterfat), chilled
    1 tablespoon instant espresso powder dissolved in 2 tablespoons
       warm water

TOPPING:

    ½ cup heavy cream (36% butterfat), chilled
    2 teaspoons instant espresso powder dissolved in 2 tablespoons
       heavy cream
    2 tablespoons sifted confectioners' sugar

OPTIONAL GARNISH:

    Chocolate Curls and Grated Chocolate (page 148) or Chocolate Leaves
    (pages 150–151)

309

Prepare the crumb crust and set in refrigerator to chill while you prepare the filling.

Put the chocolate into the top of a double boiler and melt over hot (not boiling) water. Remove from the heat just before the chocolate is completely melted and stir to complete the melting process. Turn into a metal bowl and set to cool in the refrigerator while you prepare the cream.

With a chilled bowl and beater, whip the heavy cream until it fluffs softly. Add the dissolved coffee and beat until the peaks hold their shape well; stop beating before the cream feels really stiff. Test the temperature of the chocolate: If the chocolate is too hot, it will melt the whipped cream; if too cold, it will cause the cream to become grainy when folded in. It should be comfortable to the touch when you stick your finger into it (80° to 90°F) and appear soft, satiny, and easy to stir. It it has chilled and stiffened, set it over a pan of warm water for a few seconds while you stir it until soft again. When the chocolate is comfortably cool and smooth, gradually fold and stir it into the coffee cream. Don't worry if a few flecks of solid chocolate are visible—this only adds texture to the cream.

Spoon the mixture into the prepared crumb crust, and refrigerate for at least 3 hours before serving cold, or place the pie in the freezer, uncovered, to set. When frozen hard, you can wrap it airtight in foil and store in the freezer. Thaw overnight in the refrigerator or, for an ice cream texture, leave it frozen until 15 minutes before serving.

To make the topping, whip the cream until it holds soft peaks. Add the dissolved coffee and sugar and beat until it holds firm peaks. Spread the cream in a ring around the edge of the pie, or pipe a decorative design through a pastry bag fitted with a star tip. Garnish with Grated Chocolate or Chocolate Leaves or Curls. (*Note:* The flavor of the cream is best if added shortly before serving; however, you can add the whipped cream to the pie before freezing.)

Quick Chocolate Cream Pie. Omit the coffee in the filling and in the whipped cream.

Chocolate Mousse—
Crème de Menthe Pie

· · · · · · · · · · ·

A grand-finale dinner party dessert! The rich velvety texture, heavenly flavor, and elegant presentation of this pie belie the fact that it's a breeze to prepare ahead and store in the freezer. Predictably, chocolate lovers will swoon, but the rest of the world will enjoy it too, because the mint flavor cuts the sweetness of traditional chocolate mousse. Serve topped with whipped cream rosettes and chocolate leaves.

ADVANCE PREPARATION: The chocolate crumb crust can be prepared ahead and frozen. The complete pie can be prepared ahead and refrigerated overnight. Or it can be frozen and thawed overnight in the refrigerator. Garnish with whipped cream shortly before serving.

SPECIAL EQUIPMENT: 10-inch pie plate; double boiler; chilled mixing bowl and beater for whipped cream; rubber scraper; pastry bag fitted with ½-inch star tip for decorating; plastic wrap

CHILLING TIME: Crumb crust: 30 minutes minimum; filled pie: 6 hours in refrigerator or 2 hours in freezer minimum

YIELD: One 10-inch pie; serves 8 to 10

CRUMB CRUST:

    10-inch Chocolate Wafer or Chocolate-Almond Crumb Crust (page 100)
        prepared with 1¾ cups crumbs and ½ cup melted butter

FILLING:

    12 ounces semisweet chocolate, chopped
    8 tablespoons (1 stick) unsalted butter
    4 large eggs, at room temperature
    7 tablespoons green or white crème de menthe, divided (6 tablespoons
        and 1 tablespoon)
    2 tablespoons sifted confectioners' sugar, divided (1 tablespoon and
        1 tablespoon)
    ½ cup heavy cream (36% butterfat), chilled
    ¼ teaspoon peppermint extract

GARNISH:

    ½ cup heavy cream (36% butterfat), chilled
    2 tablespoons sifted confectioners' sugar
    2 teaspoons green or white crème de menthe
    Chocolate Curls and Grated Chocolate (page 148) or Chocolate Leaves (pages
        150–151)

Prepare the chocolate crumb crust and set it in the refrigerator to chill while you prepare the filling. Put the chocolate and butter in the top of a double boiler and set to melt over hot (not boiling) water. Stir to blend, then remove from the heat.

Separate the eggs (page 34). Place the whites in a mixing bowl and vigorously whisk each yolk into the melted chocolate mixture. Stir 6 tablespoons of the crème de menthe into the yolk-chocolate mixture and set aside to cool.

Beat the egg whites until foamy, then add 1 tablespoon of the confectioners' sugar and beat until stiff peaks form. With a chilled bowl and beater, whip the cream until soft peaks form. Add the remaining 1 tablespoon confectioners' sugar, and the remaining 1 table-spoon crème de menthe along with the peppermint extract. Whip until nearly—but not completely—stiff.

To lighten the chocolate mixture, stir in about 3 tablespoons each of the whipped cream and whipped whites. Then fold in all the remaining whipped whites and whipped cream. Spoon the chocolate mixture into the prepared shell, cover with plastic wrap to protect the flavor, and refrigerate for at least 6 hours, or overnight. Or freeze the pie, then thaw it overnight in the refrigerator before serving cold.

Shortly before serving, garnish the pie. Beat the cream with the sugar and crème de menthe until stiff, place it in a pastry bag, and pipe rosettes around the pie; or, spoon the cream in a circle covering about two thirds of the center of the pie, leaving a ring of filling exposed at the edge. Stripe the spooned-on cream with fork tines. Decorate the outer edge with Chocolate Leaves or Curls or Grated Chocolate.

(*Note:* Since this is a mousse and not stiffened with gelatin, in very hot weather it is best to serve it directly from the refrigerator. At room temperature, it may become too soft to slice neatly. Return leftovers to the refrigerator or freezer.)

313

Orange Chocolate Silk Pie

. . . .

The orange lightens and refreshes, the chocolate thickens and enriches, and "silk" describes the luxurious texture. What more could you ask? This recipe can be prepared in a pie plate, or as six individual tartlets.

ADVANCE PREPARATION: The crumb crust can be prepared ahead and frozen. The complete pie can be prepared a day ahead and refrigerated.

SPECIAL EQUIPMENT: 9-inch pie plate; double boiler; electric mixer; rubber scraper; chilled mixing bowl and beater for whipping cream; plastic wrap; pastry bag fitted with ½-inch star tip, or spoon and fork, for applying whipped cream; paring knife

CHILLING TIME: Crumb crust: 30 minutes minimum; filled pie: 3 hours minimum, or overnight

YIELD: One 9-inch pie; serves 6 to 8

CRUMB CRUST:

> 9-inch Chocolate Wafer or Chocolate-Almond Crumb Crust (page 100) or six
> 4½-inch tartlet pans prepared with same crumb crust

FILLING:

> 2 ounces semisweet or bittersweet chocolate, chopped
> 8 tablespoons (1 stick) unsalted butter, at room temperature, cut up
> ¾ cup confectioners' sugar, sifted after measuring
> 2 large eggs, at room temperature
> ¼ cup orange-flavored liqueur (such as Cointreau or Grand Marnier)
> 1 cup heavy cream (36% butterfat), chilled

TOPPING AND GARNISH:

> ½ cup heavy cream (36% butterfat), chilled
> 1 tablespoon sifted confectioners' sugar
> 1 tablespoon orange-flavored liqueur (same type as above)
> Chocolate Leaves or Curls (pages 150–151 or 148)
> Thin-sliced cartwheels of fresh orange

Prepare the chocolate crumb crust as directed and set in the refrigerator to chill while you prepare the filling. Put the chocolate in the top of a double boiler and set to melt over hot (not boiling) water. Stir and set aside to cool.

With an electric mixer, cream together the butter and confectioners' sugar until fluffy. Blend in the melted and cooled chocolate. Add the eggs one at a time, beating about 5 minutes after each addition. Don't cheat; the texture developed in the beating is important. Beat in the orange liqueur.

With a chilled bowl and beater, whip the cream until medium-stiff peaks form. Fold the whipped cream into the chocolate mixture. Spoon into the prepared crumb crust. Cover with plastic wrap to protect the flavor and chill in the refrigerator for at least 3 hours to set.

Shortly before serving, whip the ½ cup topping cream until soft peaks form. Add the sugar and liqueur and beat until stiff. Decorate the pie with rosettes of cream piped through a pastry bag fitted with a star tip, or spoon mounds of cream around the edge of the pie and stripe them with a fork. Garnish with Chocolate Curls or Leaves and very thin slices of orange cut through to the center at one point, then twisted in opposite directions to form an S curve. Serve chilled. Refrigerate leftovers.

Velvet Rum Cream Pie

. . . .

This recipe was shared with me by my sister, Nancy Gold Lieberman. A delectable blend of egg yolks, cream, and rum, it is sinfully rich, and so easy to prepare you will wish you had made two. It has become a tradition in my family to serve this pie on New Year's Eve as a good luck charm for a sweet New Year. I like to decorate the pie with bittersweet Chocolate Leaves and fresh raspberries.

ADVANCE PREPARATION: The nut-crumb crust can be prepared ahead and frozen. The complete pie is best when prepared 1 day ahead and refrigerated. It can also be prepared in advance, frozen, and thawed overnight in the refrigerator.

SPECIAL EQUIPMENT: 10-inch pie plate; whisk; chilled bowl and beater for whipping cream; large mixing bowl containing ice cubes and cold water; rubber scraper; plastic wrap; pastry bag fitted with ½-inch star tip, or spoon and fork, for applying whipped cream

CHILLING TIME: Crumb crust: 30 minutes minimum (or bake for 8 minutes); filled pie: 4 hours minimum, or overnight

YIELD: One 10-inch pie; serves 8 to 10

CRUMB CRUST:

> 10-inch Graham-Nut Crumb Crust (page 100) prepared with 1 cup
> graham cracker crumbs and ¾ cup ground almonds, 5 tablespoons
> sugar, and ½ cup melted butter or one 10-inch completely prebaked
> pastry shell, recipe of your choice

FILLING:

> 2¼ teaspoons unflavored gelatin
> ½ cup cold water
> 6 large egg yolks, at room temperature
> 1 cup granulated sugar
> ⅓ cup dark rum
> 1½ cups heavy cream (36% butterfat), chilled

TOPPING AND GARNISH:

> ½ cup heavy cream (36% butterfat), chilled
> 1 tablespoon sifted confectioners' sugar
> 1 tablespoon dark rum; optional
> Chocolate Leaves (pages 150–151), or Chocolate Curls and Grated Chocolate
> (page 148)

Prepare the crumb crust and chill. Sprinkle the gelatin over the cold water in a small saucepan. Let sit for 2 minutes to soften, then place over low heat and stir constantly to dissolve the gelatin; do not boil. Remove from the heat.

In a mixing bowl, beat the yolks with the sugar until thick and light colored and the mixture forms a flat ribbon falling back upon itself when the beater is lifted. Stir in the hot gelatin, to melt the sugar, then add rum while beating slowly. Whip the cream to stiff peaks, then fold into the gelatin-yolk mixture. Set this bowl into a larger bowl of ice water and whisk for 10 to 15 minutes, until the mixture feels thick and mounds on the spoon. Immediately remove this bowl from the ice water; do not allow the mixture to set hard.

Spoon the mixture into the prepared pastry shell. Cover it with plastic wrap and chill for at least 4 hours to set. Or wrap and freeze it, but thaw overnight in the refrigerator.

Shortly before serving, whip the ½ cup topping cream to soft peaks. Add the sugar and the rum, if using, then beat until stiff. Pipe it into rosettes through a pastry bag fitted with a star tip or spoon it into a ring around the edge of the pie. Decorate with Chocolate Leaves or some Chocolate Curls and Grated Chocolate sprinkled over the cream.

Quince Pudding Pie

· · · · · · · · · ·

This unusual dessert is my autumn creation, inspired by some quince puree left after making quince paste, that glorious specialty of the South of France. If you are making quince paste or quince jam in the fall, freeze several 1-cup portions of unsweetened quince puree for later use in this recipe. The pie has the texture of a creamy pudding, though it is really a chiffon pie without gelatin. The tartness of the quince is mellowed by blending it with spices and honey in a cream custard; the flavor is rich and somewhat reminiscent of homemade applesauce with heavy cream on top. It is especially good served warm on a cold winter night.

ADVANCE PREPARATION: The unbaked pastry shell can be prepared ahead and frozen. For best texture and flavor, bake the pie on the morning of the day it is to be served.

SPECIAL EQUIPMENT: 9-inch pie plate; 2-quart heavy-bottomed nonreactive saucepan; food mill; electric mixer (preferably with 2 bowls); rubber scraper; stainless steel knife

TEMPERATURE AND TIME: 425°F for 15 minutes, 350°F for 30 to 35 minutes

YIELD: One 9-inch pie; serves 6 to 8

Unbaked 9-inch pastry shell made with All-Purpose Flaky Pastry
   (page 45) or Cornmeal Pastry (page 81)

FILLING:

   2 large ripe quinces (or 1 cup unsweetened quince puree)

   3 large eggs, at room temperature

   3 tablespoons honey

   ½ cup granulated sugar

   2½ tablespoons all-purpose flour

   ⅛ teaspoon salt, plus a pinch

   2 tablespoons unsalted butter, at room temperature

   ⅛ teaspoon ground cinnamon

   ⅛ teaspoon ground nutmeg

   1 cup heavy or light cream (depending upon how rich you wish
      the pie to be)

Prepare the pastry, roll it out, and line the pie plate (pages 52–55). Make sure the rim is fluted high enough to contain the generous filling.

Set the pastry-lined pan in the refrigerator to chill while you prepare the filling. Preheat the oven to 425°F.

To make the quince puree, wash and quarter the quinces. Place them in a saucepan with about ⅓ cup water. Cover and cook over medium heat until the quinces are tender. Drain. Put the fruit through a food mill. You should have about 1 cup pulp. (*Note:* Homemade unsweetened applesauce can be substituted for the quince puree or used to augment your puree supply.)

Separate the eggs (page 34), putting the whites into a small bowl and the yolks into the large bowl of an electric mixer. Add the honey, sugar, flour, ⅛ teaspoon salt, and butter to the yolks. Beat until creamy. Add the quince puree, cinnamon, and nutmeg and beat well. Slowly stir in the cream, then beat until combined; the mixture will be thick and creamy. If you do not have two bowls for your mixer, turn the quince mixture into another bowl and wash and dry the mixer bowl in order to use it for the egg whites.

Place egg whites in the clean grease-free bowl. Add the pinch of salt, stir, then dip a pastry brush into the whites and brush the bottom of the chilled pastry to form a moisture-proof coating. With clean beaters, whip the whites until stiff peaks form. Fold the quince mixture little by little into the whites. Spoon into the prepared pastry shell.

Bake in the lower third of the preheated oven for 15 minutes. Reduce the heat to 350°F, raise the pie to the center of the oven, and continue baking for 30 to 35 minutes longer, until the filling is puffed up and browned on top and a knife inserted in the center comes out clean. Cool on a wire rack. The filling will rise during baking but will sink down as the pie cools. Serve warm or cold. Refrigerate leftovers.

Chestnut Mousse Pie

. . . .

This velvety, rum-scented elegance is far too chic to be called simply a pie. Perhaps Mousse en Croûte would be more fitting . . . the perfect finale for a holiday dinner party.

ADVANCE PREPARATION: The completely prebaked pastry or crumb shell can be prepared ahead and frozen. The complete pie can be prepared 1 day ahead and refrigerated.

SPECIAL EQUIPMENT: 10-inch pie plate; pastry brush; 2-quart heavy-bottomed nonreactive saucepan; strainer set over a bowl; chilled bowl and beater for whipping cream; rubber scraper; pastry bag fitted with ½-inch star tip, or spoon, for applying whipped cream; plastic wrap

TEMPERATURE AND TIME: Completely prebaked pastry shell: 425°F for 12 minutes with pie weights, 350°F for 10 to 15 minutes empty

CHILLING TIME: Filled pie: 3 hours minimum, or overnight

YIELD: One 10-inch pie; serves 8 to 10

321

PASTRY:

> **Completely prebaked 10-inch pastry shell made with All-Purpose Flaky Pastry, Nut (almond) variation (page 48), or any 10-inch Nut crumb crust (page 102)**

EGG GLAZE:

> **1 large egg white (reserved from filling) beaten with 1 tablespoon water**

FILLING:

> **1 (15½ ounce) can unsweetened chestnut puree (available in many supermarkets as well as gourmet food shops)**
> **2 cups milk**
> **½ cup plus 2 tablespoons granulated sugar**
> **4 teaspoons unflavored gelatin**
> **1 teaspoon vanilla extract**
> **6 large egg yolks, at room temperature**
> **3 tablespoons dark rum**
> **1 cup heavy cream (36% butterfat), chilled**

TOPPING AND GARNISH:

> **½ cup heavy cream (36% butterfat), chilled**
> **1 tablespoon sifted confectioners' sugar**
> **1 jar candied chestnuts in syrup (marrons glacés) or Chocolate Leaves or Curls (pages 150–151 or 148)**

Preheat the oven to 425°F. If making a pastry shell, prepare the pastry, roll it out, and line the pie plate (pages 52–55). Make sure the fluted rim is high enough to contain the generous filling. Do *not* prick the pastry bottom with a fork. Chill the pastry until firm, then completely blind-bake (pages 66–67). After removing the liner and pie weights, brush moisture-proofing egg white glaze over the bottom of the pastry shell, then reduce the oven heat to 350°F and bake the shell for the final 15 to 20 minutes, or until golden brown. Cool on a wire rack. (If you are making the crumb crust instead, prepare as directed in the recipe.)

In a large saucepan, mash the chestnut puree with a fork. Add the milk and sugar and whisk until fairly smooth. Sprinkle on the gelatin, then set the pan over medium heat and bring nearly to a boil while stirring with a wooden spoon. Don't worry if there are some lumps; the mixture will be strained later. *As soon as* the mixture reaches a boil, remove it from the heat and stir in the vanilla extract.

Beat the yolks together in a mixing bowl. When frothy, stir in about ½ cup of the hot chestnut mixture while whisking constantly (to avoid scrambling the eggs). Add the warmed yolks back to the hot chestnut mixture, again stirring constantly so the eggs do not over-heat. Cook, stirring, over medium heat until the mixture thickens slightly; do not boil. When thick, remove from the heat, whisk in the rum, and pass through a strainer set over a bowl. Let the mixture cool in the refrigerator until thickened but not quite jelled. If by accident jelling occurs, simply set the chestnut mixture over hot water and stir until it softens.

With a chilled bowl and beater, whip the cream until medium-stiff peaks form. Fold the cream into the cooled and thickened (but not jelled) chestnut mixture. Turn into the prepared pastry shell, cover with plastic wrap to protect the flavor, and refrigerate for at least 3 hours, until set.

Shortly before serving, whip the ½ cup topping cream in a chilled bowl with chilled beaters. When soft peaks form, add the sugar, then beat until stiff. Decorate the pie with rosettes of cream piped through a pastry bag fitted with a star tip, or spoon mounds of cream around the pie and stripe with a fork. Cut the candied chestnuts into halves or quarters and set the pieces into the whipped cream. Or garnish with Chocolate Leaves or Curls. Refrigerate and serve chilled.

INDIVIDUAL PASTRIES, TARTLETS, AND TURNOVERS

A wide variety of single-serving pastries fits this category: Small individual Meringue Shells, or nests (page 108), filled with ice cream or pastry cream and fresh fruit; Chocolate Shells (page 104) filled with fruit sherbet or flavored frozen creams; miniature flaky pastry tarts baked in fancy shapes; individual fruit-filled pastry turnovers; and crisp phyllo dough cups filled with berries and cream. You should consider, when making tartlets, that any full-sized tart or pie can also be baked in individual tartlet shells. For example, try Blueberry-Peach Tartlets (page 173), Mincemeat Tartlets (page 188), Vermont Maple-Walnut Tartlets (page 262), Pecan Pie Tartlets (page 269), or Cranberry-Raisin Tartlets (page 227)—all made with regular pie or tart fillings. To convert a pie or tart recipe into tartlets, remember that a pastry recipe made with 2 to 2½ cups flour = one two-crust 9-inch pie = one 11- or 12-inch tart shell = approximately nine 4-inch tartlets or eight 4½-inch tartlets. Filling for a 9-inch pie = about 4 cups, enough to fill eight 4½-inch tartlets with ½ cup filling each. In addition to using flaky pastry dough, you can form individual pastry cases with quick or frozen puff pastry; see page 236.

Quick Meringue Ice Cream Tartlets

. . . .

Prepare 3-inch meringue tartlet shells (page 108). When the shells are cold, fill with your favorite ice cream and top with Rich Chocolate Sauce (page 149) or complementary fresh or frozen berries, pureed in a blender or food processor with a tablespoon or two of rum or kirsch. If you are feeling excessive, pipe a rosette of flavored whipped cream (page 131) on the top of each and garnish with a Chocolate Leaf (pages 150–151).

Angel Tartlets

. . . .

Prepare Orange Angel Pie (page 336), forming the shells into 3-inch meringue nests, as described on page 108. Fill with Angel Pie filling—Orange, Tangerine, or Lemon—and top each with whipped cream and a mint leaf. Or garnish with a slice or two of canned mandarin oranges (drained well) brushed with Plain Fruit Glaze (page 153); add a fresh mint leaf.

Pastry Tartlets
. . . .

Pastry tartlet shells can be filled with anything you would put into a large tart shell. If the shells are unbaked, or partially baked, add any regular fruit, cream, or custard filling and bake as for a full-sized pie or tart, but reduce the baking time according to tart size. If the shells are completely baked, add any chiffon or cold, cooked custard filling.

As a rule of thumb for filling tartlets: ½ cup filling = one 4½-inch tartlet;
4 cups filling = one 9-inch pie = eight 4- to 4½-inch tartlets.

Follow the instructions on page 67 to shape and completely prebake tartlet shells made with Rich Tart Pastry (page 88), Cream Cheese Pastry (page 90), or All-Purpose Flaky Pastry, Lemon or Orange Pastry variation (page 49).

Berry Custard Tartlets.
Prepare completely prebaked tartlet shells. Fill with Vanilla or other Pastry Cream (page 116) and top with fresh berries. Brush the berries with Plain or Firm Fruit Glaze (page 153 or 155) shortly before serving. Or top with any combination of berries and peeled, sliced fresh fruit. (*Note:* Canned fruits, well drained, may be substituted.)

Kiwi Cream Tartlets.
Prepare completely prebaked tartlet shells. Fill with Almond Pastry Cream (page 118). Top with overlapping slices of peeled kiwifruit. Brush with Plain or Firm Fruit Glaze (page 153 or 155) shortly before serving.

Almond-Pear Tartlets.
Prepare completely prebaked tartlet shells. Fill with Almond Pastry Cream (Frangipane) (page 122) or regular Almond Pastry Cream (page 118). Top each with half a well-drained poached pear or half a canned pear, drained and dried. Brush with Plain or Firm Fruit Glaze (page 153 or 155) shortly before serving and garnish with a sprig of mint or a sprinkling of ground nutmeg.

Whipped Cream Tartlets with Chocolate Curls or Leaves. Prepare completely prebaked tartlet shells. Fill with flavored whipped cream of your choice (page 131) and top with Chocolate Curls (page 148) or Chocolate Leaves (pages 150–151). These can be made in advance, frozen, and served partially thawed, for an ice cream–like texture.

Lemonade or Orange Juice Cream Tartlets. Prepare completely prebaked tartlet shells. Fill with Lemonade or Orange Cream Cheese Tart Filling (page 128) and top with freshly peeled orange segments or canned mandarin orange sections, well drained and dried. Brush with Plain or Firm Fruit Glaze (page 153 or 155) shortly before serving.

Strawberry Shortcake Tartlets. Prepare completely prebaked tartlet shells. Fill with sweetened whipped cream (page 131) or Lemon–Double Cream Tart Filling (page 127). Top with hulled fresh strawberries and brush with Plain or Firm Fruit Glaze (page 153 or 155) shortly before serving.

Jam Tartlets. Prepare completely prebaked tartlet shells. Fill with a thin layer of Lemonade or Orange Juice Cream Cheese Tart Filling (page 128) and top with a generous layer of your favorite fruit preserves. Sift on a light sprinkling of confectioners' sugar just before serving.

Fruit Turnovers

· · · · · · · · · · ·

These are really miniature fruit pies, as welcome and delicious as the larger versions but easier to eat, especially on picnics, or from lunch boxes. Turnovers are a good way to use up a small amount of ripe fruit or leftover pastry scraps.

ADVANCE PREPARATION: All-Purpose Flaky Pastry or Quick or store-bought puff pastry (or pastry scraps) can all be frozen. Better yet, use up puff pastry scraps by rolling out and filling them with the fruit slices, then freeze until ready to bake. Bake unthawed, but increase the baking time slightly.

SPECIAL EQUIPMENT: Pastry brush; ruler; sharp knife or pizza cutting wheel; flat rimmed baking sheet

TEMPERATURE AND TIME: 425°F for about 17 to 25 minutes

YIELD: About 6 large turnovers

PASTRY:
> Quick Puff Pastry (page 110), frozen puff pastry (page 112), or puff pastry
> scraps or All-Purpose Flaky Pastry (page 45) or Cream Cheese Pastry (page 90)

EGG GLAZE:
> 1 large egg beaten with 1 tablespoon water

FILLING:
> Half the fruit filling (about 2 to 2½ cups) for any 9-inch fresh fruit or
> berry pie

OPTIONAL TOPPING:
> Granulated sugar

OPTIONAL ICING GLAZE:
> ½ cup sifted confectioners' sugar
> 2 teaspoons milk
> ¼ teaspoon vanilla extract

Prepare the pastry. On a lightly floured surface, roll out the dough (page 52) to a thickness of about ⅛ inch. Cut as many 5- or 6-inch squares as possible. Reroll the scraps and cut more. You should get about 6 squares from a rectangle of dough 12 × 18 inches. Make 5-inch squares, or even smaller.

Brush the inner edge of each pastry square with egg glaze; if using puff pastry, don't drop any glaze along the outer edges, or the layers of dough will be glued together. In the center of each square, place between 1 tablespoon and ⅓ cup fruit filling, depending upon the size of the dough square; the filling should be generous. Fold two opposite corners together, making a triangle. Seal the edges with a fork. Brush the top with a little egg glaze, sprinkle with sugar, and cut a steam vent.

If you are using puff pastry, sprinkle a tiny bit of cold water on an unbuttered baking sheet. If you are using All-Purpose Flaky Pastry, butter the baking sheet; omit the water. Set the turnovers on the prepared baking sheet and refrigerate for about 30 minutes to firm up the dough. Preheat the oven to 425°F.

Bake the turnovers for about 17 to 25 minutes, or until the pastry is puffed up and a rich golden brown. Cool on a wire rack. To top with icing glaze, whisk together the sugar, milk, and vanilla. Drizzle on glaze. Serve turnovers warm, with ice cream or whipped cream.

Crisp Phyllo Cups with Berries and Cream

. . . .

For a summer dessert, nothing is prettier than a golden cup of crisply baked phyllo leaves filled with flavorful cream, topped by fresh berries and a light dusting of powdered sugar. The best part: very little work for the baker, because you use frozen phyllo dough and make the cream in advance. If the caloric sky is the limit, slather the phyllo with butter and fill the cups with Classic Lemon Curd; for a lighter dessert without a cut in flavor, you can reduce the butter and fill with Light Lemon Curd or low-fat Vanilla-Yogurt Cream.

ADVANCE PREPARATION: The phyllo cups should be baked on the morning of the day they are to be served. The curd or cream can be made a day ahead and chilled. Fill cups just before serving to preserve their crisp texture. Plan ahead: The day before they will be used, thaw the package of frozen phyllo leaves overnight in the refrigerator.

SPECIAL EQUIPMENT: Eight 3-inch muffin cups, preferably nonstick (2½-inch cups are too small, but 3-inch custard dishes can be substituted); small saucepan; pastry brush; aluminum foil; food processor or electric mixer for Vanilla-Yogurt Cream or double boiler for Lemon Curd; sifter

TEMPERATURE AND TIME: Phyllo cups: 350°F for 7 to 10 minutes

YIELD: 8 servings

PHYLLO CUPS:

> 4 sheets frozen phyllo dough (each about 13×17 inches), thawed
> overnight in the refrigerator
>
> 8 tablespoons (1 stick) unsalted butter, melted, or 4 tablespoons
> (½ stick) unsalted butter, melted, plus butter-flavor no-stick
> vegetable spray
>
> ¼ cup granulated sugar

FILLING:

> Classic Lemon Curd (page 120), or Light Lemon Curd (page 119), or
> Vanilla-Yogurt Cream (page 125), or Vanilla Pastry Cream (page 116)

FRUIT AND GARNISH:

> 1½ to 2 pints fresh berries (strawberries, raspberries, blueberries,
> blackberries, huckleberries, or other seasonal favorites), picked
> over, hulled, if necessary, rinsed, and completely dried on
> paper towels
>
> 1 tablespoon confectioners' sugar

To prepare the phyllo cups, stack the thawed sheets of phyllo flat on a work surface or tray and cut them all at one time, lengthwise in half, then crosswise in thirds (making 6 rectangles about 5½ × 6½ inches from each sheet). Immediately cover the stack of phyllo with a large sheet of plastic wrap topped by a slightly dampened tea towel to prevent the sheets from drying out. Keep them covered at all times. Preheat the oven to 350°F.

Lightly butter the muffin cups or coat with vegetable spray. Place 1 of the cut phyllo rectangles into a muffin cup and press gently down, easing it into the cup shape. If you are going for the full butter treatment, dip the pastry brush in melted butter and dab it all over the phyllo in the cup; or to reduce the fat, dab on a little butter, then lightly coat with cooking spray. Sprinkle on a generous pinch of sugar.

Add a second piece of phyllo, setting it on top of the first but slightly turned so the corners do not match up. Ease the second layer down into the cup and butter, or spray, and sugar it as before. Be sure some butter reaches out to the edges of the dough. Repeat with a third layer of dough. Make 8 cups, each with 3 buttered and sugared layers of phyllo.

Crumple 8 pieces of foil to make balls about the size of the center of each filled muffin cup. Fit a foil ball into each filled cup to hold the dough in place during baking.

Bake for 7 to 10 minutes, until the phyllo looks light golden brown and very crisp. Remove the tray from the oven and cool on a wire rack. Remove the foil balls, but leave the fragile phyllo cups in the muffin pans until ready to serve.

Shortly before serving, assemble the cups: Set 1 phyllo cup on each serving plate. Spoon about 2 heaping tablespoons of chilled curd or cream into each cup and top with some berries. Sift on a very faint dusting of confectioners' sugar, covering the entire plate. Serve.

Meringue Shell "Angel" Pies have a crisp meringue shell filled with any combination of ingredients your imagination suggests: pastry cream topped with fresh raspberries, softened ice cream or fruit puree, pureed berries folded into whipped cream (Raspberry Fool, see below), or citrus-flavored custards. Angel pies are indeed heavenly, especially when topped with clouds of whipped cream or even, to gild the angel, delicately browned meringue topping. Meringue Shell Tartlets (page 108) can be prepared exactly like the larger versions, with the same fillings. Here are some suggestions to inspire your creativity. Before beginning recipes, review About Meringue (page 106).

Hazelnut Meringue Pie with Raspberry Fool Filling

· · · · · · · · · ·

This elegant confection is simply a hazelnut-flavored meringue pie shell filled with a fool: a frothy blend of pureed berries and cream. You'll be anything but, if you serve this to company; the blend of flavors is delectable and it can be made well in advance of serving.

ADVANCE PREPARATION: The meringue shell can be baked ahead and kept crisp overnight in the oven with the heat off or stored for a day or two in an airtight box at room temperature or frozen. Fill the shell and refrigerate it about 3 to 4 hours before serving if you like the shell crisp; it softens but can be prepared up to 24 hours in advance. Decorate the top with whipped cream as close to serving time as possible.

SPECIAL EQUIPMENT: 10-inch pie plate; pastry bag fitted with ½-inch star tip, optional; food processor or blender; sifter; rubber scraper; chilled bowl and beater for whipping cream

TEMPERATURE AND TIME: Meringue shell: 275°F for 1 hour, plus 45 minutes in oven with heat off and door ajar

CHILLING TIME: Filled pie: 3 to 4 hours

YIELD: One 10-inch pie; serves 8 to 10

MERINGUE SHELL:

> **One 10-inch Meringue Pie Shell (page 108) made with 4 large egg whites,**
>   **¼ teaspoon cream of tartar, ⅛ teaspoon salt, ¾ cup superfine sugar,**
>   **½ teaspoon vanilla extract, plus ¾ cup shelled hazelnuts, toasted,**
>   **ground, and folded into the stiffly beaten whites (see Nuts, page 41)**
>   **(Note: Reserve 6 to 8 whole toasted nuts for garnishing the pie.)**

FILLING:

> **1 pint fresh raspberries or 1 (12-ounce) package frozen whole berries,**
>   **thawed**
> **¾ cup heavy cream (36% butterfat, chilled, plus ½ cup for**
>   **garnishing the pie)**
> **2 tablespoons sifted confectioners' sugar**
> **1 teaspoon vanilla extract**

To toast nuts, see page 41. To remove the hazelnut skins, wrap the hot toasted nuts in a textured towel for several minutes to steam, then rub off the skins.

Preheat the oven to 275°F. Prepare the meringue as described on page 108, folding in the ground hazelnuts just before turning it into the well-buttered pie plate. For a fancy shell, pipe on an edging of meringue rosettes using a pastry bag and ½-inch star tip. Bake in the preheated oven for 1 hour, then turn off the heat, prop the oven door ajar with a wooden spoon, and leave the shell in the oven for an additional 45 minutes to dry out. Or leave the shell in the oven overnight (with the heat turned off). Cool on a wire rack before filling. (See Advance Preparation, above, for storing instructions.)

In a blender or processor, puree all the thawed frozen berries or all but a handful of the fresh berries, reserving some (if fresh) for garnishing the pie top. With chilled bowl and beaters, whip the ¾ cup cream until soft peaks form, add the sugar and vanilla, and beat a few seconds longer. Fold in the pureed berries. Spread the fruit cream into the meringue shell and smooth the top. Cover with plastic wrap and refrigerate for 3 or 4 hours. If the pie stands longer before serving, the cream will soften the meringue slightly.

Before serving, whip the remaining ¼ cup cream in a chilled bowl with chilled beaters until stiff peaks form. Spoon a cream edging around the pie and garnish with fresh berries, if used, and nuts, or pipe cream rosettes through a pastry bag fitted with a star tip. Set a whole berry atop each rosette. Make a ring of cream rosettes in the center and top with the reserved whole hazelnuts.

Orange Angel Pie
. . . .

The tangy citrus custard contrasts dramatically with the crisp meringue shell in this refreshing pie. Serve topped by heavenly clouds of sweetened whipped cream, garnished with mint sprigs and orange cartwheels or long, very thin slivers of orange zest. This recipe is equally successful made into individual tartlets (page 325).

ADVANCE PREPARATION: The meringue shell can be baked ahead and kept crisp overnight in the oven with the heat off or stored for a day or two in an airtight container or frozen. Fill the shell with custard on the morning it is to be served, or at least 3 hours before serving, and chill. Pie can also be prepared a day ahead and refrigerated, though the meringue shell will soften as it stands.

SPECIAL EQUIPMENT: 9-inch pie plate; double boiler; whisk; electric mixer; rubber scraper; chilled bowl and beaters for whipped cream; knife; pastry bag fitted with ½-inch star tip, optional; grater

TEMPERATURE AND TIME: Meringue shell: 275°F for 1 hour, plus 45 minutes in oven with heat off and door ajar

CHILLING TIME: Completed pie: at least 3 hours

YIELD: One 9-inch pie; serves 6 to 8

MERINGUE SHELL:

One 9-inch Meringue Pie Shell (page 108), made with 3 large egg whites

FILLING:

4 large egg yolks, at room temperature
½ cup granulated sugar
¼ cup fresh orange juice
1 tablespoon grated orange zest
½ cup heavy cream (36% butterfat), chilled
1 tablespoon sifted confectioners' sugar

TOPPING AND GARNISH:

½ cup heavy cream (36% butterfat), chilled
2 tablespoons sifted confectioners' sugar
Fresh mint sprigs
Sliced orange cartwheels or thin slivers of orange zest

Prepare the meringue shell and bake in a buttered pie plate (page 108). Cool the shell.

In the top of a double boiler set over hot (not boiling) water, whisk the egg yolks until very light and thick, about 3 minutes. Add the sugar and whisk a minute or two, then add the orange juice and zest. Whisk constantly for 7 to 8 minutes, until the mixture is smooth, thick, and creamy. It should generously coat a spoon. Remove from the heat and set aside to cool until comfortable to the touch.

Test the custard temperature and speed cooling in the freezer if necessary; if it is too warm, it will melt the cream.

With a chilled bowl and beater, whip the heavy cream to soft peaks. Add the confectioners' sugar and beat to stiff peaks. Fold into the *cooled* orange custard, then spoon into the meringue shell. Chill at least 3 hours to set, until ready to garnish and serve.

To garnish the pie, beat the cream until soft peaks form. Add the confectioners' sugar and whip until stiff. Spoon the cream into an edging ring on top of the pie, or pipe rosettes of cream through a pastry bag fitted with a star tip. Top with very thin orange cartwheels: Cut through the rind to the center, then twist in opposite directions to make an S curve, or cut very long thin slivers of zest, twist into spirals, and place on pie top. Refrigerate pie and serve chilled.

Tangerine Angel Pie. Replace the orange juice and grated orange zest with tangerine. (*Note:* If you cannot find fresh tangerines, use frozen concentrated tangerine juice and grated orange or lemon zest.)

Lemon Angel Pie. Replace the orange juice and grated orange zest with lemon.

DUMPLINGS, COBBLERS, CRISPS, AND CLAFOUTIS

Dumplings, cobblers, crisps, and clafoutis are all old-fashioned country kitchen desserts. They are easy to prepare and casual to serve, and they have universal appeal.

Dumplings are whole fruits (apples, peaches, or nectarines, for example) baked in pastry jackets and basted with a syrup glaze. Cobblers (also called grunts, slumps, or spoon pies) are deep-dish pies with biscuit-dough topping. Crisps are deep-dish fruit pies with streusel-crumb toppings. All are enhanced by being served warm from the oven with heavy cream, plain or whipped, alongside. A clafoutis is a French country tart baked without a lining crust; it is a simple crepe batter mixed with fruit.

Apple Dumplings in Pastry

· · · · · · · · · ·

Nothing warms an icy fall evening like the sweet smell of pastry-wrapped apples baking in a maple syrup sauce. Fruit dumplings are right up there with Mom's apple pie in the comfort food department. Wherever you live, in whatever climate, this is an easy-to-make dessert everyone will enjoy, and even the youngest child can help you prepare it.

ADVANCE PREPARATION: The pastry dough can be prepared ahead and frozen. The apples can be stuffed, wrapped in dough, and refrigerated 1 day in advance. Bake the wrapped apples shortly before serving, so they are still warm.

SPECIAL EQUIPMENT: Ruler and sharp knife; pastry brush; vegetable peeler; apple corer; paring knife; small bowl; baking pan about 1½ inches deep and large enough to hold 6 apples (or 2 smaller pans with edges at least ½-inch high.

TEMPERATURE AND TIME: 375°F for 45 minutes

YIELD: 6 large pastry-covered apples

PASTRY:

> Unbaked pastry for a two-crust 9-inch pie made with All-Purpose Flaky
> Pastry (page 45), or Cream Cheese Pastry (page 90) or Whole Wheat
> Pastry (page 80)

EGG GLAZE:

> 1 large egg beaten with 1 tablespoon water
> 6 large whole cloves or six 1-inch long slivers of cinnamon sticks

FRUIT:

> 6 large firm baking apples (Ida Red, Jonathan, or Granny Smith,
>   for example)
> 6 tablespoons packed brown sugar
> 6 tablespoons black seedless or golden raisins
> ¼ cup (1 ounce) chopped walnuts
> 6 tablespoons (¾ stick) unsalted butter, cut up
> ¼ teaspoon ground cinnamon

SYRUP:

> ¼ cup pure maple syrup
> 2 tablespoons packed brown sugar
> ⅔ cup water or apple cider
> 1 tablespoon fresh lemon juice
> A pinch of ground cinnamon

Prepare the pastry (page 48). Chill in the refrigerator while you prepare the fruit. Wash, dry, and core the apples, leaving about ½ inch of the core bottom intact to hold in the filling. Then cut away about half the peel, beginning at the stem end; leaving the peel on the bottom half of the apple intact. Preheat the oven to 375°F.

In a small bowl, combine the brown sugar, raisins, walnuts, butter, and cinnamon. Pack a generous teaspoonful of this mixture into the center of each cored apple, use more filling if there is room. Set the apples aside.

Roll out the pastry dough (page 52) on a lightly floured surface to about ⅛ inch thick. Cut the rolled dough into 6 equal squares. Or, if your apples are unusual sizes, you can measure the circumference of each apple so you will know how large to cut the pastry squares. As a guide, an 8-inch-circumference and 3½-inch-diameter (medium-large) Ida Red apple needs a 7-inch square of dough.

One at a time, set an apple right side up in the center of a dough square. Moisten the edges of the pastry square with egg glaze, then bring up opposite corners of the pastry and pinch the edges to seal, making 4 pastry seams poking out around the apple. Brush the top of the pastry with egg glaze. Cut the dough scraps into oval-shaped leaves, mark veins with the back of a knife, and press 3 or 4 leaves onto the top of each wrapped apple, curving the leaves in a natural-looking way. Poke 1 whole clove, stem up, or a 1-inch length of cinnamon stick, into the center of the apple leaves, to look like the apple stem. Brush the tops of the pastry again with egg glaze, then set the apples in a well-buttered baking pan. If you have time, chill the wrapped apples about 30 minutes to firm the pastry. (They can also be baked right away.)

Bake in the preheated oven for 30 minutes. While the apples are baking, prepare the syrup: Combine the maple syrup, brown sugar, water or cider, lemon juice, and cinnamon in a saucepan. Stir over low heat until the sugar dissolves. Remove from the heat.

After the apples have baked for about 30 minutes, pour the syrup over them, then continue baking for about 15 minutes longer, while basting frequently with the syrup. Lift baked apples with a pancake turner; serve warm with basting syrup and Hard Sauce (page 143), Custard Sauce (page 144), or Maple Whipped Cream (page 133), or Crème Fraîche (page 126).

Blackberry Grunt, Blueberry Slump, Cranberry Cobbler

. . . .

Whether you call it grunt, slump, or cobbler, steaming fruit topped with biscuit dough is true country fare—easy and quick to prepare, hearty and heavenly to eat.

This recipe is a New England specialty, although cobbler, a universal term, is known to berry pickers across the country. The word is also known to my American Heritage Dictionary, which suggests it comes from mender—perhaps because of the way the dough is patched over the fruit? My 1890 Century Dictionary defines a cobbler as "something put together coarsely." This same source defines slump as a "soft, boggy place," which certainly describes the dish so-named in Maine and Vermont. Grunt is a Massachusetts term, possibly coming from the sound made by the bubbling hot fruit beneath the dough.

Colonial settlers first made this recipe in a covered pot over an open hearth and served it for breakfast. It wasn't until the nineteenth century that it became popular as a dessert. Whatever you call it and wherever you serve it, make sure it is warm, and pass a pitcher of heavy cream or serve with a dollop of Crème Fraîche.

(Note: This is a creative dish; you can use any fruit or berry or combination of the two that appeals to you. Out of season, canned or frozen—thawed and drained—fruits or berries can be substituted for fresh. Fruit canned in sugar syrup should be drained to measure and the reserved drained syrup or juice substituted for water in the recipe. Taste before adding extra sugar.)

The fruit filling is prepared on the stove top. After the dough topping is added, the cooking can be completed either on the stove top or in the oven. Select a baking dish that suits your purpose; I prefer one that can go from stove top to oven to table. In this recipe, some of the fruit juice is absorbed by the dough; if you prefer more liquid, double the fruit recipe but don't double the topping.

ADVANCE PREPARATION: Fruit filling can be made ahead; add topping to rewarmed filling and bake shortly before serving for best flavor.

SPECIAL EQUIPMENT: 2- to 3-quart stove top oven-proof casserole or 9-, 10-, or 11-inch deep-dish baking pan or oven-proof skillet. (*Note:* For cooking on stove top, be sure the skillet has a tightly fitting lid.)

FRUIT COOKING TIME: 10 minutes

BAKING TIME WITH TOPPING: 425°F for 20 to 25 minutes; or stove-top cooking time with topping: 12 to 15 minutes

YIELD: About 1½ quarts filling; serves 6

TOPPING:

> **Cobbler Topping: (page 97) made with 2 tablespoons sugar**

FRUIT FILLING:

> **1⅓ cups water**
> **⅓ to 1 cup granulated sugar (depending upon sweetness of fruit)**
> **1 tablespoon cornstarch**
> **2 tablespoons fresh lemon juice (omit if fruit is very tart)**
> **4 cups fresh berries, picked over, hulled if necessary, washed,**
>   **and dried**

In a large skillet or stove-top casserole, combine the water, sugar, cornstarch, and lemon juice. Stir, then add the fruit. Set over heat, cover, and bring to a boil. Reduce the heat and simmer for 10 minutes. Meanwhile, prepare the topping dough.

As soon as the fruit is cooked, remove it from the heat. If you plan to bake the topping in the oven, transfer the fruit to an oven-proof casserole if necessary. Preheat the oven to 425°F. Spoon the topping over the *hot* fruit. For dumplings, place separate tablespoonfuls of dough slightly apart all over the fruit; or spoon out dough in even dabs, then spread it gently into a single layer.

Bake in the preheated oven, uncovered, for 20 to 25 minutes, or until golden. Or cover the pan and bring to a boil on the stove top. Reduce the heat immediately and simmer for 12 minutes without lifting the cover. Then peek; the topping should be puffed up and dry inside. Cover and cook a little longer if necessary. To serve, spoon the topping into a dish,

344

cover with hot fruit, and serve with heavy cream poured from a pitcher passed at table or Crème Fraîche (page 126).

Raspberry-Peach Grunt. Use 2 to 3 cups peeled and sliced fresh peaches plus 2 cups fresh raspberries, picked over and washed.

Strawberry-Rhubarb-Peach Grunt. Use 2 cups fresh rhubarb stalks washed and cut into 1-inch pieces, plus 2 cups fresh strawberries, washed, hulled, and halved, plus 1 cup peeled, sliced peaches. Use ¾ to 1 cup sugar.

Apricot Cobbler. Use 1½ pounds fresh apricots, washed, halved, and pitted.

Cranberry-Apple Cobbler. Use 1 cup cranberries plus 3 cups peeled and sliced apples. Add the sugar and simmer for 15 minutes, until fruit is soft.

Other Fruit Combinations. Nectarine or Peach-Plum, Blueberry-Nectarine or Peach, or Sour or Sweet Cherry-Pear, Apricot-Apple, Apple-Pear-Plum, Plain Apple, or Peach.

Apple Crisp

· · · · · · · · · · · ·

Fruit crisps are friendly deep-dish "pies" with crisp crumb toppings instead of pastry. They are effortless to prepare and can be made with apples or any other fresh fruit, alone or in combination. Serve them warm from the oven, with a dollop of whipped or plain slightly sweetened heavy cream, or Crème Fraîche (page 126).

ADVANCE PREPARATION: The crumb topping can be made ahead and refrigerated. The fruit can be covered with topping and baked in advance, but is best when cooked no more than 1 or 2 hours before serving. It can be baked earlier, but it should be re-warmed in the oven before serving to re-crisp the topping, which softens on standing.

SPECIAL EQUIPMENT: Mixing bowl; 9- or 10-inch pie plate or 1½-quart oven-proof casserole

TEMPERATURE AND TIME: 350°F for 45 to 50 minutes

YIELD: One 9- or 10-inch crisp; serves 6. Recipe can be doubled or tripled.

FILLING:

> 4 generous cups peeled, cored, and sliced large tart cooking apples,
> or use a blend of Granny Smith and Golden Delicious, Ida Red, or
> others
>
> 3 to 4 tablespoons packed brown sugar, depending on sweetness of apples
>
> ½ teaspoon ground cinnamon
>
> 2 tablespoons fresh lemon juice

CRUMB TOPPING:

> Oat–Wheat Germ Streusel (page 138) with ½ cup chopped walnuts
> added, optional or crumb topping of your choice

Preheat the oven to 350°F. Butter the pie plate or casserole and add the prepared fruit, sprinkled with the sugar, cinnamon, and lemon juice. Add a little more sugar if needed.

In a bowl, combine the ingredients for the streusel topping. Spread the topping evenly over the fruit.

Bake in the preheated oven for 45 to 50 minutes, or until the fruit is tender when pierced with the tip of a knife and the topping is browned and crisp.

Cranberry-Apple Crisp. Use only 2 cups sliced apples, plus 2 cups whole cranberries (fresh or frozen).

Peach-Berry Crisp. Instead of apples, substitute peeled sliced peaches (or nectarines) combined with any type of stemmed fresh berries, picked over and rinsed, for a total of 4 cups prepared fruit.

347

Apple-Plum Pandowdy

· · · · · · · · · ·

As a child, I fondly remember singing "Shoofly Pie and Apple Pandowdy, make your eyes light up and your stomach say 'Howdy!' " I was always intrigued by these colorful dishes and wondered what they could possibly taste like to produce such a great reaction. Now I know—and guarantee *your* eyes will light up as soon as you try them.

Shoofly Pie (page 272) is of Pennsylvania Dutch origin, but pandowdy is a down-home New England farm recipe, related to cobblers, slumps, and grunts. Pandowdy consists of a layer of cut-up fruit—traditionally apple, though I like nectarines or peaches as well, or combinations such as the apple-plum in this recipe—sweetened with brown sugar or maple syrup and topped by either a biscuit or short-crust dough. After partial baking, the crust is cut up and pressed down into the fruit juices, a process called "dowdy-ing," which flavors and enriches the texture of the crust. When the juice-soaked crust is completely baked, it regains its crispness. Pandowdy should be served warm in shallow bowls with the fruit, juice, and a dollop of heavy cream.

ADVANCE PREPARATION: Pastry can be made in advance and frozen. Thaw before setting over fruit. Pandowdy can be baked ahead and warmed before serving, but texture of crust is best served freshly baked and warm from the oven.

SPECIAL EQUIPMENT: 10-inch pie plate; large mixing bowl; paring knife; vegetable peeler; pastry brush; spatula or pancake turner

TEMPERATURE AND TIME: 400°F for 25 to 30 minutes; "dowdy," then bake for an additional 20 to 25 minutes

YIELD: One 10-inch pie; serves 8 to 10

PASTRY:
> **Unbaked pastry for a single-crust 10-inch pie made with All-Purpose Flaky Pastry (page 45) or Butter-Lard Pastry (page 87)**

GLAZE:
> **Milk**

FRUIT FILLING:
> **4 medium-sized apples such as Granny Smith, Ida Red, or Golden Delicious, peeled and sliced (3 cups slices)**
> **12 Italian prune plums, quartered and pitted (2 cups)**
> **½ cup pure maple syrup**
> **1 tablespoon unsulfured molasses, optional**
> **2 tablespoons fresh lemon juice**
> **½ teaspoon ground cinnamon**
> **½ teaspoon ground nutmeg**
> **A pinch of ground mace, optional**
> **2 tablespoons unsalted butter, cut up**

TOPPING:
> **Granulated sugar**
> **Chilled heavy cream or vanilla ice cream**

Prepare the pastry, form it into a disk, (page 49), and set it in the refrigerator to chill.

In a large mixing bowl, gently toss the fruit with the maple syrup, the molasses, if using, the lemon juice, spices, and butter. Preheat the oven to 400°F.

Turn the fruit into the pie plate. Roll out the pastry (page 52) and fit it over the top of the fruit. With a sharp paring knife, cut the pastry off just *inside* the rim of the plate. Do not crimp the pastry edge. Brush the top of the pastry with milk and sprinkle with some granulated sugar to give it a crisp glaze. Cut several steam vents in the top (page 59).

Bake for about 25 to 30 minutes, or until the crust is a *light* golden color. Remove the pan from the oven and "dowdy" the pastry by cutting about 4 slices across the pie in each direction, dividing the crust into cookie-sized squares. Use a spatula to press these squares gently down into the fruit so the pan juices bubble up and moisten the crust. Return the pan to the oven and bake for an additional 20 to 25 minutes, or just until the crust is a deep golden brown. Serve warm, topped with heavy cream or vanilla ice cream.

Mixed Fruit Clafoutis

. . . .

The clafoutis is a casual fruit tart with a thick pancake-like batter that resembles the texture of Yorkshire pudding. Native to the Limousin region of France, where it is traditionally made with unpitted cherries, the clafoutis is one of the quickest, easiest, and most delicious of all tarts to prepare; use whatever fruit you have available.

ADVANCE PREPARATION: The clafoutis is best served freshly baked; it can, however, be prepared several hours in advance and served at room temperature or rewarmed.

SPECIAL EQUIPMENT: 10-inch heat-proof glass or pottery pie plate; bowl and whisk or electric mixer or food processor; sifter

TEMPERATURE AND TIME: 350°F for 35 to 40 minutes

YIELD: One 10-inch clafoutis; serves 8 to 10

FRUIT:

> 3 cups prepared mixed fresh fruit (such as 4 or 5 prune or other type
> ripe plums, pitted and thinly sliced, plus 1 banana, peeled and sliced,
> plus 1 large pear, cored and sliced; or sliced peaches or nectarines and
> blueberries; sliced apples and cranberries; or sliced pears and
> raspberries)
>
> 3 tablespoons granulated sugar
>
> 2 to 4 tablespoons rum, brandy, or fruit-flavored liqueur

BATTER:

> ¾ cup milk
>
> ¼ cup light cream or half-and-half
>
> 3 large eggs, at room temperature
>
> 2 teaspoons vanilla extract
>
> 3 tablespoons granulated sugar
>
> A pinch of salt
>
> ⅔ cup unsifted all-purpose flour
>
> A pinch of ground nutmeg

TOPPING:

> Confectioners' sugar

Preheat the oven to 350°F. Generously butter a pie plate and set it aside. Prepare the fruit and combine it in a mixing bowl with the sugar and rum, brandy, or liqueur. Macerate the fruit for about 15 minutes, or at least while you prepare the batter.

Combine and whisk together the milk, cream, eggs, vanilla, sugar, salt, flour, and nutmeg. If the batter looks too lumpy, strain it.

Spoon the prepared fruit and all its sweetened and flavored juices into the pan, then pour on the batter. *Note:* If there seems to be excess fruit juice, use only about half. Bake for about 35 to 40 minutes, or until the top is golden and puffed up. The clafoutis will flatten as it cools. Set it on a wire rack. Just before serving, sift on a fine dusting of confectioners' sugar. Cut into wedges and serve warm or at room temperature.

Cherry Clafoutis: For the fruit, use 3 cups fresh sweet cherries, washed, dried, stemmed, and pitted. Or substitute drained canned sweet Bing or tart cherries; macerate the cherries in kirsch plus sugar.

STRUDEL

. . . .

Of all the creations made with fruit and pastry, strudel is surely one of the most delightful. Ideally served warm from the oven, it is pure pleasure to crunch through its golden buttery flakes of sugared pastry to the rich, lightly spiced sweet-tart fruit filling. Austrians, who take their strudel seriously, serve it with coffee late in the afternoon, without other culinary distractions. I recommend it at any time of day, or night; if you serve your warm homemade strudel as a dinner party dessert, don't be surprised if you receive a standing ovation!

Apple-Apricot-Nut Strudel
· · · · · · · · · · ·

This recipe, made easily using store-bought frozen phyllo (filo) dough, is enough for two strudel rolls, to serve twelve, but you can also bake one and freeze the other for another occasion. This fruit filling is especially flavorful because it combines fresh fruit with the concentrated sweetness of dried fruit. You can be creative with the blend of fruit; replace the apricots with whole fresh cranberries or Craisins (sweet dried cranberries), for example; or combine peaches or nectarines with plums; or use plums, pears, and apples.

Before beginning the recipe, read About Phyllo (page 113). Be sure to keep thawed phyllo leaves completely covered at all times, or they will quickly dry out. For authentic strudel, follow the recipe as written (using about 12 tablespoons butter), brushing each sheet of phyllo with melted butter. For Reduced-Fat Strudel, use only 2 tablespoons of butter, melted and stirred together with 2 tablespoons canola oil. Dab each sheet of phyllo very lightly with the butter-oil, then spray it with butter-flavor vegetable cooking spray before sprinkling with some of the bread crumbs. Repeat with each layer, then fill and bake as directed.

Advance Preparation: Frozen phyllo must be thawed overnight in the refrigerator before using, so plan ahead. Strudel is best when freshly baked, but can be assembled early in the day and baked a couple of hours before serving. Fruit filling can be prepared several hours ahead and kept refrigerated. To freeze one of the strudel rolls, leave it unbaked, place on a stiff cardboard base, double-wrap in plastic, and then slide into a heavy-duty resealable plastic bag. To use, bake, unthawed, for about 10 to 15 minutes longer than specified.

Special Equipment: Baking sheet with edges, such as jelly-roll pan, at least 14 × 18 inches; 2 small saucepans; tea towel about 14 × 18 inches; plastic wrap or aluminum foil; pastry brush; broad spatula or pancake turner

Temperature and Time: 425°F for 15 minutes, then 350°F for 15 to 20 minutes

Yield: Two 13-inch-long strudel rolls; each serves 6

PASTRY:

    8 sheets frozen phyllo dough (each about 13×17 inches), thawed, see
        Advance Preparation, above. (*Note:* Frozen phyllo is available in most
        supermarkets, as well as Eastern European or Greek specialty markets.)

FILLING:

    1¼ cups apricot preserves
    2 tablespoons applejack, brandy, or fruit juice
    8 to 12 tablespoons (1 to 1½ sticks) unsalted butter, at room temperature
    ½ cup golden raisins
    ¾ cup seedless black raisins
    ½ cup dried apricots, cut into ¼-inch slivers
    1 cup dried peaches or pears, cut into ¼-inch slivers
    2 large Golden Delicious or other eating apples, peeled, cored, and cut
        into ¼-inch dice (about 2 cups)
    Grated zest and juice of 1 lemon (about 2 teaspoons zest and 2 to 3
        tablespoons juice)
    ½ cup packed light brown sugar
    ½ teaspoon ground cinnamon
    ¼ cup unflavored dry bread crumbs or graham cracker crumbs
    ¼ cup granulated sugar

TOPPING:

Confectioners' sugar

Be sure the phyllo sheets are thawed and flexible; set the package out at room temperature now, but do not unwrap the sheets at this time. Preheat oven to 425°F. Coat the baking sheet with butter or vegetable spray. In a small saucepan, combine the apricot preserves with the applejack, brandy, or juice and stir over low heat until melted and spreadable. Remove from the heat and set aside.

In another small saucepan, melt the butter over low heat; remove and set aside. In a large bowl, toss together all the fruit, the lemon zest and juice, brown sugar, and cinnamon. In a cup, stir together the crumbs and granulated sugar.

Unwrap the phyllo sheets and set them flat on a tray. Cover them immediately with a sheet or two of plastic wrap or foil large enough to reach slightly beyond pastry edges; top with a large slightly damp tea towel.

Remove 1 sheet of phyllo, re-cover the rest, and place it on a work surface with a short edge toward you. Brush it all over lightly with melted butter and sprinkle with some of the crumb mixture. Place a second sheet directly over the first and add butter and crumbs as before. Repeat with third sheet; with the fourth, add butter but no crumbs.

Spread *half* the warmed preserves all over the top of the fourth sheet *except* for a 1-inch-wide border all around, which should be left plain. Spread *half* the fruit mixture evenly over the preserves, keeping the border plain.

To roll, fold the top edge of the pastry over the filling and roll over twice, then fold in each of the side borders, to hold in the filling. Continue rolling, as compactly as possible, to the bottom edge. Seal the bottom border with a little melted butter. Place the strudel roll seam side down on the buttered baking sheet. Brush the top of the roll with butter and sprinkle with a little of the crumb mixture. Repeat, using the remaining 4 sheets dough and the rest of the filling to make the second roll. Place it on the baking sheet, or freeze (see Advance Preparation, above).

Bake the strudel for 15 minutes, then reduce the oven heat to 350°F and bake for 15 to 20 minutes longer, or until golden brown and crisp. Use a long wide spatula to slide the strudel onto a wire rack or board to cool. Just before serving (preferably while still warm), sift a light dusting of confectioners' sugar over the strudel, then cut into 2-inch-wide segments using a serrated knife; cutting straight across or on a sharp diagonal.

FROZEN PIES

. . . .

The following pies are designed for easy entertaining; they can be prepared well in advance and frozen until a few minutes before serving. For easy slicing, be sure to remove frozen pies from the freezer 15 to 20 minutes before serving.

Baked Alaska Pie

· · · · · · · · · ·

The mystique of Baked Alaska lingers from the days of ice chest coolers. With today's excellent home freezers, the making of this dessert is a breeze, although the magical effect of combining fire and ice is as stunning as ever.

This dazzling finale is really a busy cook's secret weapon: It comes almost entirely from the freezer and is ready to serve in only a few minutes. For best results, the meringue really should be made and baked on the pie immediately before serving, and as the entire process takes no more than fifteen minutes, it's good enough to ask your guests to wait for. However, if the last-minute idea makes you feel too pressed, you can complete the entire procedure and return the pie to the freezer before sitting down to dinner. Serve as soon as possible.

ADVANCE PREPARATION: Pie shell can be made ahead and frozen, or it can be filled with ice cream, covered airtight, and frozen for a minimum of 4 hours, or as long as convenient. Prepare meringue just before serving, for best flavor, or return the pie to the freezer after browning the meringue. Remove from the freezer about 10 minutes before serving.

SPECIAL EQUIPMENT: 9- or 10-inch metal pie plate; plastic wrap; electric mixer for meringue; spatula; pastry bag and ½-inch star tip, only if making meringue scrolls or latticework; wooden board slightly larger than the pie plate (to set it on in the oven so heat will not be conducted to pie) optional; aluminum foil

YIELD: one 9- or 10-inch pie; serves 8 to 10

PASTRY:

9- or 10-inch pie shell made of either side-by-side slices of
store-bought ladyfingers or sponge cake sprinkled with sweet sherry,
brandy, rum, or a completely prebaked pie shell made with the
pastry of your choice or baked crumb crust of your choice
(see Index)

FILLING:

1 quart ice cream, any flavor, or 2 pints different flavors, softened at
room temperature for about 5 minutes; chopped nuts or chopped
fruits spread between the ice cream layers, optional

MERINGUE TOPPING:

Read About Meringue (pages 106–107), made with 4 large egg
whites, ¼ teaspoon cream of tartar, a pinch of salt, and ½ cup
superfine or granulated sugar

OPTIONAL GARNISH:

Chopped pistachio nuts or sliced almonds

Prepare the cake, pastry shell, or crumb crust ahead and be sure it is well chilled, or frozen, until just before it is lined with ice cream.

Bring the ice cream to spreading consistency, then smooth it into the shell. To make different layers, you may need to return the pie to the freezer to harden between each layer. Smooth the top, cover with plastic or foil, and freeze hard, at least 4 hours, or as long as convenient.

Just before serving, preheat the broiler. Prepare the Meringue Topping. Use a spatula to spread a smooth ¾-inch-thick coating of meringue over the top of the pie and seal it to the edges of the crust and pie plate all around. Then add the remaining meringue and decorate the pie top by making peaks with the back of a spoon, or pipe scrolls or latticework of meringue over the top using a pastry bag fitted with a ½-inch star tip.

Sprinkle with finely chopped pistachio nuts or almonds if you wish, and set the pie on wooden board if you have one.

(*Note:* Wood is not essential, but since it does not conduct heat, it prevents the hot oven shelf from melting the ice cream.)

Brown the meringue under the preheated broiler for about 3 minutes, but watch! Cover any quick-browning spots of meringue with pieces of aluminum foil to prevent burning. Turn the pie around under the broiler if necessary for even browning. Remove the pie as soon as the meringue turns golden, and serve at once. Or, if you must, return the pie to the freezer, but remove it about 10 minutes before serving.

359

Frozen Mud Pie

. . . .

This easy-to-prepare ice cream dessert comes entirely from the freezer, is a perfect last-minute concoction, and tastes infinitely better than its name would suggest.

ADVANCE PREPARATION: Keep an extra crumb or nut-crumb crust on hand in the freezer for making this pie. This crumb shell can be filled with ice cream, wrapped, and stored frozen until needed. To serve, simply add Rich Chocolate Sauce and whipped cream, if you wish.

SPECIAL EQUIPMENT: 9- or 10-inch pie plate; plastic wrap; foil

CHILLING TIME: Crust: 30 minutes minimum; filled pie: 2 to 3 hours minimum in freezer, or longer

YIELD: One 9- or 10-inch pie; serves 6 to 8

CRUMB CRUST:

9- or 10-inch Chocolate Wafer or Chocolate-Pecan Crumb Crust
  (page 100)

FILLING:

1 quart coffee ice cream (or 1 pint dark chocolate and 1 pint coffee),
  softened at room temperature for about 5 minutes
1 cup (4 ounces) pecan halves, broken, optional

TOPPING:

Chocolate Icing (page 152)
Grated Chocolate (page 148)
Rich Chocolate Sauce (page 149), warmed
Sweetened plain or Maple or Butterscotch Whipped Cream
  page 133), optional

Prepare the crumb shell and chill it well, or freeze. Soften the ice cream to spreading consistency. Line the shell with ice cream and top with pecans, if desired, or line with half the ice cream, spread a layer of pecans over it and, then top with the remaining ice cream. If you are using two different flavors, put the pecans between them. Cover the pie with plastic wrap and fast-freeze until hard.

Wrap the pie in freezer foil and store frozen until about 20 minutes before it is needed. To serve, top with Chocolate Icing, or Grated Chocolate, or warm Chocolate Sauce, and whipped cream if desired.

361

· · · · · · ·

Bridge Kitchenware
214 East 52nd Street
New York, NY 10022
(800) 274-3435 Fax: (212) 758-5387
Catalogue
Domestic and imported baking pans,
equipment, and utensils, including wire
pastry blender
www.bridgekitchenware.com

The Broadway Panhandler
477 Broome Street
New York, NY 10013
(212) 966-3434
(no catalogue)
Wide variety of pie baking supplies
including pie birds

Chukar Cherry Company
320 Wine Country Road
P.O. Box 510
Prosser, WA 99350
(800) 624-9544 Fax: (509) 786-2591
Wide variety of excellent dried cherries,
berries, and cranberries
www.chukar.com
e-mail: chukar@chukar.com

Dean & DeLuca
560 Broadway
New York, NY 10012
(212) 226-6800
Catalogue (800) 221-7714
www.dean& deluca.com
Wide variety of baking equipment and
utensils, dark and white chocolate and
cocoa, dried fruits, dried berries,
cranberries, cherries, nuts, flour

Dean & DeLuca
3276 M Street, NW
Washington, D.C. 20007
(202) 342-2500
(800) 925-7854

Frieda's Inc.
4465 Corporate Center Drive
Los Alamitos, CA 90720
(800) 241-1771
www.Friedas.com
Tropical fruits (mangoes, blood oranges,
etc.)

King Arthur Flour Baker's Catalogue
P.O. Box 876
Norwich, VT 05055
(800) 827-6836 Fax: (800) 343-3002
Catalogue
Baking equipment and utensils
(including pie birds, nonstick baking pan
liners, baking parchment, feather pastry
brushes, instant-read thermometers,
rotary-style nut mills), baking
ingredients (including variety of flours,
chocolate [dark and white], cocoa, nuts,
seeds, pure extracts, coarse and pearl
sugar, orange oil, Key lime juice,
meringue powder, dried buttermilk
powder, nuts, chocolate-covered coffee
beans)
www. kingarthurflour.com

New York Cake and Baking Distributor
56 West 22nd Street
New York, NY 10010
(808) 942-2539
Wide variety of baking supplies

Penzeys, Ltd.
P.O. Box 933
Muskego, WI 53150
(414) 679-7207 Fax: (414) 679-7878
Catalogue
Exceptional selection of herbs and spices
(especially good cinnamon), pure
extracts, Tahitian and Madagascan vanilla
beans and extracts, Dutch-processed and
natural cocoa
www.penzeys.com

Simpson and Vail
P.O. Box 765
3 Quarry Road
Brookfield, CT 06804
(800) 282-8327 Fax: (203) 775-0462
Catalogue
Key lime juice, Tahitian vanilla beans and
extract, flavored citrus oils, Venezuelan
El Rey chocolates (dark and white),
hazelnut and walnut oils, honey
www.svtea.com

VIP Foods
Kojel Food Company
137 Gardner Avenue
Brooklyn, NY 11237
(718) 821-5330
www.vipfoodsinc.com
Kojel Koshen gelatin; call for local sources

Williams-Sonoma, Inc.
Mail-Order Department
10000 Covington Cross
Las Vegas, NV 89134
(800) 541-2233
Wide variety of baking equipment and
utensils, baking ingredients
www.williams-sonoma.com

INDEX

. . . .

366

· · · · · · · ·
369

373

374